Mystery Cults, Theatre and Athenian Politics

Also available from Bloomsbury

Behind the Mask, Angela M. Heap
Parody, Politics and the Populace in Greek Old Comedy, Donald Sells
The Materialities of Greek Tragedy, edited by Mario Telò and Melissa Mueller
The Politics of Youth in Greek Tragedy, Matthew Shipton

Mystery Cults, Theatre and Athenian Politics

A Reading of Euripides' Bacchae and Aristophanes' Frogs

Luigi Barzini

BLOOMSBURY ACADEMIC
LONDON • NEW YORK • OXFORD • NEW DELHI • SYDNEY

BLOOMSBURY ACADEMIC
Bloomsbury Publishing Plc
50 Bedford Square, London, WC1B 3DP, UK
1385 Broadway, New York, NY 10018, USA
29 Earlsfort Terrace, Dublin 2, Ireland

BLOOMSBURY, BLOOMSBURY ACADEMIC and the Diana logo are trademarks of
Bloomsbury Publishing Plc

First published in Great Britain 2021
This paperback edition published 2023

Copyright © Luigi Barzini, 2021

Luigi Barzini has asserted his right under the Copyright, Designs and
Patents Act, 1988, to be identified as Author of this work.

For legal purposes the Acknowledgements on p. x constitute an extension
of this copyright page.

Cover design: Terry Woodley
Cover image: A bronze statue of the god of wine Dionysos, early 2nd century CE.
By permission of the Ministry for Cultural Heritage and Activities and
Tourism – National Roman Museum.

All rights reserved. No part of this publication may be reproduced or transmitted
in any form or by any means, electronic or mechanical, including photocopying,
recording, or any information storage or retrieval system, without prior
permission in writing from the publishers.

Bloomsbury Publishing Plc does not have any control over, or responsibility for, any
third-party websites referred to or in this book. All internet addresses given in
this book were correct at the time of going to press. The author and publisher
regret any inconvenience caused if addresses have changed or sites have
ceased to exist, but can accept no responsibility for any such changes.

A catalogue record for this book is available from the British Library.

Library of Congress Cataloging-in-Publication Data
Names: Barzini, Luigi, author.
Title: Mystery cults, theatre and Athenian politics : a reading of Euripides' Bacchae and
Aristophanes' Frogs / Luigi Barzini. Description: New York : Bloomsbury Academic, 2021. |
Includes bibliographical references and index.
Identifiers: LCCN 2021005479 (print) | LCCN 2021005480 (ebook) |
ISBN 9781350187320 (hardback) | ISBN 9781350187337 (ebook) |
ISBN 9781350187344 (epub)
Subjects: LCSH: Euripides. Bacchae. | Aristophanes. Frogs. | Greek drama--History and
criticism. | Greece--Politics and government–To 146 B.C.
Classification: LCC PA3978 .B277 2021 (print) | LCC PA3978 (ebook) |
DDC 882/.0109—dc23
LC record available at https://lccn.loc.gov/2021005479
LC ebook record available at https://lccn.loc.gov/2021005480

ISBN: HB: 978-1-3501-8732-0
       PB: 978-1-3501-8739-9
       ePDF: 978-1-3501-8733-7
       eBook: 978-1-3501-8734-4

Typeset by RefineCatch Limited, Bungay, Suffolk

To find out more about our authors and books visit www.bloomsbury.com
and sign up for our newsletters.

This book is dedicated to my patient wife Paula and to the memory of Constantinos Gouzelis

... εἰδότες δὲ τὴν πόλιν τῶν μὲν περὶ τοὺς θεοὺς μάλιστ' ἂν ὀργισθεῖσαν, εἴ τις εἰς τὰ μυστήρια φαίνοιτ' ἐξαμαρτάνων, τῶν δ' ἄλλων εἴ τις τὴν δημοκρατίαν τολμῴη καταλύειν ...

... knowing that in religious matters the polis would be incensed if any man should be shown to be violating the mysteries, and that in other matters if any man should dare to attempt the overthrow of the democratic constitution ...

Isocrates De Bigis 6.

Contents

Acknowledgements	x
Map of Attica	xi
Preface	xii
Definitions	xiii

Part One Summary and Context

1 The Plays, the Eleusinian and Great Dionysia Festival … 3
   1.1 The plays … 3
   1.2 The Attic cult of Demeter and Persephone at Eleusis … 6
   1.3 The Great Dionysia … 10

2 Mysteries and Mystery Initiation in Athens … 13
   2.1 Mystical initiation in a world context … 14
   2.2 The Athenian mystery cults … 16
   2.3 Plutarch's initiation experience … 23
   2.4 Mysteries, ethics and the afterlife in Plato … 25
   2.5 The imagery of the mysteries … 27
   2.6 Modern visions of the afterlife … 31

3 Initiates and Theatre Audiences in Athens … 35
   3.1 Initiates in Athens … 35
   3.2 Theatre audiences in Athens … 40
   3.3 Women in theatre audiences … 44

4 Mystery Rituals and Theatre Performances … 49
   4.1 Theatre and poetic inspiration … 50
   4.2 Music and divinity … 53
   4.3 Catharsis and theatre reception … 57
   4.4 Ecstasy and the *aulos* … 59
   4.5 Dance, chorus and audience … 62

5	The Polis, Mystery Cults and Civic Ideology	67
	5.1 Political implications of the *Homeric Hymn to Demeter*	67
	5.2 Mystical/political values in Aeschylus' *Oresteia*	73
6	Historical Context and Episodes	81
	6.1 Stasis	82
	6.2 Epimenides, the Initiation of the Polis and Solon	85
	6.3 Demeter, Miltiades and Telines	89
	6.4 The Herms' and Eleusinian mysteries' scandal	92
	6.5 Aeschylus, Diagoras and *Asebeia*	97
	6.6 Religion, the demos and the Arginusae trial	99
	6.7 The overthrow of the Thirty and civic reconciliation	105

Part Two The Plays

7	Audiences, Similarities and Scholars' Misapprehension of Pentheus	117
	7.1 *Bacchae* and its audience	117
	7.2 Similarities between the *Bacchae* and *Frogs*	119
	7.3 Politics and scholarship	121
	7.4 The 'paradox' of *Bacchae*	124
8	Politics in the Plays	129
	8.1 The polis and *stasis*	131
	8.2 The polis and tyranny	139
	8.3 Euripides and tyranny	142
	8.4 Pentheus the tyrant	145
	8.5 The adversaries of the chorus in *Frogs*	149
	8.6 The polis and money	151
9	Mystery Cults and the Choruses	153
	9.1 Dionysus and Demeter, mystery deities	153
	9.2 Mystery cults' spaces	161
	9.3 Lights in the night, fire and torches	163
	9.4 The choruses/*thiasoi*	165
	9.5 Religious, moral and political values	169
	9.6 Interpreting *Bacchae*'s stasima	181

10 Political Implications 187
    10.1 Equality in *Bacchae* and *Frogs* 188
    10.2 The plays' political goal 192

Conclusions 197

Notes 199
References 235
Index 251

Acknowledgements

This book started its life as a PhD dissertation at the University of Exeter, presented in July 2019. Richard Seaford and Lynette Mitchell have been extraordinarily patient, perceptive and thorough in assisting me in transforming an initial intuition into a book.

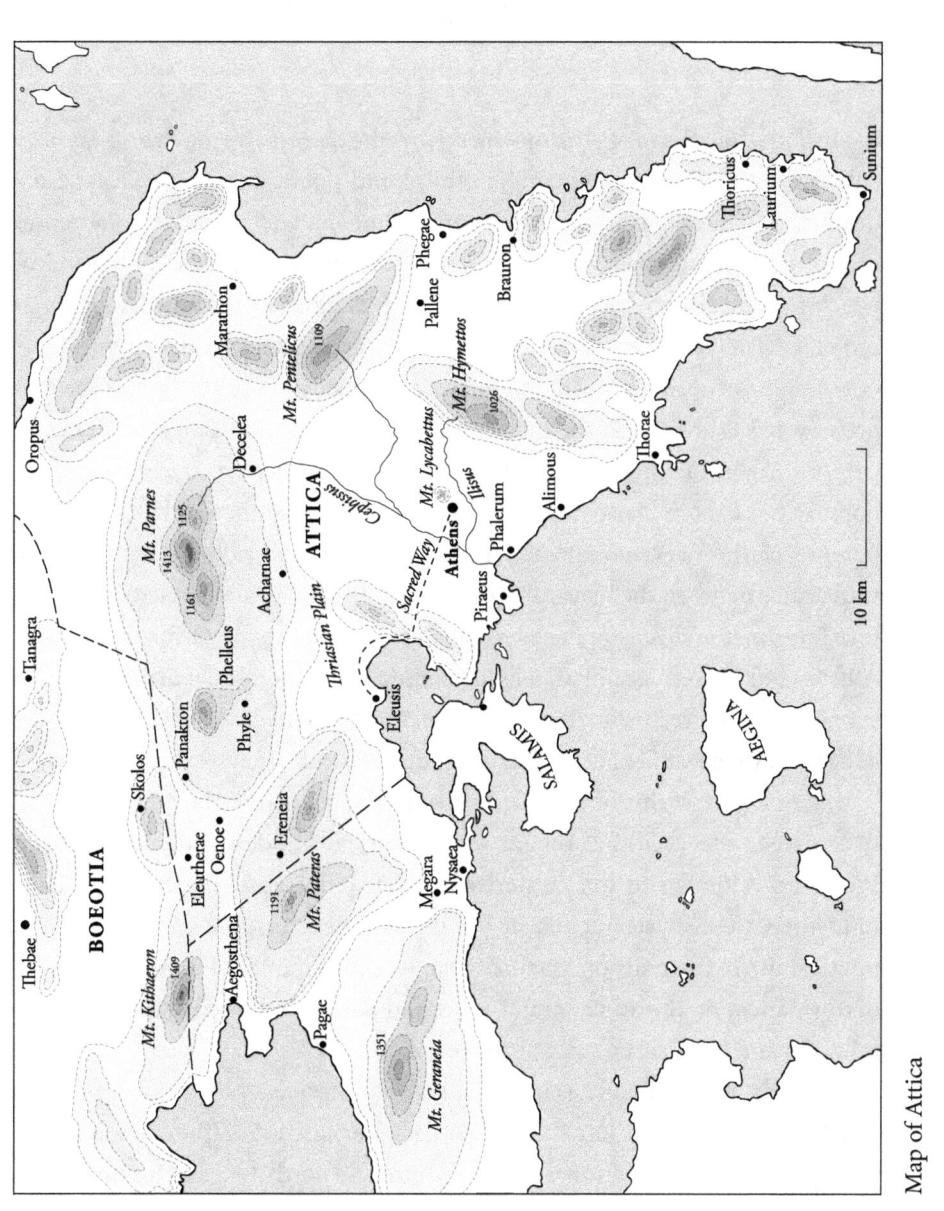

Map of Attica

Preface

In Euripides' *Bacchae* and Aristophanes' *Frogs* the themes which relate to mystery cults are intertwined with a similar ethical and political message. Despite the distinctive political positions, artistic personalities and different theatrical genres of the two authors, the two plays show significant similarities: the period in which they were composed and produced, the figure of the god Dionysus as protagonist and architect of the religious and political action and the central role of the *thiasos*/chorus that is at the same time ritualistic and theatrical. The first prize awarded to *Frogs* at the Lenaea festival in 405 and to Euripides' *Bacchae*, part of a trilogy (along with *Iphigeneia at Aulis* and *Alcmaeon*), is evidence of the popularity of these plays, not only because of their aesthetic merits, but also because of the relevance of their religious, moral and political content. The similarities between the plays, unique in extant tragedies and comedies, suggest that Euripides and Aristophanes reacted to a critical moment for the polis of Athens and shared a similar religious, ethical and political purpose, that of encouraging the reconciliation of the political tensions in Athens through the adherence to the values and rituals of Eleusinian and Dionysiac mystery cults.

The first part of this book is dedicated to the context of the plays. How did Athenian mystery cults compare with other pre-modern initiation rituals? What did initiation to the mysteries mean to fifth century Athenians? How influential were mystery cults in the development of political thought and political life in the polis of Athens? What was the emotional impact of theatre performances on the audiences? The second part is dedicated at analysing the religious and political content of the plays.

All dates refer to BC dates unless specified otherwise.

All translations are mine, unless otherwise noted. For the translation of passages in *Bacchae* and *Frogs* I have followed Seaford 1996 and Sommerstein 1997, with some amendments.

Transliteration of Greek terms and the rendition of the titles of ancient works is a notoriously disputed matter and seems to be largely a matter of personal choice. To make it consistent, I have adhered to the transliteration used by the OCD third edition, when available.

Definitions

For ease of reference, I set out below the definition of some of the essential Greek and English terms related to mystery cults and the concept of polis.

- Dionysus/Bacchus/Iacchus: this Greek deity had various appellations, of which these are the most frequent.
- Ecstasy (ἔκστασις), literally 'standing outside'. Displacement, movement outwards, distraction of mind, from terror, astonishment, anger, entrancement, astonishment, trance (LSJ).
- Initiand/initiate in the mysteries is the *mystes* (μύστης). See 'mysteries' below.
- Initiation (τελετή), from τελεῖν (accomplish, finish), originally meant 'accomplishment', 'performance'. The term is characteristically used to denote initiation in the mysteries, and in plural to mystic rites practised at initiation, such as the festival accompanied by mystic rites. This term covers a wide semantic field. Meanings include 'initiation in the mysteries' but also 'accomplishment', 'fulfilment', 'perfection' and 'completion', terms that express the spiritual weight that mystery initiation had for the Greeks in terms of the spiritual state of the individual.
- Mystery (μυστήριον), a secret religious ritual through which only the initiands became initiated. Chiefly in plural. From *myo* (μυέω): 'to close one's eyes, to close one's mouth, to initiate somebody into the mysteries, to be initiated'.
- Polis (πόλις), originally the fortified space of a city's sanctuary above the city, its heart. Hence, a religious and political community or body of citizens (opp. ἄστυ, their dwellings), state or community, free state, republic.
- *Thiasos* (θίασος), a group of worshippers of a divinity. A feature of Demetrian and Dionysiac cults.

Part One

Summary and Context

1

The Plays, the Eleusinian and Great Dionysia Festival

1.1 The plays

Euripides' *Bacchae* recounts the arrival at Thebes of Dionysus and his *thiasos*, a sacred band of Asian Bacchic women revellers, the maenads. Upon his entry on stage, Dionysus declares he has come in human disguise to Thebes, the polis where his mother Semele, daughter of Cadmus founder of the city, had been killed by her lover Zeus' lightning after giving birth to him. Having made the cities in Asia recognize his divinity and establish the rituals of his ecstatic cult, that is music making, singing and dancing in his honour, Thebes is the first Greek polis which he visits for the same purpose.

As the women of the royal family, the god's aunts, claim that a man and not Zeus was Dionysus' father, Dionysus had driven them and all the women of Thebes to perform his rituals on Mount Cithaeron. The tyrant of Thebes, young Pentheus, rejects the cult of Dionysus, and does not listen to the words of caution of his grandfather, Cadmus, and of Cadmus' old friend, Tiresias, both of whom join the revellers on Mount Cithaeron. He instead threatens to incarcerate Tiresias and has Dionysus imprisoned, who allows himself to be put in chains with a laugh. Despite a dialogue with the god, Pentheus pursues a war against the cult and chains the god up in the royal stables. Dionysus frees himself, makes the royal palace collapse, defeats Pentheus and joins his *thiasos* in front of the ruins of the palace. There he is joined by Pentheus and by a messenger who reports on the supernatural activities of the maenads on Mount Cithaeron. Pentheus is enraged and assembles his army to move against the maenads. Pushed by his prurient curiosity to watch the maenads' rituals, he is however convinced by Dionysus to disguise himself as a maenad and to follow the god to Mount Cithaeron. On the mountain, the tyrant is torn apart by the maenads led by his mother Agave, who returns to the royal palace holding Pentheus' head thinking it is the head of a wild beast, until her father, Cadmus, makes her see sense. Dionysus then appears in his divine nature, announces the establishment of his rituals in Thebes and sends Cadmus, his wife and daughters into exile.

Aristophanes' *Frogs* tells the tale of the god Dionysus who wishes to go to Hades together with his slave Xanthias to make Euripides come back to Athens to revive the art of tragedy. After receiving instructions from Heracles, Dionysus crosses the Acherusian lake and encounters a chorus of frogs that sings a comical hymn to Dionysus and Apollo. In Hades, the pair meets a chorus of mystery initiates who invoke Iacchus (the Eleusinian version of Dionysus) to join their dancing procession to the meadows of Demeter. In the parodos, the chorus then proceeds to pronounce a condemnation and exclusion of the impure Athenians who have not been initiated into the Bacchic mysteries, who kindle civic strife, are guilty of treason or do not finance theatre productions from its sacred dances and from the Dionysiac festival. The exclusion on religious and political grounds is transparently aimed at the new class of Athenian rulers, unpatriotic, irreligious and unartistic traitors. The parabasis follows some comical episodes and is a direct political appeal to the audience and to the polis of Athens. It is a curiously pro-oligarchic and at the same time a radically egalitarian manifesto, opposed to the democratic leaders of the demos, but also a defence of the well-born and well-educated class of citizens. The second part of the play contains a competition, an *agon*, between Aeschylus and Euripides, about poetry and literary critique; the winner will return to the world of the living and help save Athens from its distressed state by producing patriotic and ethical theatre performances. Dionysus is the judge, and decides in favour of Aeschylus, who is then accompanied by a torchlit choral procession to the polis.

We have no direct evidence of the date of the production of the trilogy to which *Bacchae* is a part, other than a note on Aristotle's *Didascaliae* that the play was produced by Euripides' son in Athens together with *Iphigeneia in Aulis* and *Alcmaeon,* after the playwright's death in 407/6. Some scholars, such as Webster, Cantarella and Kovacs, believe *Bacchae* was staged at the Great Dionysia of 405, about two months later than *Frogs*.[1] The political content analysis of the plays supports this hypothesis. The trilogy that included *Bacchae* won the first prize. Aristophanes' *Frogs* was produced by Philonides at the Dionysiac Lenaea festival, which took place around the twelfth day of Gamelion of the year when 'the old temple of Athena at Athens was burned, Pythias being ephor at Sparta and Callias archon at Athens' as Xenophon notes,[2] which in our calendar was around the end of January to the beginning of February 405; the plays were awarded first prize.

Most academics have neglected the significance of the probable synchronous performance of the plays, misapprehended the similarities between the plays, largely ignored the extra-textual context of them and treated them as unconnected works in the separate fields of Old Comedy and Tragedy. While the two plays are, in Lada-Richards' words, 'the two most important extant dramatizations of Dionysus in the theatre of the Athenian polis',[3] their parallel religious and political content has not been the focus of research. Despite the vast number of scholarly works separately dedicated to the two plays,[4] mystery cults,[5] Dionysus and Tragedy,[6] the development of moral and political thought in Athens during the sixth and fifth centuries[7] and the role of theatrical representations in the democratic polis,[8] no scholar has attempted a comparative reading of these two plays in their common political and religious context. Only by considering both plays in their historical, religious and political context can we hope to discard some of our 'modern conceptual hierarchies', and instead try to 'reconstruct the perceptual filters of the fifth-century Athenian audience'[9] and to properly evaluate their significance.

A common theme in the plays is their powerful religious and civic content, unique in extant Greek theatre.[10] In *Bacchae*, the choruses/*thiasoi* of Asian maenads and of Theban women are given a fundamental role as followers of the deity Dionysus and supporters of his effort to establish his cult in the polis. In the first part of *Frogs*, the chorus/*thiasos* of Eleusinian initiates establishes its authority as the polis' civic and religious sacred chorus and expresses its religious and political credo in the parodos and parabasis. The second theme of the plays is their political content. For the interpretation of the plays and of their intended impact it is essential to place them in their socio-political context that I shall briefly summarize here.

Far from addressing the military position Athens was in, as most commentators would have it, the focus of the political content of the plays is the polis' internal political situation. The plays were composed during the period of sharp and violent political division, *stasis*, in the polis of Athens that followed the regime of the Four Hundred in summer 411 and the restoration of democracy in 410. They were produced in the winter/spring of 405, a year before the seizure of power by the Thirty. During this period, despite the efforts made by the demos to strengthen its democratic rule against oligarchic conspirators and would-be tyrants, political and religious issues were still the basis of rising tensions in the polis, as evidenced for instance by the controversial trial of the Arginusae generals in the fall of 405, a few months before the production of the plays. In an atmosphere of fear and reciprocal suspicion, of extreme political and religious tension, the plays advocate collective adhesion to the ethical and civic values and rituals of the mystery cults as the way to facilitate a civic and religious reconciliation between the warring factions, in a way anticipating the Eleusinian content of the reconciliation of 403, embodied by Xenophon in the figure of the Eleusinian herald, *keryx*, Cleocritus.[11]

1.2 The Attic cult of Demeter and Persephone at Eleusis

Athenians were extremely keen attendants of the religious festivals that punctuated their lives. They were occasions for communal rejoicing, feasting on abundant food, drinking wine and making merry. Democritus said that 'a life without festivals is a long road without inns'.[12] The Eleusis festival in honour of Demeter and Persephone (the 'Two Goddesses', as they were called by Athenians) in Eleusis, where initiations were performed, and the City Dionysia, where theatre performances took place, were, together with the Panathenaea, the occasions where rituals affirming the Athenian religious and civic identity would be performed publicly by the mass of people living in the city.

Athenian mystery rituals and theatre performances shared one main characteristic: their social, gender and age inclusiveness. While Athenian society can be rightly defined as a male-dominated, patriarchal society in which women, foreigners and slaves had no political or legal rights and where political executive decisions were only taken by full-right male citizens, the

Eleusinian initiation rituals and theatre performances were open to all Athenians who could afford their relatively low prices. This allowed the polis a precious space where the whole community met and openly aired theological, ethical and political issues. In the rituals, the community periodically renewed its spiritual roots, confirmed its confidence in an easy afterlife and reaffirmed its collective cohesion.

We shall start by summarizing a well-known theme, that of the cult of the 'Two Goddesses'. This subject has been the object of several important works,[13] but it may be useful to recapitulate some of its features as it is the context of this work. Inhabited since the Early Bronze Age (2650–2200), the site of Eleusis developed into a large centre of ritual activities such as burials, offerings and sacrifices towards the end of that period.[14] The building of a large temple (Megaron B) on the site of the later Demetrian Telesterion marked an increase in cultic activity in the Mycenaean Age (1700–1200). Archaeological evidence attests that a cult involving the sacrifice of piglets took place in the temple at the same time, as in later Demetrian rituals.[15] As Cosmopoulos notes,

> the burned animal sacrifices in a restrictive setting were used by the elite group residing in Megaron B as a mechanism for consolidating the bonds between its members[16]

and may have been an early move towards using the sacrifice rituals in Eleusis as a form of religious and political initiation. The site of the sanctuary was in continuous use for religious purposes for some ten centuries, until it was abandoned following Emperor Theodosius' decree of 379 CE prohibiting non-Christian religious rituals.

The earliest evidence of the initiation cult of the Two Goddesses as a fertility cult associated with an eschatological cult is expressed in the *Homeric Hymn to Demeter*, a text probably written at some point between the middle of the seventh and the middle of the sixth centuries.

By the second half of the fifth century, the Eleusis festival had become one of the most popular festivals in Athens on a par with the Great Dionysia and the Panathenaea. The only barrier to initiation was the relatively high cost of the fee to be payed to the officiants, twelve obols or two drachmas, the salary of a skilled worker for two days' work.[17] The initiands were also expected to bring their own sacrificial victim, a piglet, that cost three drachmas.[18] All initiands went through a month-long preparatory period. The first public step took place at a festival called the 'Lesser Mysteries' in February/March of each year in the month of Anthesterion, and took place outside Athens' walls, on the hillock of the village of Agrai and in the open fields on the river Ilyssus, at the south-east of Athens.[19] The festival at the local sanctuary of Demeter was organized and run under the authority of the archon basileus, the archon who supervised all religious rituals in Athens. The rituals of purification and introduction to the mysteries of the goddesses for the initiands were run by the Eleusinian guide of the initiands, the *mystagogos*. The rituals would have involved reciting sacred texts, choral dancing and singing, and purification with the waters of the Ilyssus.

A few months later, on the fifteenth day of Boedromion (September) a crowd of some 2,000 to 3,000 initiands[20] and their mystagogues would assemble in the agora of Athens and listened to the proclamation of the religious prescription formulae, *prorrhesis* and *euphemia,* pronounced by the Eleusinian sacred herald, the *keryx*.[21] The formulae excluded murderers, those who did not speak Greek and the religious impure from the rituals; it also commanded the crowd to refrain from unholy utterances during the ceremonies. This ceremony opened the nine-day festival of the Greater Mysteries. The next day, the streets of Athens would resound with the cry 'initiands to the sea!'[22] and the initiands would march to the sea carrying a sacrificial piglet in their arms, a difficult and stressful march of some four miles as they tried to hold the squealing and struggling animals. On the beach between Phaleron and Piraeus they would bathe in the sea with their piglets, which they subsequently sacrificed to Demeter.[23]

In the early morning of the 19th Boedromion,[24] the initiands and those who had already been initiated (*epoptai*) would assemble in the agora together with masses of Athenians. From there they would start a fifteen-mile walk to bring the sacred objects and the 'mystery Iacchus',[25] probably an archaic wooden statue of Dionysus, to the Eleusis sanctuary.[26] Along the 'Sacred Road' that linked Athens to Eleusis, Eleusinian priests, officials and priestesses carrying sacred objects in baskets on their heads and wearing full ceremonial dress, would follow the initiands and *epoptai*. The religious procession would be escorted by a large crowd of armed ephebes, men on horseback, elegant women and girls in luxurious carriages,[27] festive and joyous well-wishers, families, groups of friends, slaves, rich and poor, powerful people and the destitute. The march would be accompanied by the Dionysiac cry 'Iakche! O Iakche!' to the shrill sound of the cult's core musical instrument, the double pipes (*auloi*), and followed by hundreds of mules carrying provisions and the bedding necessary for the large crowd to remain in Eleusis for the two-night duration of the ceremonies.

Crossing the bridge on the Cephissus, a small stream to the north-west of the agora, a woman would hurl insults and obscenities (*gephyrismoi*) at the important citizens in the crowd.[28] The clever and gross abuse would excite the crowd's laughter and merriment, and mark a moment of freedom from social conventions and an element of apotropaic ritual. At the bridge over the Rheitoi lake that lies in the plain of Eleusis, the descendants of Crocus ('Saffron'), the first dweller of the territory,[29] tied a saffron ribbon to the right wrist and the left leg of each initiand, as tradition dictated.[30] At dusk, with torches alight, the procession would then walk the final part of the journey. By nightfall, it would finally arrive at the sanctuary of the Two Goddesses, where participants would spend the rest of the night singing and dancing in honour of the Goddesses in the Kallichoron, the 'place of beautiful singing and dancing'. The sacred objects would then be deposited in the great hall of the sanctuary, the Telesterium, and the wooden statue of Iacchus would be deposited in the god's temple. During the rituals, initiands and *epoptai* would eat a Demetrian diet, avoiding for instance beans, pomegranates, apples and eggs or keep a fast, broken only when the initiands were offered a barley drink, the *kykeon*,[31] before entering the Telesterium. Fasting helped catharsis, the purification needed to make the mind and body ready to reach a condition akin to an altered state of consciousness necessary to approach divinity. Undernourishment helped cleanse the body, had a direct effect on the functioning of the brain and, together with the nearly total sensory deprivation of the dark, wide hall of the Telesterium/Anactoron,[32] may well have enhanced the initiands feelings of estrangement and of entering into a new reality.

During two successive nights, several rituals would take place in the darkness of the Telesterium attended by *epoptai* and initiands. Fragmentary evidence exists on some parts of the rituals, but not on their order or significance. I attempt to reconstruct the rituals in a way that seems reasonable to me, loosely following Clinton, Bremmer and Parker. The phases of the rituals would probably follow the narrative of the *Homeric Hymn to Demeter* that Clement of Alexandria calls a 'mystical drama'.³³ The first night would be devoted to a symbolic search for Persephone in Hades. The initiands and initiates would wander within the dark hall with burning torches, as Demeter had done. Stylized, mimiced sacred dances would then be enacted by the *mystai*,³⁴ vivid visions would take shape, accompanied by the music of *auloi*, cymbals and a deep-sounding drum.³⁵ The second night would see the vast hall filled with light, resounding with joy and merriment at the return of Persephone to earth and to her mother Demeter, thus re-establishing the natural course of the seasons of vegetation and the fertility of the soil. Dancing and singing would ensue, until the head priest of the rituals, 'he who unveils the sacred objects', the *hierophant*, would lead the ceremony to its climax.

Suddenly the doors of the Telesterium would open. A brilliant light would illuminate the whole hall. *Epoptai* and initiands would be in the midst of what Plato called a pure, brilliant light (ἐν αὐγῇ καθαρᾷ),³⁶ and Plutarch a great light (μέγα φῶς)³⁷ and an amazing light (φῶς θαυμάσιον).³⁸ It was perhaps at that moment that the *hierophant* would show the sacred objects of the cult to the public. This act is told by an unnamed *hierophant* in an interesting early-third century inscription: 'O mystai, then you saw me as I came to light out of the Anactoron in the white nights . . .'.³⁹ The highpoint of the ritual would emphasize its agricultural and fertility context: then, in total silence, under the awed eyes of initiands, the *mystai* and the initiates (the *epoptai*), the *hierophant* would lift his arms and show the symbol of everlasting life and death: an ear of wheat. At that point the *hierophant* would announce at the top of his voice the birth of a child by the goddess, 'Brimó ('the Terrible One') has given birth to holy Brimós' ('ἱερὸν ἔτεκε πότνια κοῦρον Βριμὼ Βριμόν).⁴⁰ The last ceremony before the crowd would return to Athens was again a reference to the fertility of nature: water contained in two earthen vessels would be poured to the west and to the east while the sacred formula 'Rain! Conceive!' would be pronounced.⁴¹

1.3 The Great Dionysia

In Athens, theatre performances took place each year at two festivals dedicated to the god Dionysus. The Lenaea festival took place in the month of Gamelion, our month of February, and included a theatrical competition between five comedies and four tragedies.[42] The Great Dionysia festival took place a few weeks later at the beginning of spring, during the month of Elaphebolion, in late March and the beginning of April.[43]

Both festivals marked moments of Athens' cult of Dionysus. As befits the deity who was honoured, the festivals were riotous, creative and colourful.[44] The Great Dionysia celebrated the legendary arrival in Athens of Dionysus from the town of Eleutherae. The arrival of the god bearing his gift of wine was marked by the natives' misapprehension or refusal of the gift, which caused the god to punish them. Several versions of the legend exist, and all have in common a punishment, sometimes described as a satyriasis disease that condemned the men to a state of perpetual sexual arousal, or as a mass suicide of Attic girls, as well as the final acceptance of the god and of his gift that cancels the punishment.[45]

In an enactment of the original legendary arrival of Dionysus from Eleutherae, an archaic wooden statue of the god would have been taken to a temple on the northern outskirts of Athens, in an area north-west of the agora, where the Academy and Ceramicus lie. Then, probably the next day, a great parade would accompany the statue of Dionysus from the temple through the agora to its final resting place in the temple of Dionysus next to his theatre.[46] The parade would have been led by sacred and civic officials, and would have included theatre performers, cult functionaries, herds of cattle, carriers of water, members of choruses, musicians, and carriers of *phalloi*[47] and sacred objects. Athenians of all classes and ages would have followed it.[48] The atmosphere would have been lively and rowdy. It would have included many phallic performers, who, free from normal rules of behaviour, would act and dance wildly in Dionysiac mode, bands of drunken men wearing satyr masks, all followed by Athenians in their thousands, who would indulge in mockeries and unbridled licence. The parade would stop at various altars where choral dances and dithyrambs would be performed. One such area where the parade would perform was that around the altar of the Twelve Gods, a site that had a special significance as symbolic centre of the polis.

In the sanctuary of Dionysus, music was played, choral dancing and singing took place, vast quantities of the new wine was consumed. As many as 400 cattle were sacrificed and the meat distributed to the population, enough to provide a kilo of meat to 80,000 people,[49] together with bread and honey cakes. For the population of Athens who probably rarely tasted meat, it would have been a feast and an occasion that would have contributed to easing sociopolitical tensions in the polis.[50] It was also the occasion for the rich to conspicuously display their wealth and artistic taste.[51] Alcibiades was said to have appeared in the parade as a producer and financier of theatre performances (*choregos*) wearing a such a splendid purple cloak, so elegant and handsome that in the theatre he was admired not only by men, but also by women.[52]

On the day after the conclusion of the Dionysiac parade, Athenian families and their friends, women and men of all classes, as well as Greeks and foreigners from all parts of the Greek world would assemble in their thousands and sit in the open for four or five days from dawn to dusk watching performances of dithyrambs, tragedies, satyr-plays and comedies in honour of Dionysus in his theatre on the south-eastern side of the Acropolis.[53] The emotional experience of theatre attendance was both an individual and collective occasion of an intensity that is difficult for us to appreciate. In the open air, the vast Athenian audiences would have felt the physical presence of the rocky side of the Acropolis at their back and of Athena's sanctuary high above them, while to their left were the walls of the Odeum, the magnificent public hall built by Pericles. In front of them, above the stage, was the view of the bay of Piraeus, where the Aegean Sea opened its ways to Athenian sailors, merchants and warriors, with all its religious, economic and political implications. In terms of space, audiences were thus at the physical, cultural and symbolic centre of their community, of its deities and rituals, of its communal civic and political spirit, while performing a religious ritual that was the acme of the festival of Dionysus.

2

Mysteries and Mystery Initiation in Athens

Most features of Greek religious cults are, perhaps, above all, their collective nature, far from our experience and spiritual feelings. In Greek polytheism, processions, sacrifices, libations, offerings, festivals, rites of passage, rituals and feasts were the way communities defined themselves and their relationship with divinity. Civic ideology and religious beliefs largely coincided. Communities and individuals considered the universe as animated by the divine. Modern readers and most commentators, heirs of centuries of Christian monotheism and of a secular civic ideology, miss the complexity and relevance of what we call 'Greek religion' and its ethical and civic implications. Modern comprehension of what the Greeks viewed as 'the divine' is impaired by our cultural framework. At the end of his introduction to his work on Andocides and the Herms, Furley for instance observes that

> there is no area of ancient society which has vanished so completely from our awareness as the feeling that the company of Olympian gods is acting behind the scenes, registering offences and worthy deeds, aiding the pious and punishing the impious ... The history of Greek religion in the modern period has suffered from a tendency to consider the object of its study as a separate and clearly defined entity within Greek society.[1]

Similarly, Sourvinou-Inwood states the need to reconstruct the perceptual filters of fifth-century Athenian audiences in order to see performances of tragedy in their essence of ritual performances.[2]

The particularly complex characteristics of Demetrian and Dionysiac cults and initiation rituals makes them difficult to integrate in a coherent vision of Greek religion. The depth of their impact on individuals, the supernatural nature of the visions they produced and their impact on the community have perhaps not been fully appreciated by scholars of either Greek religion or

Greek politics. Consequently, their role in the development of the self-identity of the Athenian polis and of its civic ideology have been somewhat neglected. However, the intricate web of interrelations between the polis and mystery cults, as well as between the polis, theatre productions and their reception, is an important factor in interpreting Greek religion, culture and political events in Athens in the fifth century. In this chapter I shall firstly study Greek mysteries from an ethnological viewpoint in order to compare Athenian mystery cults with pre-modern cults, a comparison that evidences the distinctive characteristics of Greek cults; secondly, I shall analyse Plato's and Plutarch's unique insights on initiation experiences and their exegesis; finally, I shall study the Greek cults' religious and civic pattern of polarity between initiate and uninitiated, civic virtues and vices, and happy or sorrowful afterlife as expressed by Plato, Plutarch and other Greek authors. An analysis of mystery imagery used by ancient authors to express their mystical visions follows, together with a comparison of the modern imagery used by modern near-death experiences.

2.1 Mystical initiation in a world context

To establish the specific characteristics of mysteries in the Athenian culture and spiritual life, it is necessary to review briefly the phenomenon of mystical initiation in pre-modern cultures. In the vast majority of pre-modern civilizations initiation rituals were an essential function of a community in ensuring its continuity and social cohesion, and Athens is no exception.

With perhaps the exception of Bremmer[3] and Bowden,[4] the study of mystery cults from an ethnological point of view has received limited or no attention from classical scholars. At the same time, ethnological studies have given no attention to ancient Greek rituals, but focused mainly on initiation rituals in Australia, Melanesia, Papua New Guinea, Africa, Iran and India.[5] An examination of recent scholarship on the phenomenon of mystical initiation, including its relevance for the community, reveals the similarity of initiation and ecstatic cults found in several cultures and in different ages and states of human civilization.[6] In the majority of pre-modern cultures, initiation rituals are a religious tool used by a community to maintain its spiritual and civic cohesion which connects each individual with the community's traditions, its collective imagination and its self-identity. In his analysis of the initiation rituals of Australia's aboriginal tribes, Eliade for instance comments that initiation rituals

> reactivate the connections between the human world and the divine world of the sky ... form part of a grandiose reiteration of the cosmogony, of the anthropogony ... [and] is the occasion for a total regeneration of the cosmos and the collectivity.[7]

On the other hand, initiation also marked a profound transformation in the psychology of the individual. The taste of death, characterized by an extreme physical and psychological pain to which the initiand is sometimes subjected, marks the moment the initiate has attained another mode of existence, inaccessible to those who have not undergone the initiation ordeals, as Eliade notes.[8] The ecstatic moment of a new birth, where the revelation of divinity connects the individual with the cosmos and with his own community, opens an entirely new horizon for the initiate.

For nearly a century,[9] sociologists, anthropologists and ethnologists have been analysing why some forms of religious practices in most pre-modern civilizations, such as initiation rituals, have a high emotional intensity, often involving altered states of consciousness and able to 'trigger a lasting sense of revelation'.[10] Other religious practices such as modern religious mass cults tend instead to be repetitive, to have a low emotional intensity and to cater to large religious communities. In Whitehouse's theory, the two modes of religion are defined as 'imagistic' and 'doctrinal'.[11] The 'imagistic' mode is defined by the relative rarity of initiation-ritual performances that make the experience more intense; by the use of rich ritual choreography and imagery; by the performance of a spiritual rebirth and regeneration for the individual;[12] by the deep and durable way it shapes the psyche of the individuals involved; by the perplexing encrypted symbolism of the rituals that causes spontaneous exegetical reflection, often experienced as personal inspiration or revelation; the intense social and psychological cohesion of the small group or collective involved in the rituals; the absence of religious orthodoxy or leadership; the experience of 'flashbulb memory' effect that allows initiates to re-live their experience in an extraordinarily vivid and emotional way. The 'doctrinal' mode, common to most modern mass religions, is in contrast characterized by the frequent and routinely repeated repetition of low-emotional impact rituals such as those which took place at most Athenian festivals; religious teachings by professional religious leaders who ensure some form of orthodoxy; organizational centralization by the polis of the main Athenian festivals; and involvement of a large number of people in the community.

2.2 The Athenian mystery cults

We now turn to the nature of the two Athenian mystery cults and their definition in ethnological terms. In many respects, the Athenian Eleusinian and Dionysiac mystery cults are very similar. The twin role of the deities as coming to the polis of Athens as foreigners, *xenoi*, and of their giving of gifts to mankind, the collective polis-wide mode of their festivals, their life-changing initiation rituals and their eschatological content are some of the shared elements of the two cults. In *Bacchae* and *Frogs*, we shall note the common civic and ethical tenets of the cults and the similar use of liturgical formulae and forms of rituals such as parades, dancing and singing.

Whilst the evidence of the Eleusinian mystery cults and rituals is relatively abundant, sources for the Dionysiac initiation rituals are scarcer. The bone tablets and gold leaves found in various parts of the Greek world are perhaps the earliest extant evidence. Other sources include the late-fourth century papyrus found at Derveni that contains fragments of an earlier Orphic theogony that included the birth of Dionysus as son of Persephone,[13] Euripides' *Bacchae*,[14] the well-known scene of Dicaeopolis' private procession in honour of Dionysus in Aristophanes' *Acharnians*,[15] a passage in Demosthenes' *De Corona*[16] and the first-century CE Dionysiac mystery fresco in the Villa dei Misteri in Pompeii.[17]

We shall start with the evidence offered by the places of worship. Demeter and Persephone had a sanctuary whose foundation was steeped in the legendary past and preserved in the *Homeric Hymn*. Its location in the town of Eleusis was the centre of a web of civic and religious symbols that, *pace* de Polignac, marked not only the geographical extent of the polis' power but was a key element of the self-identity of the polis of Athens.[18] Some twenty kilometres west of Athens, the ancient fortified site and sanctuary of Eleusis sat on the road that linked Attica to Eleutherae, Thebes and Delphi on one side and to Megara, Corinth and the Peloponnese on the other. The town was thus at the border of the two traditional enemies of the polis, Megara and Thebes, and at the same time it sat on the only passage from Attica to western and southern Greece. Solon's legendary conquest of the site against the Megarians marked Athens' control of the gulf of Salamis and of the large island of Salamis.[19] It also allowed Athens to control the Thriasian plain, the only large fertile plain of Attica, that could feed the population of rocky Attica with its corn. At the same time, Eleusis marked Attica's border (ἐσχατιά), the furthest limit of the polarity between the civilized and friendly world of Athenians and the wild, primitive and hostile territories beyond Attica. Eleusis sat at the outer limit of the extent of Attica's farming fields, the border between civilization and the 100-kilometre long forest wilderness of the chain of mountains that enclosed Attica from the Euboean gulf to the gulf of Corinth. The town and the sanctuary faced the other space that enclosed Attica, another space people could not submit to their control, Homer's unfarmable (ἀτρύγετος) sea.

In ethnological terms, the sanctuary at Eleusis was thus a liminal and sacred site of the deity and of its theophany, well outside the initiand's day-to-day life, time-structure and physical world. In Turner's terms, the sanctuary of the Goddesses and the great hall of the Telesterium, a liminal place in a liminal site, were a 'threshold', a period and space 'betwixt and between', marking a separation from the ordinary world onto a space where social boundaries cease to exist and the traditional patterns of thought dissolve. Thus, it was possible for the group of initiands and *epoptai* to physically feel the power of the cohesion of the cult and for the initiate to start a new spiritual and ethical life.[20]

By contrast, the main Dionysiac rituals are described as taking place in areas that were not part of the civilized world, but in forest glens, in the wilderness of the mountains such as Mount Cithaeron in *Bacchae*.[21] They therefore used what may be called 'beyond liminal' spaces, areas beyond the liminality of the Eleusinian sanctuary and beyond the borders of human agricultural activity. These spaces were the place of wild creatures, of hunters, of nymphs and other divine superhuman creatures. There, a group of worshipping maenads, a *thiasos,* would stand aside from their civic and family identity and reach a different state of consciousness, a state of ecstatic connection with the god Dionysus.

In Dionysiac rituals, the function of the god is that of dissolver of social categories, leveller of social structures, allowing society to find a new and renewed order in a controlled ritual context.[22] The same concept of liminality can also be applied to theatrical performances as they mix play, solemnity and a precise set of rules in privileged spaces and times, separate from the periods and areas reserved for work, food and sleep. In this sense, liminality is common to initiation rituals and artistic performances as it frees initiates, performers and audiences from normal social rules. It is also the scene for the emergence of a society's deepest values in the form of sacred dramas and objects, re-enacting Dionysus' aetiological myth through sacred dramas and reconstructing periodically the community's cosmogony, social institutions and religion.[23]

Initiation rituals were different in the two cults. Eleusinian rituals entailed a precise process of initiation and a complex priestly hierarchy. The first-century philosopher and mathematician Theon of Smyrna summarizes the steps of initiation in five parts.[24] The first consists of a purification of those wishing to be initiated; this involved excluding from the rituals those whose hands are impure such as murderers, those whose voice lacks the self-control necessary in all religious rituals (*euphemia*), before ritually cleansing those who pass the test. The second is the transmission of the mystery doctrine to the initiands by the mysteries' clergy. The third is the admission to the highest grade of the mysteries (*epopteia*) as overseer or witness. In the fourth, the completion of the *epopteia*, the *epoptai* wear garlands, and are called to pass the mysteries to others, in roles such as a carrier of torches (*dadouchos*), or as *hierophant*. The fifth, the crowning of the preceding steps, is the divine-given bliss (*eudaemonia*) of those who live among the gods after death. The complexity of the ritual was paralleled by that of the organization of a mass collective festival, the running of the sanctuary in financial and organizational terms. These organizational needs gave rise to a complex body that included a series of official functions, that included priestesses, the herald (*keryx*), the altar priest, the helpers of the *hierophant* (*hierophantides*), and several more layers of officials.[25]

As befits a cult where the essence of being initiated was the act of ecstatic dancing and singing in union with the god, Dionysian rituals largely consisted of dancing and hymn-singing parades wearing the masks and attire of the cult, as happened in the Great Dionysia festival. Also, well explored by Dodds and others[26] and described by Euripides in *Bacchae*, the maenadic cult involved groups of women (*thiasoi*) meeting on mountains far from the city, holding Dionysiac revelries. Maenadism was a ritual common to the whole Greek world and was exclusively performed by women, both married women and unmarried girls.[27]

Other smaller Dionysiac/initiation rituals took place in private houses in the city under the supervision of initiation masters, such as the one described by Demosthenes.[28] There the orator describes sarcastically the role of his political adversary Ctesiphon, the humble born son of a school master, in helping initiands to prepare their participation in a Dionysiac/Sebazian *thiasos* in his father's house. There Ctesiphon would help his mother, an initiation leader, in reading the sacred text while she performed the nightly rituals. Ctesiphon would help the initiands to wear a heifer skin, make libations of wine, wash the initiands and paint them with clay and bran. At the end of the initiation, he would start singing the hymn that goes 'I left evil behind, I found the better' (ἔφυγον κακόν, εὗρον ἄμεινον) and shout the cry of joy in honour of the gods that traditionally greeted sacrifices, the *ololygmos*. The culmination of those steps was the parade that took place in the streets of Athens the following day. Ctesiphon would then lead the *thiasos* of initiates through the streets, wearing garlands of fennel and white poplar branches on their heads, holding live snakes in their hands and shouting the traditional cry in honour of a deity that had taken some of the characteristics of Dionysus, namely Attis: '*Euoi Saboi! Hyes Attes!*'

Thus, in ethnological terms, the Eleusinian and Dionysiac mystery cults in Athens are examples of the religious 'imagistic' mode, while they still share some of the characteristics of the 'doctrinal' mode. The 'imagistic' mode is demonstrated above all through the physical and psychological liminality of the site and mode of the rituals, the experience of pain and near-death followed by a new birth into a new life and the highly emotional intensity of the rituals' life-changing effect. The complexity and length of the preparation of the rituals is a further common element, probably more sophisticated in Greece than in most other pre-modern societies. The preparation included the reading of sacred texts, ritual cleansing, fasting, following a special diet, praying and a period of seclusion before the ritual. The liminal separation between the initiands and the rest of the community is emphasized in both cases by the initiands wearing a common garb; the Eleusinian worshippers wore dresses made exclusively of linen while the Dionysiac cult attire consisted of the skin of a heifer that covered a loose tunic (*chiton*), whilst holding live snakes in their hands and alternately playing the *aulos*.[29] Defining the 'imagistic' mode is crucial to evaluate the impact the initiation ceremony had on individuals.

In a manner similar to most world initiation rituals, music, choral dancing and singing were entrancing means that enhanced the liminal experience of the divine and fostered the communal spirit of cohesion of the initiates, particularly in the Dionysiac *thiasos*. The secrecy that participants were called to keep about some parts of the rituals is also common to several world 'imagistic' initiation cults marking as it does the special status of the initiates in the community and their group solidarity. 'Doctrinal' features for both the Eleusinian and the Dionysiac cults include the involvement of the whole polis in the festivals, the reverence in which they were held in the polis of Athens, the regularity of their timing and the existence of a class of priests and of written sacred texts.[30]

In some respects, the mode of religiosity of Demetrian and Dionysiac initiation rituals was unique when compared with the universe of initiation rituals as reported in modern ethnology studies. What differentiates Greek initiation rituals is above all their eschatological content, their assurance of a happy afterlife for initiates, which some scholars claim to be the very focus of the rituals as it eliminates man's primal fear of death.[31] While eschatological references are absent from *Bacchae* and *Frogs*, this theme is widely present in Athenian poetry and philosophy, whose evidence we shall examine in the next sections. The Eleusinian ritual is explicit in connecting the relationship between humankind and divinity, the seasonal cycle of vegetation, the fertility of crops, herds and women, the ritual and the afterlife. In the cult's foundation text, the *Homeric Hymn to Demeter*, the promise of a happy afterlife is spelled out clearly in a *makarismos*, a formula of blessing common to religious rituals and used particularly in mystery rituals:[32] 'Blessed is the man on earth who has seen these rites, but the uninitiated who has not shared them never has the same lot once dead in the dreary darkness'.[33] While the eschatological element is absent from *Bacchae* and *Frogs*, for most ancient authors the Eleusinian mysteries are associated with the hope of a happy afterlife.[34]

In Dionysiac rituals, these eschatological themes emerged with their process of absorbing the Orphic tradition, a process that started at some point during the fifth century.[35] This theme is the subject of the formulaic words on tablets that were buried with the dead as passwords to the afterlife that have been found in various places of the Greek world. The earliest evidence we have comes from three bone tablets from the fifth century found in a temple in Olbia, a Milesian trading town on the estuary of the Bog river, in what is now Ukraine. One inscription reads 'Life death life / truth', and 'Orphic Dionysus' another 'Dionysus / Truth / Body soul', words that suggest that they dealt with a new life after death and possibly a reincarnation theme.[36] A tablet dated from around the year 400 has been found in the opposite pole of Greek colonization, in Hipponion, Calabria. It contains detailed instructions on how the dead should behave in Hades to reach the sacred road on which other Dionysiac initiates travel.[37] In a late-fourth century tablet from Amphipolis in Macedonia, the dead female initiate defines herself as pure and sacred to Dionysus Bakchios.[38] One late-fourth century tablet from Pelinna in Thessaly addresses the dead woman in these terms:

> Now you have died and now you have come into being, O thrice happy one,
>   on this same day.
> Tell Persephone that the Bacchic One released you.
> . . . .
> wine is your fortunate honour.[39]

In one from Pherae in Thessaly, dated the second half of the fourth century, a password to the netherworld is inscribed as 'man-and-child-thyrsus, Brimó / Brimó'; the thyrsus, a long stick with a pinecone at its end, is the foremost Dionysiac cult tool.[40] This last tablet suggests that by the fourth century the Dionysiac rituals, liturgy and religious tenets were amalgamating with those of the Eleusinian cult. The use of a *makarismos*, a blessing formula common to the two cults, and the reference to the Eleusinian announcement of a sacred birth are evidence of this gradual merging of the two cults, an element that is common to *Bacchae* and *Frogs*.

A second aspect of the uniqueness of the Athenian mystery cults was their emphasis of the free will of the individual to adhere to the cult and the individual nature of the after-death experience, as expressed, for instance, in the Orphic tablets. In most pre-modern tribes, mystical initiation is mostly an obligatory rite of passage, as it is the civic and religious duty of the individual to undergo rituals as part of a collective body at a stage in his life. In Athens, by contrast, individuals chose to become Eleusinian initiands with no age limits, out of their own volition.[41] In Athens, initiation entailed a religious and ethical choice of the individual rather than a tribal obligation. The very term for this fundamental step in the life of the individual is defined by the act of closing one's eyes and mouth (μύησις) that emphasizes the individual interiority of this process.

In contrast with most mystery cults, Athenian cults involved a fundamental ethical content, as they assured initiates, and initiates only, of the immortality of their divine-given soul,[42] while condemning to punishment and eternal damnation those who did not comply with the ethical tenets of the cults. Greek cults were thus structured around a contrast between initiates and non-initiates, between the just and the unjust, between happiness in this world and in the afterlife and grief and pain in either worlds. This contrast created a polarity between the collective behaviour of initiates and that of the uninitiated, between the individualistic and violent conduct of the uninitiated and the communal and cohesive conduct of the initiated: this is one of the choral themes running through *Bacchae* and *Frogs*. In common with other pre-modern cultures some parts of the Greek initiation rituals were covered in secrecy, in contrast with Athenian religious and civic rites of passage, such as those at Brauron and the Apaturia rites of passage that were open to the families and to the public.[43] Secrecy and the common shared experience strengthened the feeling of communality and cohesion of the group of initiates and of *epoptai* that characterize the mystical *thiasoi* in *Bacchae* and *Frogs,* and enhance the political message of the plays.

Central to the impact of mystery initiation in Athens was the emotional shock they provoked in the initiand and the complexity of the experience of the direct contact with divinity; this was expressed in the secret rituals through cryptic and symbolic images, spoken formulae, choral choreographies, dancing, music and songs.[44] It was an experience that famously could not be captured in words. Aristotle noted that initiates are not expected to learn anything, (οὐ μαθεῖν τι δεῖν), but to suffer pain and to alter their state of mind (παθεῖν καὶ διατεθῆναι).[45] While allusions to the theme of initiation occur in several later ancient authors,[46] accounts of the emotional experience of the initiand going through the ritual are rare. Classical authors may have largely kept away from the subject because of the difficulty of expressing complex theological concepts as well as because of the interdiction to divulge the secret part of the rituals. It is only through the use of vivid imagery and complex paraphrases that Plato and Plutarch breach the subject in some well-known passages. Both authors contrast the idyllic visions of religious purity and divine bliss with those of the uninitiated, opposing the mysteries' ethical and civic virtues to the fate of individualistic hubristic souls. It is a pattern that gives shape and meaning to Athenian mystery cults and their intertwining with Athenian civic ideology, at the base of the religious/ethical/civic content of *Bacchae* and *Frogs*. The language and the imagery the two authors use are key to comprehending this pattern: it is worthwhile therefore to explore them in some detail.

2.3 Plutarch's initiation experience

Plutarch's rendition of the experience and of its ethical and eschatological implications is probably unique in extant classical Greek literature. Plutarch's well-known fragment 178 (Sandbach),[47] and a passage from one of his philosophical works, *Quomodo quis suos in virtute sentiat profectus*,[48] date from around the second half of the first century CE. Plutarch was, together with his wife, an initiate of the Dionysiac mystery cult[49] and a high priest of the Apollo sanctuary in Delphi; he was familiar with mystery texts, rituals and liturgies, and was a passionate scholar of theology.

Plutarch's narration is worth quoting in some detail, as the images and the Greek terms he uses are key to comprehending mystical passages in Greek literature and some key passages in *Bacchae* and *Frogs*. On the point of death, as Plutarch relates in fragment 178, the soul goes through the same emotional experience of people going through the great initiation rituals (οἱ τελεταῖς μεγάλαις κατοργιαζόμενοι). During the rituals the soul goes first through

> wanderings and exhaustive running around ... uncomplete journeys through periods of darkness (διὰ σκότους τινές), ... all that is awesome and horrid, shuddering and trembling and sweat and bewilderment (τὰ δεινὰ πάντα, φρίκη καὶ τρόμος καὶ ἱδρὼς καὶ θάμβος).

After this, however, the soul is met by a marvellous light (φῶς θαυμάσιον) and received into pure places and meadows (τόποι καθαροὶ καὶ λειμῶνες) where there are voices and dances, and solemn sacred sounds and holy visions (φωνὰς καὶ χορείας καὶ σεμνότητας ἀκουσμάτων ἱερῶν καὶ φασμάτων ἁγίων ἔχοντες). There the now perfect and initiated soul (ὁ παντελὴς καὶ μεμυημένος) is free from all masters and from worldly business (ἐλεύθερος καὶ ἄφετος), celebrating the sacred mystery rituals (ὀργιάζει) in the company of holy and pure men (σύνεστιν ὁσίοις καὶ καθαροῖς ἀνδράσι), and surveying the uninitiated and impure mob of living men (τὸν ἀμύητον … τῶν ζώντων καὶ ἀκάθαρτον ἐφορῶν ὄχλον). The living, on the other hand, herded together and mired in deep mud and gloomy fog (ἐν βορβόρῳ πολλῷ καὶ ὁμίχλῃ),[50] trample one another down and, even in their fear of death, cling to their troubles, since they disbelieve in the blessings of the other world.

Plutarch uses similar mystical images and concepts in *Quomodo quis suos in virtute sentiat profectus*, where he compares the behaviour of mystery initiands and those beginning their philosophical studies.[51] Plutarch says that at the door of the Telesterion, initiands into the mysteries (οἱ τελούμενοι) throng together with great noise and shouts (ἐν θορύβῳ καὶ βοῇ) and push each other. But when the holy mysteries' rituals are performed and the sacred objects, the *hiera*, are disclosed (δρωμένων δὲ καὶ δεικνυμένων τῶν ἱερῶν) they stand in fear and silence (μετὰ φόβου καὶ σιωπῆς). The would-be philosophers behave in a similar way. The realm of philosophy is enclosed by walls with one entry. Would-be philosophers gathered around the doors to seek entrance and one can see great mayhem, talking and excitement (πολὺν θόρυβον καὶ λαλιὰν καὶ θρασύτητα), but, once the initiand into philosophy succeeds in entering the doors, he sees a great light (μέγα φῶς) as of opened shrines (οἷον ἀνακτόρων ἀνοιγομένων). His behaviour then suddenly changes. He now stands in silence and fear and astonishment (σιωπῆς καὶ θαμβος) and humbly and orderly (ταπεινὸς καὶ κεκοσμημένος) complies with Reason as he would a god (ὥσπερ θεῷ τῷ λόγῳ "ταπεινὸς ξυνέπεται καὶ κεκοσμημένος").[52]

The passage clearly defines one of the characteristics of the Athenian mystery initiation, the transformation of a crowd of disorderly individuals competing to try to gain access to the way to wisdom and to Reason, into orderly members of the collective body of initiates. As we shall see, order, humbleness, self-restraint and adherence to shared cohesion are the qualities that define the body of the initiates in religious literature, defined the behaviour of the chorus in *Bacchae* and *Frogs*, and had an influence on the development of Athenian political thought.

2.4 Mysteries, ethics and the afterlife in Plato

Plato's ethical, theological and political exegesis on the ultimate meanings of mysteries recurs throughout his whole oeuvre and particularly in *Phaedrus* and in *Phaedo*, dialogues he presumably wrote around 370. Plato's focus is on the different fate of souls in the afterlife between the initiates – pious and virtuous during their lives – and the uninitiated, godless and unholy, a contrast which Plato expresses through the use of vivid and inspiring otherworldly images. Mystical virtues coincide with the values that ensure civic cohesion: justice, piousness and self-restraint are features of the divine-inclined soul, while disregard for justice and impiousness condemn souls to reincarnation for thousands of years. Plato's influence in religious matters on Plutarch, who wrote some four centuries later, is strong.

In *Phaedrus*, a dialogue between Phaedrus and Socrates that focuses on sexual desire, *erōs*, Plato associates *erōs* with the human attraction to pure beauty, with the philosopher's quest for truth and with an initiate's visions of the afterlife. Socrates significantly describes the tone of his speech as similar to a dithyramb (238d), that is an ecstatic, divinely inspired song,[53] a balanced and religiously auspicious mythical prayer (μυθικόν ὕμνον μετρίως τε καὶ εὐφήμως) (265c) in honour of Dionysus, pointedly associating his speech to the traditional formula of *euphemia* that opened religious rituals in Athens. The religious atmosphere of the dialogue is highlighted by its setting. The two friends sit by the stream of the Ilyssus where many statues to the nymphs stand in the shade of a plane tree; with a gentle breeze and the air filled with the sound of cicadas (230b–c), it is an idyllic setting that as Socrates remarks, seems filled with a divine presence (238d).[54]

Socrates' second speech in *Phaedrus* is remarkable as it explicitly uses mystical imagery and expressions suggesting that Plato was engaged in what may be called an exegetical reflection of his own experience of initiation.[55] As was the case of Plutarch's passages, the images and terms Plato uses are of significance as they recur in mystical literature and play an important role in *Bacchae* and *Frogs*. An initial debate on the nature of the relationships between homosexual lovers and their beloved ones gives Socrates the opportunity to explore love as a form of *mania*, the greatest gift to mankind when it is inspired by the gods (244a) granting mankind the greatest happiness (εὐτυχία) (245b–c).[56] *Mania* moves the immortal souls of humans, which tend to fly after the death of the body like winged beings towards the sky, where the race of gods dwells. There the soul shares the nature of the divine, that is beauty, wisdom and moral goodness (τὸ θεῖον καλόν, σοφόν, ἀγαθόν) (246e). The soul takes its place on the outer part of heaven, where it is able to watch the colourless, formless and intangible truly existing essence, the truth that stands in the real eternal absolute where stand the respect for justice, the blessing of the gods, and self-restraint (δικαιοσύνη, εὐδαίμονια and σωφροσύνη) also exist (247d). On this plain of truth, the soul dwells in meadows (λειμῶνες) that are the best pastures for it (248b). Choruses composed by the souls that are blessed by the gods watch beauty shining in brightness, a blissful and divine vision (κάλλος τότ᾽ ἦν ἰδεῖν λαμπρόν, ὅτε σὺν εὐδαίμονι χορῷ μακαρίαν ὄψιν τε καὶ θέαν) (250b). They are initiated into that which is rightly called the most blessed of mysteries (τῶν τελετῶν...μακαριωτάτην). There, mystery rituals are celebrated in a state of perfection (ὁλόκληροι), as initiands and initiates watch perfect, simple, calm and divinely blessed apparitions which are seen in a pure light (ὁλόκληρα δὲ καὶ ἁπλᾶ καὶ ἀτρεμῆ καὶ εὐδαίμονα φάσματα μυούμενοί τε καὶ ἐποπτεύοντες ἐν αὐγῇ καθαρᾷ). Souls are then pure and not entombed in physical bodies, in which people are imprisoned like oysters in their shells (250b–c). Only select people such as philosophers have thus an instant recollection of the what creates divinity and are forever initiated in perfect rituals and achieve real perfection (τελέους ἀεὶ τελετὰς τελούμενος, τέλεος ὄντως μόνος γίγνεται) (249c), a line remarkable for its emphatic alliteration of the mystical term *tel-*.[57]

Those souls that strive to reach the upper region beyond heaven in their chariots, fall behind Zeus' flying procession and are only able to watch in part the visions of the upper world. As they are dragged down, they fight, trample and collide with each other in confusion and sweat and never reach their goal (248b). They are thus condemned to enter the cycle of reincarnation according to their degree of the respect they had for human and divine justice during their lifetime. The best among them reincarnate as philosophers and lovers of beauty, the worst as sophists, demagogues and tyrants. By contrast, among the realities manifest to the souls in heaven are the concepts of ethical adherence to human and divine justice (δικαιοσύνη), the state of bliss caused by the benevolence of the gods (εὐδαίμονια) and the civic virtue of self-control and moderation (σωφροσύνη), an expression that is repeated twice in the dialogue (247d, 250b–c). Plato thus associates ethical and civic virtues with the benevolence of the gods that ensures happiness in this word and in the afterlife, a concept that is at the same time both mystical and civic, and is at the heart of *Bacchae* and *Frogs*. Plato defines the same complex notion in *Phaedo* 69b–c. There truth, self-restraint, respect for justice and courage and common sense (τὸ ἀληθὲς . . . ἡ σωφροσύνη καὶ ἡ δικαιοσύνη καὶ ἀνδρεία καὶ ἡ φρόνησις) are identified as a source of religious purification. Consequently, the uninitiated and unaccomplished (ἀμύητος καὶ ἀτέλεστος) lie in the mire (βόρβορος), while the purified and initiated (ὁ δὲ κεκαθαρμένος τε καὶ τετελεσμένος) dwell with the gods. In both dialogues, therefore, Plato significantly associates the notion of mystical initiation allowing initiates to live an eternal happy life among the gods, with the civic, ethical and political virtues that animate the best of the citizens of the polis. In this regard, Plato can thus be associated with the development of what we may call the polis' civic and religious ideology, a long thread in Greek literature that goes from the *Homeric Hymn to Demeter* to Euripides and Aristophanes.

2.5 The imagery of the mysteries

Lights at night – stars, planets, torches and fire – are images that have a specific association with the Dionysiac and Eleusinian mystery cults.[58] As we noted when commenting on the passages in Plato and Plutarch, in Greek mystery cults the concept of the mystical rehearsal of death and rebirth was accomplished in the initiation rituals and was intertwined with the ethical and civic code of life of the community. The imagery of the polarity between darkness and light expresses the passage from near-death to a new birth in initiation and emphasizes at the same time the ethical contrast between life before and after initiation, between the pious who live a life of virtue and justice and those who do not, between those admitted to the netherworld in the company of the gods and those who are not. The terms the Greek used for the polarity between light and darkness encompass the functions of images and ritual formulae: it is worth noting them in some detail. In the passages of Plato and Plutarch which we have examined, the references to this theme are particularly clear. In Plato's *Phaedrus* 250c, the souls are immersed in a pure light, as bright as the sun (ἐν αὐγῇ καθαρᾷ) (250c); they watch beauty in its sun-like radiance (κάλλος τότ᾽ ἦν ἰδεῖν λαμπρόν) (250b), a blessed sight and vision (μακάρια ὄψις καὶ θέα), and visions blessed by divinity (εὐδαίμονα φάσματα) appear to them. In Plutarch fragment 178, a marvellous light (φῶς θαυμάσιον) startles the newly initiated, as opposed to the uninitiated soul travelling through periods of darkness (διὰ σκότους τινές) as it did in Eleusinian rituals. In those rituals, an extraordinary light appears to the initiates in the darkness of the Telesterium, marking the liturgy's zenith.[59] The climatic moment where the *hierophant* appears from the Anactoron immersed in light, is also attested by inscriptions, such as the one from the early third century, that describes the *hierophant* appearing 'in the white nights',[60] and another in which an initiate proclaims that she will never forget 'the nights shining with the beauty of the sun'.[61]

Such images are not limited to the authors we examined. They are also used with reference to mysteries probably from their establishment at some point in the seventh or sixth century.[62] In Pindar's fragment 129 the souls of the pious in the netherworld are illuminated by the might of the sun (μένος ἀελίου) while the world below is immersed in darkness. Pindar expresses this contrast elsewhere, for instance in *Olympian* 2.54–60, where the lawless souls of those who have died immediately pay their penalty; for the crimes committed on earth there is a judge in the underworld who passes their sentence. On the other hand, a brilliant star, a man's true light (ἀστὴρ ἀρίζηλος, ἐτήτυμον/ἀνδρὶ φέγγος) consists of spiritual and material wealth adorned with excellence (ὁ πλοῦτος ἀρεταῖς δεδαιδαλμένος).

Ancient authors use imagery of vegetation to express the polarity between the world of the initiated and uninitiated. Two concepts express the contrast: the meadows (λειμῶνες) of Hades, and the mire (βόρβορος), that imprisons the uninitiated after death. For the Greeks, who for the most part inhabited a dry and rocky landscape, the afterlife world of the initiates, sometimes called the

Island of the Blessed, was a lush flowery garden, and more generally evoked an other-worldly paradise far from the real world. As we noted, in Plato the plain of truth lies in meadows that are the best food for souls;[63] in Plutarch fragment 178, after death the initiates and the souls are admitted to pure places and meadows.[64] In Homer it is the place where the Sirens dwell (*Odyssey* 6.288), or a pasture beside the stream of Oceanus (*Iliad* 16.112). In the *Homeric Hymn to Demeter* (6–7, 417) the goddess' daughter is described gathering flowers in a soft meadow in an unnamed legendary land far away. The term 'meadow' (λειμῶν) seems to be especially associated with the idyllic netherworld of the initiates. In Pindar's fragment 129, after death the mystical initiates live in villas in meadows of red roses, shady frankincense trees and trees of golden fruits, leisurely exercising or playing the lyre in a fragrant breeze. In his *Olympian* 2.71–74, a lush vegetation adorns the tower of Cronus, where ocean breezes blow around the Island of the Blessed, where flowers of gold are blazing and the pious (εὐσεβεῖς) dwell in complete happiness in the company of the gods, while Aristophanes in *Frogs* 1300 defines a meadow as the dwelling place of the Muses. In Euripides' *Hippolytus*, the protagonist brings a garland to Artemis, gathered from a virgin meadow (ἐξ ἀκηράτου / λειμῶνος) where flocks do not pasture, which are untouched by the scythe and are crossed by streams (73–78.); in 210–11 Phaedra's expresses her most intimate and impossible desires including resting under a poplar tree in an uncut meadow.

A particular site in Hades is also described as being adorned with flowers and plants for instance by Plutarch in *De sera numinis vindicta* 22, different colours glazing the greenery, while a gentle breeze perfumes the air with the most surprising fragrances: there, the souls enjoy sumptuous feasts enraptured in Bacchic rituals and laughter, playing and enjoying all sorts of music (βακχεία καὶ γέλως καὶ πᾶσα μοῦσα παιζόντων καὶ τερπομένων). The association of initiates, chthonic deities and meadows also appears on one of the fourth-century golden tablets found at Thurii, containing formulae of mystical initiation, a passport for the dead, that ends with these words: 'rejoice, rejoice, you are walking towards the sacred meadows and groves (λειμῶνας τε ἱεροὺς καὶ ἄλσεα) of Persephone'; a fourth-century tablet found at Pherae carries the words 'enter the sacred meadow (εἴσιθ <ι> ἱερὸν λειμῶνα) as the initiate is redeemed'.[65]

Equally powerful images describe the contrasting world of the uninitiated.[66] Plato uses the term 'mire' (βόρβορος) in *Phaedo*, where he relates that those who established the mysteries said that whoever goes uninitiated and unsanctified into the other world will lie in the mire (ἐν βορβόρῳ), but he who arrives there purified and initiated (ὁ δὲ κεκαθαρμένος τε καὶ τετελεσμένος) will dwell with the gods.[67] We also saw Plutarch in fragment 178 describe the condition of the uninitiated as a world of mud and gloomy fog.[68] In Plato's *Phaedrus* 148e, the contrast is expressed by the fate awaiting the just and the unjust after death and reincarnation: whoever lives justly obtains a better lot, and whoever lives unjustly, obtains one that is worse. Later, in *De latenter vivendo*, Plutarch uses images of horror, as he describes the souls of those who have lived an irreligious and criminal life (ἀνοσίως καὶ παρανόμως) plunged into a place like Erebus, a pit of darkness (εἰς ἔρεβός τι καὶ βάραθρον), from which sluggish rivers of gloomy night belch forth an endless darkness, a quote from Pindar (fragment 130). In his speech about the cult and the sanctuary at Eleusis, the second-century orator Aelius Aristides defines not only the releases and liberations (λύσεις καὶ ἀπαλλαγαί) from the troubles of the past as the main gain from the festival rituals, but also the hopes of a better afterlife which the rituals inspired, as initiates will be spared the darkness and mud (σκότος καὶ βόρβορος) that awaits the uninitiated.[69]

The separation of the initiates and the uninitiated is also expressed as the contrast between order and disorder, silence and noise. The term used by Plutarch to express the order and discipline of the initiate (κεκοσμημένος) and his silence (σιωπῇ), is matched by Plato's army of daemons and gods arranged in good order (κεκοσμημένη) that follows Zeus in his ascent (Phaedrus 247a) and by the visions that the souls of the initiate possessed by divinity (ἐνθουσιάζων) (249d) watch together with the divinely blessed chorus (σὺν εὐδαίμονι χορῷ) (250b). Silence is a feature of the initiates during the rituals of the mysteries, as noted for instance by Philostratus.[70] While order and silence rule in heaven, individualism, discord and noise rule the uninitiated. In *Phaedrus*, Plato describes the souls of the unjust as being dragged down to earth by their weight, caused by an unjust life, forgetfulness and wickedness (λήθη καὶ κακία) (248d). The heavy weight and the bad nature of the horses dragging the carts makes these souls fearful and frantic, fighting each other to reach the summit. Many are lamed, wings are broken, and fighting only quickens their fall. In *Quomodo quis suos in virtute sentiat profectus*, Plutarch uses similar expressions: the initiands noisily jostle one another coarsely and violently (ἀγροίκως καὶ βιαίως) at the outset of the rituals, and so do the philosophers at the door of philosophy.

The passages we examined express the ethical, religious and political contrast between an uninitiated, disorderly and violent mankind and the well-ordered, egalitarian community of pure and holy initiates, that is, between an uncivilized and a civilized world. Some highlight the disciplined order of the blissful community of initiates, their delight in the performance of rituals and in the presence of divinity contrasts with the desperate, painful and blind wanderings of the individual in his fight. Others stress the central role of the antinomy of the collective versus the individual in mystical cults that is also at the base of the Athenian civic ideology.

This table summarizes the contrast.

Uninitiated	Initiated
Mire	Meadow
Darkness	Light
Individualism	Collective Cohesion
Reciprocal Violence	Respect, Order and Peace
Noise	Silence
Disorder	Order
Hubris	Humility
Fear	Joy
Demagogues and Tyrants	Philosophers and Initiates

2.6 Modern visions of the afterlife

The similarity of the images and of the feelings expressed by ancient authors on the subject of mystery initiation and the world of initiates in the afterlife are not a coincidence, but probably due to the neurological hardware of *homo sapiens*.⁷¹ It is interesting to note that several features of Greek initiation rituals as well as of the Orphic ritual texts of the passports of the dead closely resemble those described by the people experiencing near-death experiences (NDE) in modern times.⁷² Anecdotal evidence of over 300 NDEs has been collected, by P. Fenwick, a British neuropsychiatrist, fellow of the Royal College of Psychiatrists and lecturer at Southampton University.⁷³

The first common aspect is the difficulty nearly all modern subjects of the experience feel in expressing their complex and inspiring experience in words. One woman remarks 'all words I can think of seem limited and inadequate', and 'ineffable' is the term used by the authors to define the nature of NDE as a mystical experience.⁷⁴ The use of this term echoes that used in the Greek mysteries, 'unspoken, that cannot be expressed, unspeakable' (ἄρρητος), a term that is often used in defining the initiates' duty of silence on the rituals and their meaning.

One central visual element is common to most modern reports, in Fenwick's case in 72 per cent of them: the extraordinary light that draws the souls of the dead towards itself and illuminates the netherworld. It is a magnetic light, a bright, pure crystal clear, beautiful, radiant but not blinding, that envelops the souls in its loving warmth and creates a sense of love, joy, peacefulness and plenitude. It is not much different from the light noted in Pindar's fragment 129, in Plato's *Phaedrus* 250b–c and in Plutarch fragment 178. Souls are drawn to this immense and infinite void brimming with light, an image that recalls Plato's description of the souls flying in heaven following Zeus' procession.⁷⁵

Common to a quarter of NDEs are the images used in the description of the netherworld. It is an idyllic countryside: gardens, green lawns full of vividly coloured flowers, whiffs of wonderful fragrances, music. It is populated by young, beautiful, blissfully happy people who treated the newcomer with friendliness and love.⁷⁶ Narrating his own near-death experience, Dr Alexander, an American neurosurgeon, describes his new birth in a new brilliant, vibrant world, flying over a green lush countryside, covered with trees, fields and waterfalls, where people joyfully sing and dance in circles.⁷⁷ These visions of an idyllic netherworld closely echo the Greek mystical imagery. Pindar's description of the Island of the Blessed in his fragment 129 and in *Olympian* 2.71–74 contain the same elements of joy, flowers, music and scents. They also match the descriptions of Hades recounted by Plato in the near-death experience of Er[78] and that of Thespius of Soli narrated by Plutarch.[79]

Dr Alexander also gives also a description of the sounds he heard in the afterlife: a deep, rhythmic pounding he heard in crossing the darkness, the sound of metal against metal, as if a giant subterranean blacksmith was pounding an anvil in the far distance.[80] Aeschylus' description of the mystical ritual to the goddess Cotyto in a fragment of his play *Edonians* is remarkably similar to this description: sounds include the crashing of bronze cymbals, terrifying imitations of the bellowing of bulls, and the fearful deep sound of the drum that carries to the ear like thunder beneath the earth.[81]

The NDE leaves the majority of its subjects overwhelmingly aware of one thing: the notion of death as something to welcome and not to fear. Dr Alexander values his experience with these words: 'the knowledge given me was not taught in the way that a history lesson or math theorem would be ... insights happened directly ... knowledge was stored without memorisation, instantly and for good.'[82] This insight somewhat matches Aristotle's warning that those undergoing initiation rituals should not learn but should instead let themselves be deeply moved by the experience and be put in a state fit for the purpose (παθεῖν καὶ διατεθῆναι) that we examined in 2.2.[83]

The expression used by several NDE subjects to describe this new awareness is that death is just a moment of passage, a page to be turned to enter into a new and better reality. This realization is remarkably similar to the formula pronounced by Dionysiac initiates upon the completion of the ritual quoted by Demosthenes in *De Corona* we examined: 'I left evil behind; I found the best'. Similarly, in reference to NDE several subjects relate their awareness that physical bodies are prisons, the same paraphrase Plato famously uses.[84]

To sum this chapter up, Greek mystery initiations were far from being a phenomenon limited to ancient Greece. On one hand, they were one of the worldwide expressions of natural spirituality; on the other they were ingrained in what may be defined as the innate system of beliefs of *homo sapiens* on the immortality of the soul and the nature of the netherworld.

3

Initiates and Theatre Audiences in Athens

The public success of Aristophanes' *Frogs* and of Euripides' *Bacchae* trilogy suggests that their audiences were familiar with mystery cults, with the plays' religious and civic values being popular in Athens. Included in the audiences were mystery initiates. In this chapter I shall examine some of the evidence, mainly in demographic terms, for the population of initiates in Athens and their presence in theatre audiences

3.1 Initiates in Athens

A point rarely explored in depth by scholars is the number and influence of initiates in Athenian life, politics and theatre. Modern readers may think of initiates as a small cabal of eccentrics affiliated to a spiritualist secret cult, and of theatre-goers as a small number of lovers of dramatic arts; reality in Athens was different. While we cannot define Dionysiac and Demetrian initiates in Athens as a cohesive community sharing a common religious and political identity, it is important to note the fact that initiates were individuals united by a common deep spiritual experience and by a shared set of religious, civic and moral beliefs. They would have had a direct influence on the political ethos of the polis, particularly in moments of political division. It is therefore of some importance to try to evaluate their relative weight in the population of Athens. What evidence do we have for the demographic dimensions of mystery initiates in Athens? Is it possible to assume that initiates represented a sizable and therefore ethically and politically influential part of the polis?

No hard evidence exists to answer these questions. Some scholars have suggested that initiates would have been a considerable part of the population, but they do not expand on it. Burkert for instance writes that in his opinion most Athenians were initiated,[1] while Bérard and Bron, in their article on the relationship between the Dionysiac *thiasos* and politics in the polis, write: 'Mais si, à Athènes il n'y a jamais eu crise dionysiaque, c'est bien parce que au départ, la cité toute entière était initiée' (If in Athens a Dionysiac crisis never happened, it is because the whole city was initiated since the start).[2] As Parker puts it, 'it seems to have been the norm for Athenians who could afford it to undergo initiation',[3] while Sourvinou-Inwood notes: 'There is every reason to think that the large majority of Athenians were initiated ... The large majority of fifth-century Athenians, I assume, were initiates of the Eleusinian Mysteries.'[4]

As the question has otherwise been largely ignored by scholars despite its relevance to the impact of mystery cults on the polis of Athens, it is worth examining it briefly. We shall examine some demographic and archaeological evidence in order to produce an estimate of the ratio of initiates/total population which may support the views of Burkert, Bérard and Bron, Parker and Sourvinou-Inwood. To do so, we shall assess first the question of the population of the urban agglomeration of Athens/Piraeus in the second half of the fifth century. Because of the difficulty of extrapolating the small amount of extant data in Thucydides and in the corpus of inscriptions, and of estimating the number of women, metics (foreigners living in Athens) and slaves that would have been admitted to the rituals, the matter is still highly controversial and has been discussed by scholars for decades. A consensus is difficult to find. Gomme, for instance, estimates the total inhabitants of Athens and Piraeus in the time of Pericles at some 155,000.[5] Raaflaub suggests a total of 150,000–240,000,[6] and Scott quotes the figures of 120,000–150,000,[7] while Hansen estimates the total population of Attica in the same period at some 300,000 or more and the number of male full-right citizens in 431 at some 60,000. Some consensus, however, exists on the estimates for Athens' population at the end of the Peloponnesian war. Hansen estimates the post-war and post-plague number of full-right citizens at some 30,000 by 406/5,[8] while for Strauss the total population of Athens in the same period amounted to a total of 56,000–65,000.[9] The two figures are not incompatible as the women, metics, slaves and children who are included in Strauss' estimate may well have represented half of the total population. We shall retain the figure of 60,000 as an acceptable estimate for the population of Athens at the end of the fifth century, when *Bacchae* and *Frogs* were produced.

Out of this number, how many mystery initiates were there in Athens? Unfortunately, we have no evidence that could lead us to any estimate of the number of Dionysiac initiates in Athens, apart from some later evidence of the maenadic cult in the polis.[10] The Eleusinian cult of Demeter offers some more data; firstly, there are the dimensions of the sanctuary of Demeter and of the Telesterium, a factor that has been ignored by scholars but one that provides an important clue to the popularity of the cult in the context of Attica's collective religious life. The sanctuary was very large, covering an area of some 24,000 square metres (equal to two football fields) and comparable to the whole area of the Acropolis; roughly half the size of the open-air area of the Athenian agora which measured some 50,000 square metres. Aelius Aristides probably overstated it when he wrote that the full complement of the polis (τῆς πόλεως πλήρωμα) attended the festival in the sanctuary of Eleusis,[11] equating the population of Athens and that at the festival; nevertheless, the crowd must have been very large indeed.

Equally unexplored by scholars is a possible answer to the key question of the number of Eleusis initiands, which modern theories base upon on the number of people the Telesterium, the initiation hall in the sanctuary, could accommodate. The Telesterium, rebuilt in Pericles' time by the architects Coroebus, Metagenes and Xenocles, measured 51.55 x 51.20 metres, with a surface of 2,640 square metres. The Telesterium was thus an extremely large religious building by Athenian standards,[12] second in Pericles' Athens only to the Odeum, the large, covered public structure adjacent to the theatre of Dionysus that covered 4,280 square metres;[13] it served several other public functions, such as musical performances, choral rehearsals, public meetings, and occasionally even as a military barracks. A study by Still, Professor of Crowd Science at the Manchester Metropolitan University, establishes the space needed by one person in a comfortable and loose standing crowd as 1–1.5 square metres.[14] If filled to this level, the Telesterium would have been large enough for some 1,800–2,600 initiates and *epoptai*.

This estimate strengthens the case made by some scholars, such as Clinton and Cavanaugh. On the basis of his analysis of the epigraphic records and of a later inscription,[15] Clinton estimates that a 'reasonable total' of some 2,150 *mystai* had been initiated in the year 408–407.[16] It is the only year for which some data for the sanctuary's income exists, but this figure may lead to an underestimation, as the annual land procession to Eleusis had been interrupted because of the Spartan military presence at Decelea which in turn may have prevented some initiands participating in the rituals. Based on the same evidence Cavanaugh comes to a similar total of 2,200.[17] Parker later corrected his total to 2,400.[18] Bremmer believes that *mystai* and *epoptai* present at the rituals numbered at some 3,000.[19] It is obviously impossible to speculate further on these figures as the Telesterium may not have been full each year and as we have no evidence of the number of *epoptai* participating in the rituals, but this hypothesis, however, offers grounds that initiates in Athens numbered a comparatively large number of people being larger as a percentage of the population towards the end of the century, with the war losses hitting the full-right citizens more than women, slaves or metics. Adopting Parker's 2005 figure of 2,400 new initiates per annum on a post-war population of 60,000, we may tentatively imagine that the Eleusinian initiates in Athens were in the region of 40 per cent of the population in the final years of the Peloponnesian war, which would confirm the insight of Burkert, Bérard and Bron, Parker and Sourvinou-Inwood.

How influential were initiates in Athens' political scene? Initiates were not a homogeneous political group with definite beliefs and goals, but individuals connected by shared eschatological, moral and civic beliefs that influenced the public opinion of the Athenian polis in some crucial moments of its history. Hard contemporary evidence of their direct political influence does not exist, apart perhaps from an observation of Andocides on the composition of the political decision-making body of the polis, the ecclesia.[20] According to Andocides, the ecclesia discussed the imminent expedition to Sicily in the presence of the expedition's generals Nicias, Lamachus and Alcibiades. One Pythonicus then rose and cried that one of the leaders of the dangerous expedition, Alcibiades, had been holding mystical rituals in his home with others, and offered to produce a witness. Alcibiades defended himself vigorously before the Prytanes, the court members of the polis' supreme judicial court, the *Boule*. The Prytanes decided to clear the meeting of non-initiates, in order to be able to listen to the witness' evidence of the sacred matter of sacrilege against the goddesses. This account suggests that the initiates within the ecclesia were not a small crowd, which would have made such deliberations irrelevant, and may have represented a substantial part of the 6,000 attendees at the ecclesia meetings.[21] This does not imply the existence of a party of initiates acting in concert in the ecclesia but suggests that intellectually active Athenians were at the same time mystery initiates and active participants in the polis' political life. Thus, the group of new *mystai* and existing *epoptai* may be thought as a sizable and influential minority in the population of the city.

One such initiate was the archon *eponymos*[22] whose role was to choose authors and plays for the Lenaea and Great Dionysia festivals in the spring of 405, including *Bacchae* and *Frogs*.[23] His name was Callias,[24] and he belonged to the genos Kerykes, high priests of Demeter's sanctuary at Eleusis, to whom the office of *dadouchos* belonged hereditarily.[25] Other members of the genos included Cleocritus, who, according to Xenophon,[26] had accompanied Thrasybulus in the anti-oligarchic campaign to overthrow of the Thirty and had made a speech inspired by Eleusinian themes to the troops after the battle of Munichia, a theme we shall observe in 6.7. Callias was *proxenos* of Sparta, a man who represented the interests of Sparta in Athens, a friend of Socrates and of Alcibiades, host to Plato's *Protagoras* dialogue and to Xenophon's *Symposium*, and later Andocides' adversary in court. His family had a close relationship with the anti-tyrannical genos of the Alcmaeonidae and with Pericles.

Callias was the son of Hipponicus and Agariste, who belonged to the Alcmaeonidae genos and who later married Pericles: Pericles' sons, Paralus and Xanthippus, were Callias' step-brothers.[27] Callias' sister Hipparete married Alcibiades.[28] As his paternal family leased slaves to the silver mines in Laurium for one *mina* a day,[29] Callias inherited a large fortune and was one of the richest men in Athens.[30] Plato calls his house the *prytaneion* of Greece's wisdom.[31] He was, Xenophon writes, Eleusinian *dadouchos* in 371, when he was part of an embassy to negotiate terms of peace with the Spartans.[32] According to Xenophon, Callias made a speech to the Spartans centred on an Eleusinian theme. Demeter's mysteries and her gift of grain were common to Athens and Sparta, and therefore war between the two poleis was incompatible with their brotherhood in Demeter's cult. Callias also pointed out that Triptolemus, his legendary ancestor, had revealed the secret rituals of the goddesses to Heracles, the mythical founder of Sparta, and to the Dioscuri, who were Sparta's citizens; he had also asked whether it was just for the Spartans to destroy the harvest of those from whom they had first received the seed of grain, and for Athenians not to wish abundance of food for those to whom they had first given the seeds.

To sum it up, Callias was a complex and somewhat contradictory figure. If one is to judge by his family roots and connections, he was a wealthy member of the oligarchy, an anti-tyrannical Alcmaeonid, and an intellectual, friend of the sophists, and an *aulos* player.[33] His attachment to his priestly role in the Eleusinian cult, his defence of the cult's veneration for peace, his cultural sophistication and the immense wealth he spent as an Athenian Maecenas suggest he was open to new ideas and devoted to Athens' religion and to mystical cults. The same combination of traditional religious and advanced political ideas can be found in *Frogs* and *Bacchae*; it is thus tempting to suggest the hypothesis that Callias' choice of those plays in 405 may have been motivated in part by the politico-religious beliefs that he shared with the authors of the plays.

If one extrapolates the same estimated ratio of initiates/total population of around 40 per cent for theatre audiences, the part of the audiences particularly sensitive to the mystical allusions and ritual enactments in plays such as Aeschylus' *Oresteia*, Euripides' *Bacchae* and Aristophanes' *Frogs* would have been sizable. For instance, Heraclides Ponticus relates how Aeschylus was almost lynched on stage by the audience of one of his plays, who suspected him of having divulged some of the mysteries' secrets, with Aeschylus having to take refuge at the altar of Dionysus to save his life.[34] Only initiates would have been able to recognize the secrets Aeschylus had breached, and their number was large enough for them to be credibly identified as the whole audience. The experience of initiation, their sharing of mystical and ethical values, may have made the number of initiates sufficient to influence the success of any play, by applauding or booing plays and by swaying its judges.[35] It is thus tempting to imagine that the initiates in the audience may have influenced the first prize result awarded to *Frogs* and to *Bacchae* in 405.

3.2 Theatre audiences in Athens

In considering the religious/political impact *Bacchae* and *Frogs* had on their audiences as well as on the polis of Athens at large, we must first address some basic issues. How large were theatre audiences compared to the polis' population? How representative of the polis community was a theatre audience at the Lenaea or Great Dionysia festival? How large was the group of initiates in theatre performances?

How many Athenians would watch theatre performances? We have no hard evidence of the capacity of the theatre of Dionysus, whose ruins sit at the base of the Acropolis, other than its extant dimensions and the archaeological research on its various reconstructions since archaic times. The outlines of the theatre that we can visit today, spread out on the south-eastern slopes of the rock of the Acropolis, are in fact the ruins of a later version of the theatre, built in marble in the late fourth century where the original theatre had been. The theatre was first built around 500 BC, was rebuilt in the second half of the fifth-century BC at the same time as the construction of the odeon of Pericles, and then again, some 120 years later. Contemporaries give some estimates on its capacity, such as Plato who in his *Symposium* has Socrates praise the author and actor Agathon whose wisdom was 'shining forth from your youth, strong and splendid, in the eyes of more than thirty thousand Greeks' in the theatre of Dionysus.[36] In his *Ion*, however, Plato has the rhapsodist standing 'before more than twenty thousand friendly people'[37] in a space that is unnamed, but likely to be the theatre of Dionysus. Both figures are highly dubious, especially as Plato may just have used the term 'more than twenty/thirty thousand' to define a very large crowd.[38]

Pickard-Cambridge called the audience capacity of the theatre of Dionysus 'by modern standards very large'.[39] During the last forty years his estimate of 14,000–17,000 available seats has been taken as authoritative, despite the fact that it was based on the foundations of the larger theatre rebuilt by Lycurgus a century later than the one that was used in Pericles' times. Other scholars share this opinion, such as Csapo and Slater[40] and Wiles.[41] Kawalko-Roselli includes spectators sitting outside the benched area and reaches the figure of some 8,000.[42] Whatever the capacity of the theatre, demand for seats was high, probably much higher than supply. If the estimate of Pickard-Cambridge for the later Lycurgian theatre's capacity is right, it is evidence of the need for the new theatre to accommodate twice as many spectators as it may have done in Pericles' time, even though the population of Athens may have actually declined.[43]

While attendance at theatre performances was open to all, including metics, slaves and foreign visitors,[44] two main factors had a limiting effect on theatre attendance: the price of tickets and the availability of seats. A large attendance at public theatrical performances was a political priority for the polis. The price of tickets was a politically sensitive issue, so much so that, according to some of our sources, Pericles had established the practice for the treasury of the polis to purchase tickets and distribute them for free to those in need, a practice called *theorika*.[45] The date at which the two-obols *theorika* became custom is uncertain;[46] only an appraisal of its relative cost can give an indication of the social inclusivity of theatre performances before the introduction of the *theorika*. Theatre tickets were priced at two obols, a level that most Athenians could afford. Two obols were one-third of a drachma, the cost of two orders of meat stew,[47] of six *kotylai*, one-and-a-half litres of wine,[48] of a litre of olive oil,[49] or of one book sold in the agora,[50] whilst the piglet which each initiand had to offer to Demeter cost eighteen obols, or three drachmas.[51] Soldiers and sailors were usually paid half to one drachma a day (three to six obols),[52] while jurors were paid three obols per day, a rate thought sufficient to compensate the juror and his family for daily expenses.[53] So, the price of tickets allowed most people in Athens, including metics and some slaves, to watch the shows performed in the theatre of Dionysus for a relatively affordable price.

The official social and political structure of the polis of Athens was reflected in the way some of the seats were allocated in the theatre of Dionysus, but not all of them.[54] Male full-rights citizens would have had the majority of the seats granted by the polis. The city's archons and the members of the *Boule* were provided with seats free of charge, as were civic magistrates and officials, foreign ambassadors, distinguished individuals, the high priest of Dionysus Eleuthereus,[55] and successful generals. But other social strata were also present in audiences and widened the range of issues raised and discussed by tragedies and comedies.

Starting with the metics, a number of them and their families lived in Piraeus and were active in industrial manufacturing, such as Lysias' father, a large manufacturer of shields for the army.[56] Given their relative wealth and their relative proximity to the theatre of Dionysus, they would have been able to pay for their tickets and attend theatre performances. The conflict between their important role in the economy of Athens and their lack of political voice is attested to by, for instance, Xenophon. In his early fourth-century *Ways and Means* 2, Xenophon makes a plea on behalf of metics residing in Athens.[57]

They provide, Xenophon writes, the best source of revenue for the polis as they are self-supporting, do not receive subsidies from the polis and instead contribute to the community welfare and war effort by paying a special tax.[58] As such, Xenophon pleads, they should be encouraged to stay in Athens, and measures should be taken to attract other metics to reside in Athens, such as the right to own land and to serve in the cavalry. Metics can thus be considered to have a natural affinity with an egalitarian and democratic, anti-tyrannical and anti-oligarchic political stance; Lysias clearly shared this stance as he was said to have supplied money, mercenaries and shields to the democratic forces at Phyle.[59]

Theatre productions, in both the comedy and tragedy genres, paid particular attention to metics. At the high point of the *Oresteia* trilogy, in the solemn finale of the exodos of *Eumenides* (1028–1029), in a sign of the high respect Athenians had for metics, Aeschylus has Athena invite the chorus escorting the *Semnai Theai* to wear purple-dyed garments, such as those ritually worn by metics at the Panathenaea procession. In Aristophanes' plays, metics were an integral part of the polis, yet different from full citizens and in a sense, aliens: for instance he describes metics and citizens as the chaff and the ear of corn,[60] and often imitates in scorn their garbled and mispronounced Greek.[61] In his *Pax*, the protagonist Trygaeus addresses the audience to summon all people to help free the goddess Peace from her prison (296–300) among them farmers, merchants, carpenters, craftsmen, metics as well as people from the islands in the Aegean, details that help us to understand the composition of audiences at the performances of comedies. A few lines later (545–549), it is stated that among the spectators are men involved in industrial production, in all likelihood metics: among them a helm crest maker; a maker of hoes or mattocks, a blacksmith, a maker of swords, a maker of sickles and a spear-maker. The passage obviously emphasizes those who will suffer most from a state of peace, that is, arms manufacturers, while it invites farmers to go back to their farms and start working again as peace allows them to resume their activities in the fields of Attica. In Aristophanes' *Frogs*, the theatre audience is defined twice in opposite ways: as Euripides' spectators, they are muggers and pickpockets, parricides and burglars (771–772), but as the knowledgeable, literate, intellectually sophisticated people watching the play's *agon*, the play's competition between Euripides and Aeschylus (1109–1118).

Despite their size as a proportion of the population, the number of slaves attending the theatre may have been small. Those working in the fields of Attica or in the mines at Laurium often lived far away from Athens and were poorly paid, if at all. Only the most educated of slaves attended, some as pedagogues of children; Theophrastos attests to a shameless man who takes foreigners and even his children and their (slave) tutor to performances without paying.[62]

The relative inclusiveness of its performances made theatre an important tool in the creation of the democratic self-identity of Athenians. Athenians of all classes would have considered their perceptual universe in the theatre as composed of the re-enactment of Greece's mythological past, of the here-and-now presence of divinity, and of the polis' moral, civic and political issues. Theatre performances were the unique forum where the whole community could watch and react to the publicly aired and discussed essential ethical and religious themes of the day. The mass participation of a large portion of the polis to collective rituals of high emotional impact would have the effect of creating a communal feeling of ethical and political cohesion and of bolstering Athenian egalitarian self-identity.

3.3 Women in theatre audiences

Given the prime religious and political role of the *thiasoi* of women in *Bacchae* and the explicit presence of women in the *thiasos* of initiates in *Frogs*, were women present in the audiences? This controversial and much-debated issue is particularly relevant in evaluating the impact of *Bacchae* and *Frogs* upon their audiences. The religious and political content of the plays is centred on the Dionysiac cult (in *Bacchae*), where it is the theme of the choral odes of female maenads, and on the Demetrian cult (in *Frogs*), where the chorus is composed of Eleusinian initiates, both women and men.[63] While the choruses in the plays point at a traditional role of women in mystical rituals, their ethical and political pleas to the audience would be less significant if women had not been among the spectators. In *Bacchae* and *Frogs*, the role of women is both carefully chosen and essential: in *Bacchae* as the maenads who abandon the polis, execute the tyrant and recreate the cohesion of the polis; in *Frogs* they are an explicit part of the god-blessed *thiasos* (165–166) that gives the polis political advice in the parodos (354–371) and in the parabasis (686–737), greets Aeschylus' victory in the agon and escort him to Athens (1528–1533).

Among the evidence of the presence of women in theatre performances two passages of Plato have a particular significance.[64] In *Laws*, Plato writes that if anybody in the polis were to be a judge of public artistic performances, children would give the prize to puppet showmen, older boys to comedy producers, well-educated women, young men and the mass of the public to tragedies,[65] while old men would very likely take most delight in listening to a *rhapsodos* giving a fine recitation of the *Iliad* or the *Odyssey* or of a passage from Hesiod. While it establishes a connection between well educated women and tragedy, which would be unthinkable if women had not been allowed in the theatre, the passage is still based on the idea of the freedom of choice to all, a freedom that may not have reflected reality.

Much clearer is a passage in Plato's *Gorgias*.[66] Plato notes that, in Athens, sacred and wonderful tragic composition (σεμνὴ καὶ θαυμαστὴ ἡ τῆς τραγῳδίας ποίησις), had ceased to be a work destined to educating its audiences and was devolving into the mere gratification of spectators. Poetry in theatre had become a kind of popular harangue addressed to men, women, and children, slave and free alike;[67] Plato's Socrates observes he rather disliked this form of theatre, as it serves only to flatter the audience. Plato then significantly contrasts theatre audiences in Athens to those in other cities, where the audiences are only composed of free men. Other evidence of the presence of women in theatres is admittedly sparse; of note is Plutarch's observation, admittedly written in the second century AD, in a letter to his wife, that her simplicity had won admiration at religious ceremonies, sacrifices, and theatre performances.[68] The much later author of *Vita Aeschyli*[69] mentions miscarriages that happened at the sight of the Erinyes appearing on stage in Aeschylus' *Eumenides*; while this could have been an apocryphal anecdote, it would have had no credibility if women had been officially excluded from theatre performances. A final piece of evidence is Athenaeus' description of the figure of Alcibiades, whose elegance, wealth, and beauty were admired in the theatre not only by men, but also by women.[70]

While arguments such as these for the presence of women in the performances of both tragedies and comedies seem convincing, several scholars have maintained a sceptical position. Perhaps driven by his vision of Athenian democracy, Goldhill for instance puts great emphasis on the function of tragedy in the structure of Athenian democracy as an exclusively male citizen preserve. 'The issues of the play are focused firmly through the male, adult, enfranchised perspective … the Great Dionysia in all sense represents democracy', writes Goldhill.[71] Were theatre audiences a copy of ecclesia meetings? Goldhill thinks so: 'as a civic event, the scene in the theatron would be much closer to the ecclesia than to the Panathenaea'. As Kawalko-Roselli points out, the very theme of the role of women in the polis may well have been 'a bone of contention' on a disputed issue, namely that of the danger to democracy in Athens posed by mass theatre audiences that included women, slaves and metics.[72] The issue is complex and perhaps in need of a radical redefinition of the role of women in Athens' public and private life, mired as it is in our modern views of women's role in society and our preconceptions on Greek history and society, involving what Kawalko-Roselli calls our 'drastic simplification of ancient culture'. In Goldhill's words, 'if citizen women did walk through the streets, sit in the theatre, watch plays, be watched, walk home, much modern writing on the role of women in the *oikos* and polis would need a new emphasis'.[73] I believe that my reading of *Bacchae* and *Frogs* supports Henderson's vision, who writes that, as theatre audiences were more inclusive than ecclesia meetings, 'in theatre, citizen males may have been surrounded, perhaps even outnumbered, by the "others" on whose behalf they ran the polis'.[74]

We may try to put this issue in its Athenian context, as it has been influenced by modern contrasting positions on politics and gender. We shall start by briefly examining the role of women in some aspects of Greek religion such as religious rituals, as it helps to establish the role of women in Greek society, an argument that supports the presence of women in theatre audiences.

Greek civilization was certainly patriarchal, with women's freedom and civic rights strictly limited and political rights non-existent. But society rarely follows a perfectly equilibrated and unilinear model, often using polarities and conflicts as ways to air its tensions, test its limits and reaffirm its identity. The Greek antinomy between male and female, order and disorder, public and private served to make this process function. Religious rituals, and particularly ecstatic and mystical rituals, gave women an exclusive space to develop their identity as a community, thus creating a gender polarity which had a fundamental role in making the polis work.[75]

Women priestesses had an important role in the Eleusinian festival of Demeter and Persephone,[76] with some festivals of the cult of Demeter and Persephone being famously restricted to women.[77] The Demetrian festival, the Thesmophoria, for instance, was reserved for the female community, a prohibition mentioned by Aristophanes in *Thesmophoriazousae* (1148–1154) where the chorus of women celebrating the Thesmophoria festival invokes Demeter and Persephone to come to their precinct, where men are forbidden to watch the initiation rituals. Narrated only in one late source,[78] the Athenian festival of the Haloa was another space for rituals reserved for women. The Haloa festival is of interest as it was a festival jointly dedicated to Demeter, Persephone and Dionysus, coinciding with the tasting of wine that had been kept in storage as well as with the celebration of the myth of Icarius and the adoption of wine making and Dionysiac rituals in Athens.[79] Evidence also points to Athenian women playing a primary part in the rituals of Dionysus, such as their role as maenads, well attested both in Athens and throughout the Greek world.[80] As Euripides notes, women had a prime role in religious rituals as in those of Apollo, those in Dodona, while the initiation rituals of the Fates and of the Revered Goddesses (*Semnai Theai*) were promoted exclusively by women.[81]

Among existing evidence are abundant iconographic evidence attesting to the close and almost exclusive association between Dionysus and women, whether nymphs, maenads or worshippers. Women, Parker writes, 'were the god's [Dionysus'] privileged congregation'.[82] In Carpenter's vast list of images, Dionysus is always accompanied by women, and nearly never by men, and then only by satyrs, i.e. phallic, comical caricatures of men.[83] Some of the so-called Lenaea vases show groups of women drawing wine from large vessels into smaller ones, a scene that could refer either to a scene from the *Choes* day of the Anthesteria Dionysiac festival that celebrated the pitchers (*choes*) that were used to offer wine libations to the gods, or from Dionysiac celebrations at the Lenaea festivals.[84] Dillon analyses them in conjunction with two other vases. One is a red-figure *stamnos* attributed to the Villa Giulia painter, now in Boston,[85] where women dressed in plissé *peploi* draw wine from a crater before a statue of Dionysus. The second is a red-figure cup by the painter Macron, now in Berlin,[86] that shows women, similarly well-dressed but with hair falling on their shoulders, dancing in ecstasy, playing *auloi*, and shaking *thyrsoi* in the company of the god in Bacchic revelry scenes, elements common to Dionysiac scenes in ancient Greek iconography. Whatever ritual or festival the vases refer to, they are evidence of the close and restricted ritual relationship between women and the god Dionysus, and the absence of men from the scenes confirms the exclusivity of that relationship.

One of the rituals of the Anthesteria festival that celebrated the maturing of the new wine and the end of winter was one of the Dionysiac festivals in Athens involved a woman. The male-dominated (and 'remarkably women-unfriendly', as Parker calls it)[87] Anthesteria festival bears some traces of an ancient, special ritual role reserved for a noble Athenian woman, the wife of the king-archon. Accompanied by a group of fourteen mature priestesses she would proceed to the ancient royal palace called the Boukoleion, became engaged to the god in the effigy of an archaic wooden statue, and then had sex with him.[88] It is the only attested ritual enactment of a marriage between a Greek god and a mortal and celebrated the union between Athens and Dionysus.

We have noted that women played a pre-eminent role in both these Athenian mystery cults, that of Dionysus and that of Demeter. One of the characteristics shared by these two cults was the active role of women in the performance of rituals. Women were free to attend the most important moment of Demeter's cult, the initiation rituals at her festival in Eleusis, where women priestesses were among the top clergy.[89] It is thus highly unlikely that women were barred from attending the climax of the Athenian festival of the deity who had a special affinity with them, Dionysus, at the god's own theatre.

To summarize, I would argue that the audiences of drama and comedies in Athens at the end of the fifth century were both socially and gender inclusive, even though the price of theatre tickets excluded the poor. Audiences also comprised sizable numbers of mystical initiates. Women would have also been present. Audiences were not composed of passive spectators; they were an essential, active component of the collective phenomenon of theatre performances and of their success.

4

Mystery Rituals and Theatre Performances

Social and gender polarities in the classic Athenian world can be seen as paradoxical. Only Athenian full-right citizens had the right to attend the meetings of the ecclesia, work as polis officials and man the courts. However, two fundamental institutions admitted everybody, women, metics and slaves influencing the working of the polis: mystical initiation rituals and theatre performances. These institutions were more closely interrelated than we may suppose; mystical rituals have a strong association with theatre performances in most pre-modern cultures. Anthropology scholars have focused their research for some time on the affinity between mystical rituals and theatrical performances. Schechner for instance, an anthropologist and theatre director with a particular interest for Greek tragedy, found that the pattern of theatrical performances is analogous to that of initiation rituals in many world pre-modern cultures. While focusing mainly on the nature of theatrical performances, Schechner notes that both involve the separation of the performers/initiands from their community, where initiands and performers go through rituals of cleansing and preparation, endure training and rehearsals, live a moment of transition/rebirth in a liminal space/time, and are rewarded with a final re-incorporation in the community. The only difference between initiation rituals and dramatic performances, Schechner notes, is that the first changes people permanently, while with the latter the change is only temporary. Performances and rituals share the same pattern, both having the function of transforming the individual's identity while reaffirming the cohesion of the community, its beliefs and its cosmological vision. The effect of performances and of initiation rituals is to transport and transform both performers and audience, initiands and initiates.[1]

It is curious to note that, perhaps as a reaction to the first half of the twentieth century 'Cambridge ritualists' such as Harrison, Murray and Frazer, the notion of theatre performances being performed as religious rituals in Dionysus' theatre by a Dionysiac chorus playing Dionysiac music and performing Dionysiac ritual dances has been overlooked by many classical scholars. Among the few scholars who explore the subject, Sourvinou-Inwood for instance rightly focuses on the issue of modern reading of ancient perception of theatre performances as modern readers are mired in modern 'rational' perceptual filters, a perspective vitiated by the traditional 'rationalistic' reading of Aristotle's *Poetica*.[2] Scholars such as Seaford[3] and Kowalzig[4] have correctly examined the subject in the wider context of the general theme of the theatrical chorus as an expression of the religious and political collective essence of the polis, as well as the role of aetiological myths in tragedy and how it contributes to the building of self-identity of the Greek poleis, but have not fully developed the application of their theories to a concrete case such as the one represented in 405 by *Bacchae* and *Frogs*. In her work on emotional and cognitional audience response in classical drama as applied to Aristophanes' *Frogs*, Lada-Richards examines this theme, acknowledges the work of Schechner; however, she mentions it only as a preamble to her main argument, that the central figure of Dionysus in the play is allegorically undergoing an initiation ritual, an interpretation of the structure of the play that I find ultimately unconvincing.[5]

4.1 Theatre and poetic inspiration

The evidence we shall examine confirms that for the Athenians the participation in theatre performances was akin to an act of collective worship. It was a ritual in which the divine would interact with each of the performance's constituents, the author, the chorus, the actors and the audience, and in which each constituent interacts with each other. In this context, it is significant that in the authors we shall consider, the emotional experience of spectators of public performance is expressed in terms that echo the experience of mystical initiation.

We shall firstly examine Gorgias' famous fragment dedicated to the power of human language in his *Encomium of Helen*. In his peroration in favour of mythological Helen, victim of the powers of Paris' seductive language, Gorgias interestingly focuses on the power of public poetry readings over listeners owing to its supernatural power (9–10). The element emphasized by Gorgias is the power of music as a psychotropic medium. All poetry, writes Gorgias, is a speech in rhythm (λόγος ἔχων μέτρον); music and words cause in listeners the same fearful shuddering (φρίκη περίφοβος), tearful pity (ἔλεος πολύδακρυς), and a feeling of yearning and longing for something that is not there (πόθος φιλοπενθής)[6] as people empathize with the good fortunes and catastrophes of the actors on stage. Compassion and longing can be transformed by the power of songs, as divinely inspired songs (αἱ ἔνθεοι ἐπωιδαί) are bearers of pleasure (ἐπαγωγοὶ ἡδονῆς) and banishers of pain (ἀπαγωγοὶ λύπης).

The passage establishes the supernatural powers of poetry and music as both inspiring fear and compassion and curing them. Some notes are necessary on some of the terms Gorgias uses. The term 'shuddering' (φρίκη) has religious connotations as it marks the awe, the shivering fear felt in the presence of the divine, as was the case of Miltiades facing Demeter's theophany in her sanctuary on the island of Paros (see 6.3). With its cognate verb φρίττειν it is often used to define the initiand's reaction to initiation rituals,[7] typically defining the thrill and terror of numinous or supernatural sights in Greek literature.[8] The ἐπωιδαί are ἔνθεοι, 'full of god', 'god-inspired', 'god-possessed', a term we shall also encounter in Plato's definition of poetry further in this section,[9] while the terms φόβος and ἔλεος are also significantly defined as the negative emotions that drama creates in their audiences, as in Aristotle's famous definition of tragedy in *Poetica*.[10]

Plato expands this concept into a 'strikingly new theory',[11] wider and more radical than his previous ones. According to Diogenes Laërtius, before banning poets and tragedians from his ideal polis in his *Republic* (595a–b), Plato had in his youth written 'poems, first dithyrambs, afterwards lyric poems and tragedies'[12] and had therefore experience of creating and performing poetry and drama for a public as well as of evaluating the public's reaction. In *Ion*, a dialogue between Socrates and Ion, a celebrated rhapsodist, on the subject of artistic inspiration, Plato's thoughts on the power of poetry and music run along similar lines to Gorgias. Plato stresses Gorgias' concepts and makes the interaction between divinity, poets' inspiration, actors, *mousike* and their audience more explicit and closely interrelated. The interaction is compared to an electromagnetic attraction as happens in nature to a certain type of mineral, such as magnets. Similar to Gorgias, Plato has Socrates define it as a divine power (θεία δὲ δύναμις) that has the power to attract iron rings (ἡ λίθος ... αὐτοὺς τοὺς δακτυλίους ἄγει τοὺς σιδηροῦς) and gives them the power to attract other rings in his exploration of the reason for Ion's excellence in his art as *rhapsodos*. In the same way, the Muse makes poets divinely inspired (ἐνθέους ποιεῖ), this inspiration attracting and being attracted by others in an interconnected divine-inspired magnetic chain composed of the spectator (ὁ θεατής), the *rhapsodos*, the theatre actor (ῥαψῳδὸς καὶ ὑποκριτής), and a chain of choral performers and masters and under-masters (ὁρμαθός χορευτῶν καὶ διδασκάλων καὶ ὑποδιδασκάλων).[13] For Plato, just as for Gorgias, the good epic or lyric poets are not defined by their technical skills, but because they are inspired and possessed by divinity (οὐκ ἐκ τέχνης ἀλλ' ἔνθεοι ὄντες καὶ κατεχόμενοι) as a Corybant or a maenad.[14] As the maenads draw honey and milk from rivers, so do poets as they bring to their audiences the honey they cull from springs like bees in Muses' gardens and glades, possibly a reference to Euripides' *Bacchae*.[15] The poetry of rhapsodists inspire in their spectators (θεωμένοι) an extraordinary passion (ἔκπληξις), as the rhapsodists are out of their senses and possessed by divinity (ἡ ψυχὴ ἐνθουσιάζουσα).[16]

A few notes on the expressions Plato uses are needed here. The use of the terms actor (ὑποκριτής), member of the chorus (χορευτής) and producer, trainer (διδάσκαλος) are terms that belong to the organization of theatrical performances and suggest that Plato associated the divine magnetic ring beyond Ion's rhapsodies applying it to the theatrical performing arts in general, such as dithyrambs and the performance of tragedy and comedy.[17] The term extraordinary passion (ἔκπληξις) is worthy of some exploration of its semantic field, as it is often associated with a kind of mystical rapture. In the *agon* of *Frogs* for instance, the character of Euripides contrasts his own poetic style with that of Aeschylus: 'I did not use pretentious expressions, nor did I tear my spectators from their reason, nor did I drive them out of their senses' (οὐδ' ἐξέπληττον αὐτούς). In his *Symposium*, Plato has Alcibiades praise the extraordinary power of Socrates' speech, comparing him to Marsyas, the legendary player of the *aulos*, Dionysus' spellbinding musical pipes, that leave its listeners astounded and entranced (ἐκπεπληγμένοι καὶ κατεχόμεθα), as if possessed by a Corybantic ecstasis.[18] In *Phaedrus*, Plato associates 'ἔκπληξις' with the ecstasy produced by Dionysiac rituals. Describing his reaction to Phaedrus' speech Socrates says: 'I was enraptured (ἐκπλαγῆναι) and followed you and joined you in your Dionysiac frenzy (ἑπόμενος συνεβάκχευσα μετὰ σοῦ τῆς θείας κεφαλῆς)'.[19] The association of 'ἔκπληξις' with initiation rituals is made explicit in the fourth-century orator Demetrius. While discussing allegories in literature, which are more terror-inspiring (φοβερώτεροι) than plain discourse, Demetrius notes that this is why the mysteries are expressed in allegories, in order to inspire divine-inspired passion and the divine shuddering that we noted in Gorgias (πρὸς ἔκπληξιν καὶ φρίκην), such the feelings aroused by darkness and night (ὥσπερ ἐν σκότῳ καὶ νυκτί).[20]

4.2 Music and divinity

There is one other element that theatre performances have in common with initiation rituals and religious festivals: the performing arts. We unfortunately know very little about music, singing and dancing in Greek theatre, and the little evidence we have comes from ancient texts and iconography. As was the case with the phenomenon of mystical initiation, the role played by performing arts in religious rituals and in theatre has been extensively studied in ethological terms in pre-modern world cultures, but nearly ignored in Greek classical culture.[21] We shall start by a brief exploration of some aspects of the Athenian perception of music.

The association of music, its rhythm and harmony, to divine inspiration and its psychological impact on spectators is central to the way the Athenians recognized the phenomenon of poetic performances. This theme is of some importance in understanding theatre productions in Athens, but despite its significance, it has been mostly neglected by classical scholars.[22] But ancient authors are more explicit, however. The Greeks used two terms related to our notion of music: '*mousike*' (μουσική) is a term that encompasses all the arts inspired by the Muses, but especially poetry sung to music and dancing, and 'tune, melody' (μέλος), that designates instrumental music accompanying sung poetry, choral dances and the instrumental interludes that came between choral strophes. In *Frogs*, Aristophanes for instance has Euripides exclaim that speech and poetry accompanied by music are the sinews of tragedy (τἄπη, τὰ μέλη, τὰ νεῦρα τῆς τραγῳδίας),²³ while Plato defines poetry sung to music (τὸ μέλος) as composed by speech, harmony and rhythm (ἐκ τριῶν ἐστιν συγκείμενον, λόγου τε καὶ ἁρμονίας καὶ ῥυθμοῦ).²⁴ For Isocrates for instance, the decisive component of poetry is music, powerful beyond verbal expression: 'though poets may be deficient in style and thoughts, yet by the very spell of their rhythm and harmony they bewitch their listeners'.²⁵ Plato defines tragedy as the artistic genre most capable of bewitching (ψυχαγωγικώτατον) its audience.²⁶ Plato and Isocrates use the same term for bewitch (ψυχαγωγέω), 'to lead or attract the souls of the living, win over, persuade, allure' (LSJ). The term is an early aknowledgement of the psychological impact of music, that, together with the visuality of choral singing and dancing, would have helped the spectators of a tragedy to feel detached from their day-to-day life and enter into a new frame of mind.

Rhythm was an essential element of Greek poetry and music, and the Greek conception of it was probably similar to ours, as some scholars argue.²⁷ In ethnological terms, the rhythmical sound of drums and chanting affects the central nervous system and causes both performers and listeners to behave unusually and even to fall into a trance-like state.²⁸ The Greeks associated the influence of rhythmical music with divine possession, and particularly with Dionysiac mystical rituals.²⁹ In Plato's vision, where music accompanies public performances of poetry in *Ion*, lyric singing, *melos*, is explicitly associated with ecstatic rituals. When lyric poets (οἱ μελοποιοί) enter into the world of harmony and rhythm (εἰς τὴν ἁρμονίαν καὶ εἰς τὸν ῥυθμόν), in whatever poetic genres they may express themselves: the one in dithyrambs, another in eulogies, another in songs accompanied by dancing, another in epics, another in iambic poems. They all abandon their senses as Corybantes, and revel in the frenzy of Dionysus, possessed by the god (βακχεύουσι καὶ κατεχόμενοι).³⁰ The second-century author Lucian of Samosata calls the rhythmic nature of music and dancing an important and inspiring element in mystical initiation rituals, a passage that is worth quoting in full.

> ... not a single ancient mystery-cult can be found that is without dancing, since they were established, of course, by Orpheus and Musaeus, the best dancers of that time, who included it in their prescriptions as something exceptionally beautiful to be initiated with rhythm and dancing (σὺν ῥυθμῷ καὶ ὀρχήσει μυεῖσθαι).³¹

Music, Aristotle notes in the Politica, has the power to make souls possessed by divinity (ποιεῖ τὰς ψυχὰς ἐνθουσιαστικάς) particularly when it is composed in the Phrygian mode, a Dionysiac musical mode characterized, particularly when played by the *aulos*, by causing mystical frenzy (ὀργιαστικὰ) and wild excitement (παθητικά). Music is also a means of catharsis, of relaxing tensions and giving rest (πρὸς διαγωγὴν πρὸς ἄνεσίν τε καὶ πρὸς τὴν τῆς συντονίας ἀνάπαυσιν), a concept he famously develops in Poetica. Music is capable of raising compassion, fear and yet divine possession (ἔλεος καὶ φόβος, ἔτι δ' ἐνθουσιασμός), of producing catharsis and lightening souls from their burdens (κάθαρσιν καὶ κουφίζεσθαι).[32]

Music and rhythm had an impact on modes of religiosity. The association of music with mystery rituals is particularly clear in a passage of the late first-century author Strabo. Strabo has *mousike*, which he defines as choral dancing (ὄρχησις) as well as rhythm and melody (ῥυθμὸν καὶ μέλος), help in turning the minds away from their day-to-day occupations and instead to the divine (τὸ θεῖον), often causing participants to enter divine possession (ἐνθουσιασμός) and connecting them to divinity (τὸ θεῖον συνάπτει) by the delight it provides and by its artistic beauty. Human beings act most like the gods when they are doing good deeds for others, and when they are happy and favoured by divinity (ὅταν εὐδαιμονῶσι); such happiness consists of rejoicing, celebrating festivals, pursuing philosophy, and engaging in *mousike*.[33]

Aristotle's famous definition of the nature of tragedy in *Poetica* as composed by music and by the recitation of verses in metre is key to comprehend the relationship between *mousike*, Athenian religious feelings, and theatre performances in the perception of his contemporaries. The passage has famously produced a wide range of conflicting interpretations[34] and is worth quoting in full (my translation).

> Tragedy is, then, the artistic representation (μίμησις) of an event that has gravity, completeness and greatness (πράξεως σπουδαίας καὶ τελείας μέγεθος ἐχούσης), by means of a narrative structure composed of several different elements (ἡδυσμένῳ λόγῳ), each used separately in the different parts of the play . . . and by inspiring compassion and terror (*in the audience*) (δι' ἐλέου καὶ φόβου) as it cleanses it from these and similar emotions (περαίνουσα τὴν τῶν τοιούτων παθημάτων κάθαρσιν). By 'narrative structure in which several different elements are parts', I mean the dramatic

expression created by rhythm and tune (ῥυθμὸν καὶ ἁρμονίαν), and by 'used separately' I mean that some effects are produced by verse alone (διὰ μέτρων μόνον) and some again by poetry sung to music (διὰ μέλους)... the essential element of a tragedy (πρῶτον ... μόριον) is its spectacular effect (ὁ τῆς ὄψεως κόσμος) and, besides that, its creation of poetry sung to music as well as speech (μελοποιία καὶ λέξις). For these are the means of the artistic representation. By 'speech' I mean here the metrical arrangement of words; and by 'poetry sung to music' I use the full, obvious sense of the word.[35]

For Aristotle, music is thus an integral element of tragedy's impact on the audience. It is composed of different elements (ἡδυσμένος). This is an important term that I believe has been mostly misread by scholars. The term that I translate as 'composed of several different elements' (LSJ), has led commentators to misinterpret the passage. Far from being, for instance, a mere 'ornament' (Fyfe)[36] and 'embellishment' (Halliwell),[37] I argue that the term expresses a closer connection between music and tragedy than is apparent.[38] The semantic field of the term 'make pleasant' (ἡδύνω) has stronger connotations in describing the association between musical and non-musical parts of tragedy in ancient Greek than it does for modern readers. The metaphor belongs to the world of Greek food and cooking.[39] Greek base food (σῖτος) was rough and tasteless: mostly unsalted gruels of coarse ground grains such as barley or wheat, akin to English porridge and Italian polenta, and/or bread, mostly made of barley. It would have been virtually inedible without an accompanying serving of some sort that made the meal pleasant (ἡδύς) to the palate, some sort of relish (ὄψον): salt, olives, fish, cooked vegetables, as essential part of a meal as bread (σῖτος) and wine.[40] Thus, far from being an accessory to action and dialogue, Aristotle implies that the music and songs performed by the dancing chorus and by the music players were separate but integral components of tragedy, without which the mere action and dialogue of actors would have been of little interest and attraction. Plutarch, writing on the topic of the need to accompany music with sung words in *symposia*, used the same metaphor: 'We should regard melody and rhythm as a relish added to the lyrics (τὸ δὲ μέλος καὶ τὸν ῥυθμὸν ὥσπερ ὄψον ἐπὶ τῷ λόγῳ) rather than using or prizing them for their own sake'.[41]

In a way that is revelatory of the ancient perception of the connection between theatre and mystery cults, the first century AD orator Dio Chrysostomus describes a mystery initiation where the initiand would watch mystical sights (μυστικὰ θεάματα) and listen to mystical voices in an alternation of light and darkness (σκότους τε καὶ φωτός). In the ritual of the *thronosis*, the initiands would sit and those already initiated would sing and dance round and round them. Similarly, Dio says, in nature immortal gods initiate mortal men, and both in sunlight and under the stars they dance around them forever. There, the whole initiation spectacle is led by a leader of the choir who directs a chorus composed of the entire heaven and the whole universe.[42]

4.3 Catharsis and theatre reception

The notion of catharsis in the passage of Aristotle's *Poetica* we are examining needs some discussion here.[43] The semantic field of the term is vast and may have been chosen by Aristotle because of 'its range and reference to a wide area of psycho-physical responses'.[44] The meaning of the term concerns primarily ritual and religious cleansing.[45] Aristotle uses it in the sense of purification from pollution in a religious ritual: the term appears only twice in *Poetica*, the first in the passage we are examining, and the second in his mentioning Orestes' ritual cleansing from the pollution caused by the slaying of his mother,[46] (a term Aeschylus uses for the same episode).[47] Catharsis is connected with mystical initiation on one side and with civic virtues on the other. For instance, the term is used to describe the collective purification rituals Epimenides made the polis of Athens go through to vanquish the polis' pollution (*agos*).[48] It also appears in the parodos of *Bacchae* (73–77) linked to the Dionysiac cult, where the chorus of Asian maenads sings a blessing to the initiate, a person who has a pure lifestyle (βιοτὰν ἁγιστεύει) and performs Bacchic rituals with holy purifications (ὁσίοις καθαρμοῖσιν), two concepts that are at the centre of the play's theme of religious purity and civic virtue. In Plato's passage in *Phaedo* that we examined for instance,[49] the mystical eschatological link between catharsis, initiation, civic virtues and a blissful afterlife is explicit: catharsis consists of separating the soul from the body, and Plato associates it with eminently civic virtues, such as self-restraint, respect for justice and courage.[50] In Plato, the lack of catharsis defines the fate of the dead: whoever goes uninitiated and unsanctified to the other world will lie in the mire. Only he who arrives there purified and initiated (ὁ δὲ κεκαθαρμένος τε καὶ τετελεσμένος) will dwell with the gods. Plato thus directly associates catharsis with the concept of truth and with those mystical and civic values, self-restraint, obedience to the laws, valour and common sense that are a way of cleansing one's soul – the religious and civic virtues that characterize the association between the initiate, divinity and his community.

Jungian analysts have covered the subject of catharsis in ways that illuminate the complex interrelationship between theatre performers and audience. Saban, for example, interestingly focuses on the theatrical aspect of psychotherapy and on theatre's therapeutic/cathartic function. Jung defines theatre as a 'psychotherapeutic institute where complexes are staged', and Saban goes further in defining the virtual world of the theatrical event as a world of dynamic complex and reciprocal relationships between audience and actor, actor and role, actor and actor. In the theatrical world the ego engages in mutual dramatic and dialogical relations with internal others, and by re-enacting the dramas each partner is re-acquainted with parts of itself that have split-off, been forgotten or never even met.[51]

I argue that catharsis, psychotherapy and initiation share a similar therapeutic role for individuals and the community. In his famous definition of tragedy's impact on its audience Aristotle defines a process not unlike that of that of mystical initiation we noted in Plutarch's fragment 178. Echoing Gorgias' definition of the influence of poetry, Aristotle notes that it is by having the audience experiencing a strong empathic compassion with the emotions of the characters on stage and with the terror they inspire that tragedy accomplishes its goal: to free the spectators from these emotions. As Segal correctly points out,

> Greek tragedies often direct the emotional response of the audience towards a resolution in a spirit of community and continuity ... Aristotle may have felt the affinity between that the emotions of group participation in rituals and the emotions of an audience gripped by the painful events in a tragedy.[52]

One of the effects of this relief is that it created a sense of cohesion and communality among the spectators who shared the same feelings and sentiments.

To summarize, Gorgias' definition of the magic power of public readings of poetry accompanied by music, Plato's divine magnet metaphor in *Ion* and

Aristotle's definition of theatre performances as catharsis are powerful notions that help us to reconstruct what the Athenians felt as the impact of drama and comedy on audiences. Following Plato's cue, we may then be tempted to compare the experience of the individual spectator of drama, part of a community of spectators in a magnetic chain of reactions, sentiments and feelings, to the single initiands undergoing the intense individual and collective experience of initiation in the presence of hundreds of *epoptai*.

4.4 Ecstasy and the *aulos*

According to ancient authors, the psychological effect of music and *mousike* played to a public audience is generally associated with their capacity to influence the mood of the spectators and to enrapture them into a kind of stupor, inducing watchers into something akin to what ethnomusicologists call an 'altered state of consciousness', or define as 'trance music'.[53] In the ancient Greek world, altered states of consciousness may well have been a part of the experience of theatre performers and audiences as well as that of participants in initiation rituals. Both rituals used music, singing and dancing as psychological tools to enthral their audiences, initiands and spectators and to bring them to a state of rapture.

In the Greek context, this state was called in various ways that are worth examining. The term ecstasy (ἔκστασις) means literally 'to be outside oneself', hence 'trance, entrancement' (LSJ). It was a state associated with mystical and ecstatic rituals, which were particularly connected to the cult of Dionysus. Far from being marginal ritual acts, such performances were at the heart of the functioning of the Athenian polis. The anthropologist Bourguignon, for instance, notes that in most world cultures the institutionalized altered states of consciousness in religious rituals have a significant impact on the functioning of society and in particular by functioning as mediators or initiators of social and cultural change. It is not a marginal phenomenon: Bourguignon states that in a sample of 488 world societies at the time of his writing, 90 per cent have culturally patterned forms of altered states of consciousness.[54] The ethnologist Whitehouse would define these theatrical performances as examples of 'imagistic' mode of religious rituals. The intensity of the audience's theatrical experience would have been amplified by their rarity and concentration in a short lapse of time, by their rich choreography, imagery, songs and dances and in some cases, such as in Aeschylus' *Oresteia*, *Bacchae* and *Frogs*, by the allusions to, and enactment of, mystical rituals. Under the influence of rhythmical music and chanting, the mystical initiates among performers and spectators may have experienced moments of 'flash-bulb memory', experiencing vividly the panoply of emotions they had felt during initiation rituals.

The principal musical instrument associated with ecstasy, the cult of Dionysus and with theatre performances was the *aulos*. The *aulos* is still frequently translated as 'flute': 'a deplorable habit of literary scholars', notes M.L. West.[55] Unlike the flute, the *aulos* is in fact a reed instrument usually composed of two cane pipes and its sound is totally different from the suave and mellow tone of flutes.[56] Instead it is shrill, sharp, and high in volume, amplified by a second pipe that may have emitted a single and continuous accompanying low note like a drone or played in unison with the first pipe.[57] Its sound is described by Pindar, in Pythian 12, as a many-toned melody, a loud wailing sound (πάμφωνον μέλος ... ἐρικλάγκταν γόον). One of the earliest reed instruments to be created,[58] variants of the *aulos* are still played today. Some use bags of hide to pump air into the instrument such as Scottish bagpipes, some, like the Sardinian *launeddas*, are probably a direct descendent of the ancient Greek double *aulos* (*diaulos*) instrument, having three cane pipes played by keeping the cheeks constantly filled with air to allow the instrument to be played without pauses. It is often accompanied by tambourines and castanets,[59] as they were in ancient Greece. I suspect that the music played with it in Athens may have been rather similar to that of the *launeddas*: highly rhythmic, insistent, resonant and hypnotic, playing infinite variants of a single musical theme in a fast succession of notes, and accompanied by the pulsing, quick beat of tambourines, bells and castanets – instruments fit to express extreme emotions.[60]

In Athens, the *aulos* was considered a foreign musical instrument, alien to the polis' values of the sacredness of the human mouth, voice and speech, alien to civic and rational behaviour. Its players were outsiders, often slave girls and, in Euripides' day, its playing was taken up by sophisticated avant-garde intellectuals such as Alcibiades, Critias and Callias.[61] It was Dionysus' instrument, opening the mind and body of listeners to the god's ecstasy, as alien to the polis as the god was thought to be, but yet an integral part of its culture.[62]

In the performances of tragedy, music was played by one or more *aulos* players who stood amidst the members of the chorus in the orchestra and played while the chorus danced, also accompanying the sung lyrics of the actors. In Sophocles' *Trachiniae*, the chorus of women from Trachis exult in joy at the news of Heracles' return, in a particularly vivid description of dancing to the tune of the *aulos*. The chorus' jubilation starts in a collected way, with a traditional appeal to Apollo, Artemis and the nymphs expressed as an Apollonian paean. Then the mood of the chorus suddenly changes with the abrupt burst of sound from the *aulos*, a Dionysiac gust of ecstatic energy. The jubilation turns to ecstatic dancing as the chorus leader is lifted into the air in dance by the *aulos*, an instrument invoked as 'tyrant of my heart' (ὦ τύραννε τᾶς ἐμᾶς φρενός).[63] The hypnotic power of the *aulos* is also the subject of an interesting passage of Plutarch.[64] There an *aulos* player's performing before a symposium, Plutarch narrates, has his audience so entranced (καταυλεῖν καὶ ἀκολασταίνειν) with the music of his instrument that they leapt from their seats and joined the player's dance, as music can inebriate more effectively than any wine. The author then quotes Pindar's experience of being so galvanized in dancing by the lovely tune of *auloi*, that he felt like a dolphin dancing in the deep sea.[65]

When addressing the issue of the role of the music played on the *aulos*, Plato associates Dionysiac *aulos* music with mystical initiation rituals. In the *Symposium*, Plato discusses the music of the *aulos*, and its powerful impact on the listener. Whether played by an excellent artist or by the humblest performer, it bewitches (ἐκήλει) men, and has no equal in being able to cause divine possession. By the divinity that is in the *aulos*, it can reveal who are most in need of the deities and their initiation rituals (τῶν θεῶν καὶ τελετῶν δεομένοι).[66] In his discussion in *Politics* of whether *mousike* should be part of the educational curricula of young people, Aristotle interestingly starts by associating Dionysiac rituals with the liberating power of music, quoting the second stasimon of Euripides' *Bacchae*, where the chorus invokes Purity, queen of the gods (Ὁσία πότνα θεῶν) to come to the defense of Dionysus, the deity who joins in choral dances, laughs with the *aulos* and brings an end to cares (ἀναπαῦσαί μερίμνας) with his wine.[67] Aristotle too explicitly connects the Phrygian musical mode with the *aulos*, the dithyramb and Dionysiac revelry and dancing (βακχεία καὶ πᾶσα ἡ τοιαύτη κίνησις), and for this reason excludes the playing of the *aulos* from the education of children.[68]

4.5 Dance, chorus and audience

Scholars have been debating the role of the chorus in tragedy for years, but only relatively recently has 'the chorus begun to be given its due recognition not only at the centre of any attempt to understand drama in its original context but as a major form of Greek cultural, social and religious life'.[69] *Choraea*, 'the practice of dancing and singing as a social collective to the words and music of a poet', was the fundamental tool through which the community shaped its ethical, religious and political principles.[70] While the practice of choral dancing and singing was associated in other parts of Greece with various deities, in Athens it was principally associated with the cult of Dionysus.[71] Choral performances in tragedy, comedy and dithyrambs were Dionysiac religious rituals at the apex of the festival of the Athenian festival of the god.

The chorus had a pivotal role in the dramatic construction of the play and in the process of self-definition of the polis through its religious, emotional and artistic impact on the audience.[72] As already noted, Aristotle affirms the unity of the components of a tragic performance and the primary importance of the role of the chorus, regarding it as important as that of the actors; it was an integral part of the whole performance and of the action,[73] a role that is at the same time religious and dramatic, political and fictional. The interaction between the chorus and the audience connects the polis and the deity, thus encompassing the realm of politics, religion and dramatic fiction. One well-known example may suffice to define the complex role of the chorus. In a highly dramatic choral song in Sophocles' *Oedipus Tyrannus*, the chorus expresses its religious and performing role in its anguished question after Jocasta's denial of the veracity of Apollo's oracles. If oracles are untrue, if devotion for divinity ceases, if injustice rules, why should I dance? (τί δεῖ με χορεύειν;) (895): the world of divinity is dead (ἔρρει δὲ τὰ θεῖα) (910).[74] If the actors on stage pronounce an oracle untrue, the notion of divinity crumbles, not only on stage, but in the real world. Therefore, both the stage and the real role of the chorus ends. The chorus' dancing and singing in the theatre of Dionysus has no meaning anymore.

While the connection between the theatrical role of the choruses and the polis has been widely explored, the specific political nature of the connection has mostly escaped the attention of scholars, such as Kowalzig, who, in her

2007 works on choral music and dancing in Greek culture,[75] explores in detail the connection between myth and communal rituals, choral music and Greek society, religion and choral performance, and aetiology and ritual, but somehow overlooks the socio/political function of the chorus. On the other hand, Seaford in his 2013 work on the subject of politics, dancing and singing of the mystical chorus,[76] convincingly argues that choral activity was connected on the one hand with the arousal of ecstasy and the experience of cosmic interconnection and, on the other, with its expression of a communal political action; Seaford defines this as a contrast between autocratic individuals and the solidarity and cohesion of the chorus, a pattern we shall observe in *Bacchae*. Seaford rightly establishes an association between public choral performances, initiates-only ritual choruses and dithyrambs, examining briefly the possibility that the chorus may have been a 'bridge between mystical secrecy and public display'.[77] However, he does not explore the way in which the chorus in *Bacchae* and *Frogs* may be seen as constituting, along with the audience, a single body politic, with mystical values forming a common, civic and religious discourse between the chorus, the audience and the polis.

How representative of the polis' social composition were choruses? At the Great Dionysia, the membership of tragic choruses and the role of *choregoi*, the wealthy individuals who financed, trained and lead the chorus, was restricted to Athenian adult citizens, although the membership of the choruses was probably widened at the Lenaea to include boys and metics. Some 1,200 chorus members,[78] males under thirty years of age,[79] were chosen among the polis' tribes (φυλαί) to man dithyrambs' choruses,[80] but we have little or no their composition or their representativity.[81] In view of the number of members the choruses needed each year, it seems unlikely that they would have been chosen exclusively among aristocratic, wealthy families, but would have included numbers who came from families of the demos, as the 'Old Oligarch' notes.[82]

The education of Athenian men and boys in choruses made them trained and cultured, as Plato observes,[83] and created one of the bases of the polis cohesion.[84] Their training lasted months, from the appointment of the *choregos* by the archon *eponymos* during the summer to the performances in the following winter-spring. The *choregos* was chosen amongst the wealthiest men in Athens; he housed the members in a schoolroom, sometimes in a part of his own house, feasted them with the choicest foods, hired instructors for voice and dance training, paid them or their families a salary, and provided them with rich costumes for the performance during what may have amounted to well-organized male bonding camp under the auspices their tribe.[85] The length and intensity of their physical and artistic training suggests that the performance of the choruses' dancing and singing was probably more complex than we may imagine. Synchronized choreography and singing executed by dozens of players, led by the chorus' leader, the *coryphaeus*,[86] suggest it was like a highly skilled pantomime involving quasi-acrobatic acts. These actions provide evidence of the choruses offering a highly sophisticated and expressive spectacle, 'in a fluid succession of emblematic, stylised poses'.[87]

As Golder convincingly argues, tragic dancing evolved from perhaps a form similar to the archaic crane-dance, the *geranos* dance, similar to its description in Homer and to the modern *syrtos*, to a form that had been transformed by the mid fifth-century into a form of tragic acting, where 'the choreography was coeval and coextensive with a particular postural and gestural style of tragic acting'.[88] Through the use of poses (σχῆματα), and of gestures of arms and hands (χειρονομία), chorus members were able to vividly impersonate complex mythical figures and passions.[89] Particularly in the mix of mystical, ethical and political themes expressed in *Bacchae* and *Frogs* by the choruses, the spectacle, what Aristotle calls the *opsis*, must have been a remarkable experience. We unfortunately can only rely on the evidence provided by the copious iconography to imagine the dance movements and poses of the *thiasoi*/choruses of maenads and initiates in *Bacchae* and *Frogs*, a field where I believe the work of Lawler still stands alone.[90] The spectacle may well have been inspired by Dionysiac maenads and satyrs dancing which we can observe in the iconography: the dancers are enthralled, making wild movements with their bodies, often jumping high from the dancing floor, their faces facing the sky or the soil in ecstatic elation and concentration, their loose hair flowing in the air, their *chitons* flowing freely around their bodies,[91] banging their tambourines or castanets to the rhythm of an *aulos* and brandishing the ritual Dionysian staff, a *thyrsus*.[92]

The impact of the plays on their audiences would have been intense. The audience, far from being a motley crowd of unconnected individuals passively watching these theatrical performances, may have been largely composed of people who had a direct experience of collective dancing, singing and playing music, a group of people, 'a high proportion of which would also have joined *en masse* to make crucial decisions in assembly and lawcourts'[93] and who shared the same intellectual sophistication of Aristophanes' audiences.[94] This implies that a part of the audiences would have been familiar with the experience of choral performance: as Revermann notes, the impact of drama, comedy and dithyrambs on audiences can only be appreciated on the basis of the fact that some spectators had been performers themselves:

> As anyone who has ever acted himself or herself will confirm, this experience fundamentally shapes how theatre is viewed, perceived, and eventually evaluated as a spectator ... Performing in the orchestra provides a feel for ... the dynamics of actor-audience interaction and the difficulties of winning and sustaining the interest of large audiences.[95]

Among the spectators there would have been a sizable number of Dionysiac and Eleusinian initiates that may have influenced the whole audience in their participation to mystical rituals enacted on the stage. The chorus would then involve the audience in an integrated performance, one in which the choral performance in the orchestra merges with the performance of religious rituals in the action.[96] Thousands of spectators would then share the same reactions in their deepest emotional ramifications, creating what Wiles calls 'an osmosis passing through the bodies of the spectators'.[97] Athenian audiences may therefore be thought of as representing an influential group of people in the polis, a medium between theatre performances and public opinion, between drama and the political decisions in the ecclesia.

In summary, the affinity between mystical rituals and theatre performances ran deeper than we may imagine. Its pivot was the chorus, which personified the civic and mystical values through which the polis of Athens identified itself. The synchronicity, order and discipline we noted in the ancient definition of the world of initiates applies to the chorus' movements on the stage. Through this medium, the fundamental harmony of religious fervour and ethical and civic values was re-enacted before the community, a factor that will be the focus of my interpretation of the religious and political content of *Bacchae* and *Frogs*.

5

The Polis, Mystery Cults and Civic Ideology

The works that I take to best represent the establishment of the Eleusinian cult, the *Homeric Hymn to Demeter*, and that best representing the early development of the Athenian civic ideology, Aeschylus' *Oresteia*, express the mystical and political values that permeated Athenian political consciousness. I will argue that mystery cults came to be an integral part of the way the polis defined itself as an ideally pious, egalitarian and democratic community ruled by law.

5.1 Political implications of the *Homeric Hymn to Demeter*

Ethical and civic themes animate the *Homeric Hymn to Demeter* (the '*Hymn*'), a text probably written between the middle of the seventh century and the middle of the sixth century,[1] which narrates the establishment of the mystical rituals of Demeter in Eleusis by the goddess herself. It is the earliest textual evidence of the Eleusinian mystery cult and connects diverse elements in the aetiological social and political logic of the polis, elements that clarify the influence of mystery cults on the development of the polis which we shall find developed later in Aeschylus' *Oresteia* and in *Bacchae* and *Frogs*.

The *Hymn* recounts the tale of Demeter, goddess of vegetation and agriculture, and of her daughter, Persephone. One day Persephone, a young girl, was abducted by Hades, Zeus' brother, the lord of the Underworld, while picking flowers in a remote field with the young daughters of Ocean, far from her mother. Demeter grieved when she heard the news and left her abode with the gods in her anger with Zeus, who she knew had given her daughter to Hades. Demeter searched the earth and sea for her daughter for a long while, until she came to Eleusis, disguised as an old woman, where the young daughters of Celeus, the ruler of the city, brought her to the palace of Celeus' wife Metanira, who had a baby of nursing age. Under the care of his divine nurse, the baby thrived extraordinarily until Metanira, frightened at the magic methods of the nurse, withdrew the child from her care. Demeter, enraged, revealed her divine status and ordered all the people of Eleusis to build her a temple where she could teach the people her rituals. Demeter, still grieving for Persephone, caused a widespread famine that threatened the survival of mankind. Zeus then sent Hermes to persuade Hades to let Persephone go, which he did. Zeus then decreed that Persephone must spend a third of the year underground, during which time Demeter's grief will freeze the world. But for the rest of the year, Persephone may live with the gods on Mount Olympus, and the earth will spring to life again. Demeter agreed and taught the rulers of Eleusis her secret mystery rituals which give happiness to the initiates in their life and in the afterlife.

While focusing exclusively on the polis of Eleusis and not mentioning Athens, an omission that can be assumed as deliberate,[2] the *Hymn* binds together several fundamental religious and political elements about the way Athenians conceived their community.[3] While Burkert defines Greek religion as having 'no founding figures and no documents of revelation, no organisation of priests and no monastic orders,'[4] this does not seem to apply to the Eleusis rituals and to the *Hymn*, a document perhaps unique in the main body of Greek religion; it establishes the aetiology of an eschatological cult, its ritual liturgy, the clerical order of the Eumolpidae and Kerykes families, and some of the main elements of the egalitarian ideology of the polis of Athens. As already noted, this is one of the elements that mark the uniqueness of the mystical cult of Eleusis among the world's initiation cults.

Until Strauss Clay's 1989 and Foley's 1994 study of the *Hymn*,[5] the attention of the interpreters of it mainly focused on themes linked to the relationship between the *Hymn* and the stages in the agricultural year on the one hand and on its religious content on the other, while largely overlooking its political implications. In his admirable work on the *Hymn*, Richardson for instance writes that the declaration which opens the cult to all men on earth (ὅς ... ἐπιχθονίων ἀνθρώπων) (480) 'does at least suggest universality', adding however that 'the development was rather in the opposite direction, i.e., *barbaroi* were later excluded because of anti-Persian feelings after the Persian

Wars'. This exclusion is in fact contradicted by Euripides, who in *Bacchae* has Dionysus mention that he has established his rituals in the *poleis* of Asia where barbarians and Greeks mix together (17–22).[6] Richardson also overlooks Demeter's call to the 'whole demos' (πᾶς δῆμος) (270), briefly noting instead that the cult was open to the whole community of Eleusis in Celeus' assembling the people (λαός) (296); however, he does not explore the issue of the cult's egalitarian allusions further.[7] Parker, too, devotes little attention to the socio-political implications of the *Hymn*, while exploring the its theme which expresses the aetiology of the Athenian Panhellenic mission and focuses on the eschatological significance of the Demophöon episode and of the finale of the *Hymn*.[8] Seaford, writing in the same year as Foley, takes an entirely new direction in interpreting the *Hymn*, and convincingly relates its main underlying theme to the tragic pattern of the tension between the enclosed royal household and the demos, between the maenad Demeter (385–386) and the male-dominated socio-political order of the community, tension that is resolved by the goddess' gift of renewed fertility of the land and of the Eleusinian mystery cult.[9] While the theme of the aetiology of the liturgy of Eleusinian mystical rituals is certainly at the centre of the *Hymn*, it has to a certain extent jeopardized the exploration of other dimensions of the work,[10] such as the transformation of the social structure which the goddess institutes and inspires, which is the theme to which this section is dedicated.

In the *Hymn*, the crisis is cosmic and imperils the relationship between mankind and divinity. The whole cosmos is separated: Demeter leaves Olympus in search of her daughter; Persephone leaves her mother and disappears into Hades; Demeter stops the growth of vegetation threatening the survival of mankind and the continuation of those sacrifices that ensure the goodwill of divinity towards mankind. Only the establishment of a new interconnection within the cosmos by the renewal of the fertility of nature and the establishment of initiation rituals can save both mankind and Olympus.[11] The *Hymn* creates, in Strauss Clay's words, 'an irreversible alteration in the organization of cosmic space ... its concerns are the relations among the gods, their relations with mortals, and the repercussions of both on spatial and temporal realms'.[12]

In the *Hymn*, this ultimate cosmic crisis can only be overcome by the collective effort of the polis in establishing the cult of Demeter. The social inclusiveness of the rituals is made clear by the terms δῆμος and λαός used to designate the people of Eleusis. Demeter establishes her cult in Eleusis with these words: 'Let all the people build for me (ἄγε μοι ... πᾶς δῆμος) a great temple with an altar (νηόν τε μέγαν καὶ βωμόν) beneath the sheer wall of the city under the rising hill above Callichorum' (271–273). The expression is an order to the πᾶς δῆμος that has fundamental socio-political implications for the nature of the Eleusinian cult and for the polis of Athens. In Homer, the word δῆμος means those living outside the city, and defines the common people engaged in farming, as opposed to the oligarchic families of the polis who live within the city walls.[13] The expression πᾶς δῆμος thus involves the whole population of Eleusis and stresses the polarity between the enclosed families of Celeus and of the other rulers with all the common people who are specifically called upon to build her temple. It thus accentuates the direct relationship between the goddess and the city's population, her future cult and the polis' body politic. It also implies the well-ordered and coordinated collective activity of the whole people in building as complex a building as a temple: marble had to be quarried, trees felled, and all the elements prepared to exact specifications and installed.

In contrast, the term defining Celeus' innumerable people (πολυπείρων λαός) (296–300) whom he calls to assemble in the agora and obey his bid to build the temple, is the term λαός. This implies an uncoordinated mass of individuals: in the *Iliad* it marks the mass of soldiers as opposite to their leaders,[14] while in Athens it later designated people assembled in the ecclesia[15] or in theatres.[16] The *Hymn* thus emphasizes the cohesive and organized 'whole people', whom the goddess calls to be in charge of the construction of the temple: these are the characteristics of the initiates' collective behaviour we noted in the passages in Plato and Plutarch we examined.

The *Hymn* emphasizes the concept of divine justice as the central value of its socio-political order, as the aetiological myth of one of the central tenets of Athens' civic and religious ideology. In a prefiguration of the rulers of the polis-to-be after the institution of Demeter's cult, the polis' kings are called lawgiving (θεμιστοπόλοι) (103, 215, 473). The term, unique to the *Hymn*, defines the authority of rulers who act to guard traditional customs in accordance with divine authority (θέμις),[17] not yet Solon's human law (νόμος). The main moral traits of the heads of the city of Eleusis' ruling families, notes Metanira, are respect for the feeling or opinion of others, sense of honour (αἰδώς) and kindness (χάρις) (214–215). Their great power (μέγα κράτος) derives from their sense of honour (τιμή), as they protect the city and its walls with the civilian arts of their counsel (βουλή) (150–152), and from their art of giving the right judgement (ἰθεῖα δίκη).[18] Their role in the polis changes with the establishment of the goddess rituals, as their law-administering powers and responsibilities now extend to ensuring the organization and performance of the goddess' mystical rituals. The *Hymn* is particularly emphatic on this point, as it repeats the list of the city's leaders: it is to Triptolemus and Diocles, and mighty Eumolpus and Celeus, leader of the people, that Demeter revealed the conduct of her rites (δρησμοσύνην θ' ἱερῶν) and taught her secret initiation rituals (ὄργια) (470–479).

The aetiology of the religious and political role of choral public dancing and singing in the civic and religious life of the polis is suggested in the *Hymn* by reference to the maiden's well (παρθένιον φρέαρ) (99), the well near the house of Celeus the site where the goddess first sat after arriving at Eleusis, a communal place where young girls and women meet to fetch water. While revealing her divine nature to Metanira, the goddess calls the place above which her temple shall stand 'the place of beautiful dances' (καλλίχορος), and thus interprets the place in terms of *mousike*, the choral communal activity that is essential to the cohesion of the polis (272).[19] In fact, female choruses in Eleusis may have survived for a long time, as Pausanias (1.38.6) attests in the second century AD that Eleusinian women would gather at the place of beautiful dances to sing and dance for the goddess.

The cult's egalitarian horizon is wide, as the goddess, in her rage after being interrupted while making Celeus' and Metanira's son Demophöon immortal, addresses all humankind, as all men are equal before the divine, ignorant and foolish, unable to foresee destiny, incurably misled by their lack of sense, whose only hope is performing the rituals of the goddess she institutes (256–258). The gifts of the goddess are the same for all: fertility of the soil (469) and the blessing of the rituals (480). The *Hymn's* author thus extends the concept of equality in her cult and in the community of her worshippers from the demos of Eleusis to the whole mankind.

Still, the sense of restored cohesion of the community through the newly-instituted Eleusinian rituals, what Seaford calls 'the resolution of the crisis' that the *Hymn* creates through a new 'interconnection of the sectors of the cosmos',[20] marks also an early expression of that polarity that inspires Greek religious and political thought. The new order separates the community into two parts, those whom Demeter defines as the believers who perform due rituals (εὐαγέως ἔρδοντες) (274), and those whom Hades defines as failing to appease the goddess' power with sacrifices, rites and offerings. Hades uses the same terms for worshippers that Demeter uses (εὐαγέως ἔρδοντες), while he defines non-believers as those who have done wrong (ἀδικησάντες), and will receive retribution (τίσις) (367–369). The term 'justice, law' (*dike*) here prefigures the notion of justice as a religious and political concept which is at the core of Athenian civic ideology.

In the double *makarismos* at the end of the *Hymn*, the polarity between initiates and non-initiates involves both their afterlife and their earthly life (480–489). Firstly, the blessing extends to any mortal on earth who has watched these rituals (ὄλβιος, ὃς τάδ᾽ ὄπωπεν ἐπιχθονίων ἀνθρώπων): the uninitiated, who have not participated in the rituals, never has the same lot as his (initiated) equals (οὔποθ᾽ ὁμοίων αἶσαν ἔχει),[21] even when he is dead in the dreary darkness. In the second and stronger *makarismos*, the emphasis is on the rewards the goddesses offer to any mortal on earth they favour with their love (προφρονέως φίλωνται) (487), as they will send to his house Plutus, the god who gives abundance to mortals.[22] Another factor that separates initiates from non-initiates in the *Hymn* is the secrecy of initiation rituals (ὄργια σεμνά) that are not to be transgressed, pried into, or divulged (478–479). Secrecy, obedience to the cult's rules and the restrictions to its access helped the self-definition of initiates in contrast with non initiates, the division we noted in Pindar, Plato, and Plutarch.

The contrast between light and darkness we noted in section 2.5 and that we will find animates Aeschylus' *Oresteia* as well as *Bacchae* and *Frogs*, finds an early expression in the *Hymn*. In the *Hymn*, the polarity between the two realms structures the division of the universe caused by Persephone's abduction by Hades. The realm of Hades and Demeter's grief are expressed by dark colours and night. Demeter is grieving and puts a dark mourning shawl (κυάνεον κάλυμμα) on her shoulders (42); the world Demeter explores in search for her daughter is dark, as she carries blazing torches (αἰθομένας δαΐδας μετὰ χερσὶν ἔχουσα) (48, 61) just as Hecate carries a torch as she delivers the message of the sun (Helius) (52). Persephone is carried away beneath the earth (431) into the misty darkness (ὑπὸ ζόφον ἠερόεντα) (80), by the dark-haired (κυανοχαίτης) Hades (347). Demeter enters Celeus' palace as an old woman (101), wearing a veil and a dark peplos (πέπλος κυάνεος) (182–183) but, as the goddess enters the royal hall to meet Metanira, her head reaches the roof filling the doorway with a divine radiance (σέλαος θείοιο) (188–189). It is only after Metanira interrupts Demeter's rituals with Demophöon that the goddess reveals her divinity: she throws off her guise as an old woman and appears in her divine semblance. With her robes diffusing a delicious fragrance, light beaming out from her skin and her golden hair flowing over her body, her beauty floods the palace with the full radiance of lightning (αὐγὴ ἀστεροπῆς ὥς) (275–280).

To summarize, the *Hymn* establishes some of the fundamental values of the Eleusinian cult. The first is the political role of Demeter, the goddess who comes from afar to the polis of Eleusis as a stranger and causes a development in the social structure of the polis, a role similar to that of the god Dionysus in *Bacchae*. The second is the collective and ordered response of the socially and gender inclusive polis that, through the adhesion to the goddess' mystical cult and the construction of her temple, resolves a universal crisis that threatens both mankind and the gods. The third is the radical change of the social structure of the community where the goddess establishes a direct contact with the demos, while the rulers become the cult's ministers. This transformation expresses an early form of a democratic community that is ruled by the values of mystical cults, a theme that dominates the political content of *Bacchae* and *Frogs*.

5.2 Mystical/political values in Aeschylus' *Oresteia*

Let us examine the intertwining of mystical, ethical and political themes in Aeschylus' *Oresteia*, a dramatic trilogy that is an early theatrical expression of the religious and political ideology of the Athenians. Aeschylus' *Oresteia* was performed at the Great Dionysia in Dionysus' theatre in 458, some 100 to 150 years after the *Homeric Hymn to Demeter* and a half-century before *Bacchae* and *Frogs*. The political atmosphere in Athens was then particularly tense, as the conflict between partisans of the status quo and some of the leaders of the demos became strained after the second Persian war, in the polis that was gradually advancing to a democratic constitution (ἡ πόλις, ἅμα τῇ δημοκρατίᾳ κατὰ μικρὸν αὐξανομένη).²³ For seventeen years after the war, the political power in Athens remained in the hands of the aristocratic-dominated *Boule* sitting on the hill of the Areopagus, although its powers were gradually eroded. Ephialtes then became the leader of the demos and in 462 stripped from the *Boule* of most of its remaining political powers. The polis was divided and in violent turmoil: the following year Ephialtes was assassinated by a man who possibly acted on behalf of aristocratic circles²⁴ and in a retort, his opponent, the aristocratic pro-Spartan Cimon, was ostracized.²⁵

In a manner analogous to that of Euripides, who would set his *Bacchae* drama in Thebes, Aeschylus applies his thoughts on the political crisis he witnessed in Athens to the polis of Argos. His political message for a civic reconciliation is intertwined with mystical themes, often expressed in imagery of darkness and light, a complex subtext perhaps evident to a contemporary audience but less so to a modern.²⁶ A few scholars have explored what they call 'mystical allusions' in the work, but in fact the *Oresteia* can be considered as a complex metaphor for mystery rituals being the solution to Athens' political crisis, similar to that proposed by Euripides in *Bacchae* and Aristophanes in *Frogs*. Mystical imagery of darkness and light, similar to that of Pindar, Sophocles, Plato and Plutarch which we already examined, dominates the trilogy as it expresses mankind's passage from darkness to light, from the night surrounding the watchman in the opening of *Agamemnon*, through the black and ominous atmosphere of *Choephoroe,* to the final sunlight evoked by Athena as a blessing of the *Semnai Theai* in *Eumenides* (906, 924). The way Aeschylus builds up a crescendo in his treatment of the issue of light/liberation from the Erinyes/darkness/evil is complex and allusive. The progression of mystical imagery needs to be followed in some detail.

The multi-layered prologos of *Agamemnon* (1–39), creates a sharp contrast between the unhappy state of the watchman, with the night surrounding him, and images of mystical lights. The watchman lies on the roof of the royal palace on his bent arm, like a dog, enjoying no rest on his restless bed, wet with dew, fearfully standing at his post instead of asleep (φόβος ἀνθ' ὕπνου). In the night, under the stars and the radiant powers (λαμπροὺς δυνάστας) of planets, the watchman is looking out for a signal of light, a dawn of fire (λαμπάδος τό σύμβολον/αὐγὴν πυρός), as he prays for deliverance from evil for himself and for the royal house of Atreus (ἀπαλλαγὴ πόνων). Terms belonging to the λαμπ- family, expressing the notion of humanly lit fires are repeated in a crescendo.[27] The watchman awaits the fire signals, which would bring the good news of Agamemnon's victory in Troy appearing as a fire in darkness (εὐαγγέλου φανέντος ὀρφναίου πυρός). A part of Aeschylus' audience would have connected these images of light and fire with the mystery imagery we have examined. Light in the night suggests a hope for a solution to the polis' crisis, but fires are also ominous images of war, of Troy's temples desecrated, of the city sacked and burnt to the ground, of religious pollution.

Then the beacon-light finally appears, to the joy of the watchman. The fire of night is a light as bright as day (λαμπτὴρ νυκτός, ἡμερήσιον/φάος). This is a complex, ambivalent image that associates the torches in darkness which were signalling the ill-omened victory from Troy to Argos, to an allusion to the marvellous light illuminating the night in the experience of mystical initiation. This light, the watchmen then exclaims, will cause the performance of many a dance in Argos (χορῶν κατάστασιν πολλῶν). May the queen shout in joy, may the king come back to his palace and may I clasp his hand in mine (γένοιτο δ' οὖν μολόντος εὐφιλῆ χέρα/ἄνακτος οἴκων τῇδε βαστάσαι χερί), exclaims the watchmen. It is a vision of peace and of deliverance from evil for the royal house and the polis. The mention of choral singing and dancing, that collective act of religious worship and civic unity of a polis, a theme that we noted in the *Homeric Hymn to Demeter*, is also significant here, suggesting the civic cohesion created by the choral dancing and singing as well as that created by initiation rituals illuminated by a mystical light.

But the ominous image associating Troy with fire lingers on. The watchman's images of a liberation light soon turn into disappointment, as the chorus watches the city of Argos aflame with sacrificial fires as high as heaven (οὐρανομήκης λαμπάς), reiterating the flames engulfing the city of Troy and its sullied temples. The slaying of Agamemnon and Cassandra confirms the ominous and ambiguous sign given by the fires, as it is welcomed by Aegisthus with an image of light, as a 'kind light, day of just reward' (φέγγος εὔφρον ἡμέρας δικηφόρου) (*Agamemnon* 1577) as he ominously salutes the slaying of Agamemnon. In *Choephoroe*, the second play in the trilogy, the audience is pushed further into darkness and fear. The House of Atreus, and with it the polis, is in ruin, enshrouded by darkness that men loathe (ἀνήλιοι βροτοστυγεῖς/δνόφοι καλύπτουσι δόμους) (*Choephoroe* 50 ff.). This polarity between light and darkness continues, as Orestes enters the palace as night is falling (*Choephoroe* 660–661), and the chorus expressing its hope for the radiant light of freedom to come (ἐλευθερίας φῶς λαμπρόν) (*Choephoroe* 810), only to be met with the news of Aegisthus' death, followed by Clytemnestra's. The chorus nevertheless continues to be optimistic, saluting the new slayings with a shout of triumph (942) and with the exclamation 'The light has come!' (961). The tyrants may be dead, but the divine law of retribution continues, with Orestes noting that his victory has produced a pollution that can only be cleansed by his own death (1017). The reversal is complete in the very last scene of *Choephoroe*, when the audience is plunged into the horror of the appearance of the Erinyes, unseen by the chorus and by the audience but seen and described by the terrified Orestes.

In *Eumenides'* exodos, the conversion of the Erinyes into *Semnai Theai* ('Revered Goddesses') following their defeat at Orestes' trial is also marked by powerful images of light. In their answer to Athena's exhortation, the chorus of *Semnai Theai* exclaims its wish that the bright light of the sun (φαιδρὸν ἁλίου σέλας) may be beneficial to Athens' life (922–926). Terms used in the prologos of *Agamemnon* shed their ominous tone and friendly terms for light, torches and fire (λαμπάς, σέλας, φέγγος, πῦρ, φῶς) illuminating the scene. Light in darkness is now sacred, as Athena exclaims to the tamed Erinyes, as they go to their new dwellings by the sacred light (πρὸς φῶς ἱερὸν) of the polis' processional escorts (1005). The goddess declares a few lines later that she will escort them in the procession by the light of blazing torches (φέγγει λαμπάδων σελασφόρων) (1022) and orders the light of fire (τὸ φέγγος πυρός) to illuminate them (1028–1029). The chorus of escorts closes the scene and the trilogy, with another vivid image of light as it exhorts the *Semnai Theai* to delight at the fire that devours the torches (πυριδάπτος λαμπάδα) (1036–1042) and to intone the ritual choral scream of joy (ὀλολυγμός). This formula is used for the third time in the trilogy, this time in its proper ritual implication as it accompanies the choral dance and singing act, a scene that would have connected the audience to the Panathenaea procession and to the atmosphere of the Eleusinian night rituals. The light of torches accompanies the tamed Erinyes to their new dwelling in *Eumenides'* exodos, as it accompanies the cortege escorting Aeschylus to Athens in *Frogs'* finale.

In parallel with the imagery, the expression of deliverance from evil (ἀπαλλαγὴ πόνων), an expression associated with mystery rituals, connects the whole trilogy from its introduction in the prologos of *Agamemnon*, through the narration of the religious purification and judicial acquittal of Orestes, to the liberation of the polis of Athens from domestic strife, *stasis*, under the protection of the Eumenides in the exodos of *Eumenides*. As Thomson points out, deliverance from evil is a concept that, while in common use as a proverb, is also used in mystery cults as denoting the state of spiritual bliss granted to initiates. Thomson's list of examples of the use of this expression in this way is exhaustive: it is perhaps sufficient to limit it to Plato's mention of the soul in heaven as free from these evils (ἀπηλλαγμένη τούτων τῶν κακῶν)[28] and to Aelius Aristides describing the gain to be obtained from participation to the Eleusinian rituals as not only joy (ἡ εὐθυμία), but releases and liberations (λύσεις καὶ ἀπαλλαγαί) from the troubles of the past.[29] In *Agamemnon*'s parodos the watchmen prays for his own deliverance from his pains (*Agamemnon* 1), but the concept widens after a few lines to the pollution enveloping the house of Atreus (*Agamemnon* 18) and by implication the polis of Argos. In *Eumenides*, the same term is used by the god Apollo in his recommendations to Orestes. There Aeschylus deliberately connects Orestes' ultimate ritual cleansing (ἀπαλλάξαι πόνων) from the Erinyes with the notion of human justice produced by judges and a legal dialectic process (*Eumenides* 81–84).

In the *Oresteia*, the political theme of the polis as a cohesive community is gradually built up. In the prologos of *Agamemnon* the term 'polis' is not used, but we saw the theme evoked by the expectation of dancing and singing in the city of Argos at the good news of victory at Troy (23–24). In *Choephoroe* the term polis is mentioned only twice, once in expressing the exile from his polis for who is pursued by the Erinyes (389), and by the chorus' significant exultation at the death of Clytemnestra and Aigysthos, bringing a new freedom to the polis (1044–1047). In *Eumenides*, however, the term appears some twenty-two times. The polis of Athens is presented as the polis of the goddess Athena and associated with the institutions Athena will establish (79, 475, 524, 572, 617, 687, 698, 701, 733 etc.). In the goddess' words to the herald opening the trial of Orestes in the announcement of her ordnances (θεσμοί), the whole polis must learn and apply them for everlasting time (εἰς τὸν αἰανῆ χρόνον) (571–572). It is an openly political plea, recognizing the people of Attica

(Ἀττικὸς λεώς) (681) as a coherent community, responsible in judging Orestes. The judges the goddess will choose will be the best of her citizens, Athena declares (487), they will 'represent the whole polis, being the flower of its manhood'.[30] It is thus by a human, egalitarian and judicial process that Orestes is able to escape his fate as victim of the unending cycle of divinely ordained revenge, a series of killings that had seemed unstoppable.

The second part of *Eumenides* is dedicated to a solution of Athens' political crisis and violent strife, defined as the greatest enemy of the polis and is the subject of Athena's answer to the menaces of the Erinyes. Athena, the personification of her polis of Athens (474, 487 etc.), asks the Erinyes to refrain from encouraging blood feuds (μὴ βάλῃς/μήθ' αἱματηρὰς θηγάνας), feuds that madden the young with drunkenless fury, and not to excite in citizens the spirit of war among relatives that emboldens them to fight each other (Ἄρη/ἐμφύλιόν καὶ πρὸς ἀλλήλους θρασύν) (858–863). The converted *Semnai Theai* accept Athena's plea: they solemnly pray that civil war (στάσις), insatiable cause of evils (ἄπληστος κακῶν), may never rage in the polis, and that the blood of citizens may never be spilt as a consequence of murders in revenge for blood (ἀντιφόνοι ἄτας). The newly found communal spirit of the polis is expressed in the wish of the *Semnai Theai* for the people of Athens to unite in common love and in shared hatred of the enemy (χάρματα δ' ἀντιδιδοῖεν/κοινοφιλεῖ διανοίᾳ/καὶ στυγεῖν μιᾷ φρενί), sentiments that will cure many evils (975–987).

In the last scene of the *Oresteia* (1003–1047), a short passage of forty-two verses, Aeschylus brings the imagery motifs of the trilogy to completion, bringing all its complex issues to their religious, ethical and political solution. It is a scene of great communal rejoicing: the Athenians are free from the threat of the Erinyes and have succeeded in establishing a new civic order for the polis based on a divine-ordained but human judicial system; the *Semnai Theai* have been accepted by the polis of Athens as deities and have their own dwelling on the Acropolis near the temple of Athena, where the citizens of the city will worship them. Their power will benefit the city and assure its prosperity and victory in war. The scene uses mystery-cults images on a background linked to the Panathenaic procession, merging the main civic and religious cults of the polis of Athens.[31] In addition to the associations of the images of light and torches we examined earlier, some elements link the scene to religious rituals, such as the twice-repeated religious ritual formula of *euphemia* that opens the procession escorting the *Semnai Theai* to their new dwellings (εὐφαμεῖτε δέ, χωρῖται) (1035–1039).

A second political theme may be considered as a subtext of *Oresteia*, the antinomy between democracy and the powerful politically negative Athenian connotation of tyranny. The evil from which that the community of Argos suffers derives from what the watchman calls the misfortune (συμφορά) of the royal house, which has not been managed as admirably as it was in the past (*Agamemnon* 18–19). The allusion obviously refers to the absence of the king and obliquely to the love affair between Clytemnestra and Aegisthus, but in *Agamemnon* the figure of the queen progressively develops the features of a tyrant-like figure. Upon her appearance on stage her power (κράτος) is defined by the chorus as absolute, and the sacrifices for the victory at Troy are hers, and hers alone (258–263, 587, 594, etc.).

Aegisthus is, together with Clytemnestra, the tyrant of the land (*Choephoroe* 973). In the powerful scene that follows the slaying of Agamemnon, Aeschylus emphasizes the contrast between the two tyrants with the orderly democratic debate of the members of the chorus.[32] Orderly, but ominous: the talk of angry citizens is as dangerous, warns the chorus, as a public curse, one that would have caused the death or the exile of the tyrants (456). In their discussion on how to react to the slaying of Agamemnon, a member of the chorus charges the unnamed slayers of Agamemnon with planning to set up a tyrannical regime in the polis of Argos (1346–1371). The audience, aware of the identity of the slayers, would have associated the crime of kin-slaying with that of would-be tyrants and would have shared the chorus' preference for death rather than life under tyrants (1362–1365).

Aeschylus powerfully concludes the association between the polis and its anti-tyrannical essence in the second stasimon of *Eumenides*, where the Erinyes state their divine status and the benefits to mankind brought by religion, pleading for mankind to follow the middle way and not the two extremes of anarchy or tyranny, to respect the unwritten laws, and to avoid hubris (526–537). This note is significant, as it summarizes the chorus' moral and political stance on moderation and civic reconciliation in *Bacchae*. The plea is again stressed by Athena, who wishes to establish the Areopagus as the political body that will grant the application of justice and dissuade citizens from seeking either anarchy or tyranny (696–698).

In conclusion, Aeschylus merges religious and civic elements in *Eumenides* to provide a solution to the trilogy: the divine law of blood retribution is replaced by the human code of laws administered by the polis' *Boule* on the Areopagus; the chthonian punishers of pollution become the *Semnai Theai*, goddesses who will keep civic unrest, *stasis*, under control and bring reconciliation to the polis; and the light of the once ominous torches is now accompanying the grand and solemn procession to the temple of Semnai Theai.

6

Historical Context and Episodes

Classic Athens' civic ideology was a combination of notions that were simultaneously religious, ethical and political. In this section I focus on the timing of this process of amalgamation of these concepts: the beginning of the sixth century, a period that some scholars call the 'Solonian' period. Several factors came to significantly coincide with this phase of Athenian history, which help to explain the development of civic concepts that encompassed the political and religious dimension. I argue that beliefs of mystery cults, the anti-tyrannical stance of the demos and its horror of political strife played a crucial role in rallying the polis of Athens in its most critical moments, such as the attempt of Cylon to proclaim himself tyrant of Athens in the 590s, the scandal of the Herms and mysteries in 415, the persecution of poets and philosophers under the accusation of irreligiousness, *asebeia*, the opposition to the regime of the Thirty in 404 and the final reconciliation and restoration of democracy in 403. Whenever the socio-political division of the polis was felt to jeopardize its survival, the Eleusinian and Dionysiac cults provided a spur for a renewal of its unity, cohesion and solidarity.

Several aspects of the association between the mystery cults and politics in Athens can be elucidated by a brief summary of the structural changes that Athens went through in a period between the end of the seventh century and the end of the sixth. Firstly, the socio-political polarization between the haves and the have-nots, was exacerbated in the mid-sixth century by the introduction of money in the form of coinage, which followed a more thorough exploitation of the silver mines at Laurion.[1] Money in liquid form helped wealth to be concentrated in just a few hands and also broke the traditional reciprocity of gifts, thus weakening a prime factor of stability in the polis, the solidarity between citizens. This stimulated the Athenian continuing political strife that lasted until the reconciliation between the oligarchic circles and the demos in 403.

Secondly, the push by Athenians for the control of Attica was put into effect by the strategic conquest of the island of Salamis, of the large fertile Thriasian plain on the west side of the Aegaleus mountain ridge, as well as of the ancient town and sanctuary of Eleusis that became a deme of Athens in the early sixth century. The control of Attica and its policy of bringing the communities of Attica under the same political roof, *synoikismos*, made Athens the richest and most powerful polis in mainland Greece.

Thirdly, in the early sixth century, Solon took power in Athens, established a new egalitarian constitution and set of laws, and established the organization of the mysteries in Eleusis.[2] The figure of Solon, who saved the polis from political strife and founded the egalitarian polis, was to accompany the development of Athenian political thought in the fifth century.

Fourthly, in the same period, the archaic agrarian cult at Eleusis came then to embrace an eschatological dimension, becoming an initiation mystery cult and the *Homeric Hymn to Demeter* was written.[3] This development is also evidenced by archaeological data that show that an extensive building activity took place in the area of the Eleusis sanctuary, where the terrace to the south of the existing temple to Demeter was expanded and a new temple to Demeter and Persephone, the Telesterion/Anactoron, was built.[4] Eleusinian cultic ties with Athens were then strengthened with the construction of the City Eleusinion.[5]

6.1 Stasis

A few notes on the concept of political strife, *stasis,* are now necessary. Among other meanings *stasis* designates 'party, faction, sedition, discord, division, dissent, strife, quarrel, contention' (LSJ). It is a term that defines a large variety of different phenomena: political altercations between citizens, dissension on civic matters, social unrest, political assassinations, insurrection against the government, socio-political revolutions and fully fledged civil war.[6] While for modern readers organized political dissent and conflict are part of the democratic process, for the Athenians it was the enemy of the community, and the moral duty to reject it has ancient roots in Greek ethical and political thought.[7] In a manner similar to the perception of the threat of tyranny, the concept of *stasis* as enemy helped the community define itself and its civic goal of harmony and concord, *homonoia*.[8]

Stasis was considered a phenomenon which prevented the orderly workings of the polis that operated through the harmonization of dissimilar but fundamentally homogeneous elements. For instance, in *Politicus* 310e–311c, Plato famously compared the polis as 'the product of the art of ruling by weaving together' (βασιλικῆς συνυφάνσεως ἔργον) different ethical values, beliefs and opinions into 'a smooth, well-woven fabric' (λεῖον καὶ εὐήτριον ὕφασμα), a magnificent cloth that covers all the inhabitants of the polis, both slaves and free, and holds them together.[9] Aristophanes uses this metaphor as a way to bring the cohesion back to the polis in *Lysistrata* 574–586, where Lysistrata explains to a magistrate how Athens' women would proceed to bring harmony to the polis:

> Imagine the polis as a fleece just shorn. First, put it in a bath and wash out all the sheep dung; spread it on a bed and beat out all the riff-raff with a stick, and pluck out the horns; as for those who clump and knock themselves together to snag government positions, card them out and pluck off their heads. Next, card the wool into a sewing basket of unity and goodwill (κοινὴν εὔνοιαν), mixing in everyone. The metics and any other foreigner who's your friend, and anyone who owes money to the people's treasury, mix them in there too ... So take all these flocks and bring them together here, joining them all and making one big bobbin. And from this weave a fine new cloak for the people (τῷ δήμῳ χλαῖναν ὑφῆναι).[10]

Stasis takes precedence over external war in Plato's *Laws* as the main danger facing a community. The only solution to a divided family is reconciliation (διάλλαξις), Plato writes,[11] using the term we shall see Xenophon use in his rendition of the Spartan appeasement strategy in Athens in 404. Internal concord can only be reached by the establishment of mutual friendship and peace by conciliation and takes precedence over external war, Plato concludes. Lysias observes: 'concord is the best thing a polis has, and stasis is the cause of all evils' (ὁμόνοιαν μέγιστον ἀγαθὸν εἶναι πόλει, στάσιν δὲ πάντων κακῶν αἰτίαν) (18.17).

This approach to the issue of *stasis* has ancient roots. In Homer for instance, anybody expressing public political dissent is defined as impious and deserving of exclusion from the community. At the beginning of Book 9 of Homer's *Iliad*, the Achaean army has retreated before a successful sortie commanded by Hector.[12] A bitter discussion takes place in the assembly between Agamemnon, who wishes the army to sail back to Greece, and Diomedes, who accuses Agamemnon of cowardice. The old *mantis*, Nestor, then intervenes, warning Diomedes of the gravity of breaching the unwritten laws governing the community. He who thirsts for the chilling war among his own people shall be deprived of his tribal links (ἀφρήτωρ), Nestor says, and shall find himself outside the law (ἀθέμιστος), with no family and no home (ἀνέστιος).[13] The warning is clear: a man deprived of his tribe, of his legal rights, of his family and of his home has no reason to live. Spoken by the wise Nestor to one of the army's leaders, the warning expresses in full the Greek rejection of internecine conflict on religious, moral and civic grounds that continued through the centuries.

In Hesiod, *stasis*' synonymous deity, Strife (ἔρις), is presented in the darkest theological terms as daughter of Deadly Night (Νὺξ ὀλοή), and sister of Nemesis, Treachery and Old Age. In her turn, Strife is mother of a series of deities, personifications of evil: among them Toil, Oblivion, Famine, Fight, Murder, Quarrel, Treachery, Lawlessness and Ruin.[14] In Solon, several political and moral concepts are connected with *stasis*. Hubris, unrestrained greed and lack of self-control bring to the polis an inescapable wound, that of falling into the slavery of a tyrant, which awakens civil strife and tribal war (στάσις ... ἔμφυλος πόλεμος).[15] Among other authors,[16] Herodotus notes that civil strife (στάσις ἔμφυλος) is worse than war waged on the basis of common consent, just as war is worse than peace.[17] A similar concept also characterizes the definition of *stasis* in Aeschylus' *Eumenides* 864–866, where external war is blessed, but only if there is no battling of birds within the home.[18]

It is in Thucydides that we find the deepest analysis of what *stasis* represented for a fifth-century Athenian. One of the threads of Thucydides' narration of the Peloponnesian war are his reflections on the way *stasis*, a term he uses twenty-five times in his work, is a social and political phenomenon that destroys the ethical and moral fabric of society. While often perceived as a religious sceptic,[19] Thucydides, in his well-known detailed description of the effects of *stasis* in Corcyra and by extension on the whole of the Greek world[20] notes the disruption *stasis* brings to the observance of civic and religious rituals.[21] For Thucydides, the terrible sufferings that *stasis* brings to communities are part of human nature: they have occurred and will continue to occur as long as human nature is what it is (ἕως ἂν ἡ αὐτὴ φύσις ἀνθρώπων ᾖ).²² Still, as long as religious rules are observed, citizens will maintain their abhorrence of civil strife: in the strife between the Four Hundred and the body of hoplites who had marched on Athens from Piraeus in 411 that Thucydides describes (8.93), the hoplites' goal was not the seizure of power for themselves, but the restoration of *homonoia* to the polis.

6.2 Epimenides, the Initiation of the Polis and Solon

In the following sections we shall examine some instances where the ancient Greeks wrote about the relationship between mystery cults and the polis. I have taken this evidence not as a literal historical record, but as an expression of what mystery cults represented in the collective religious and civic consciousness of the Athenians. For this reason, these episodes in Athens' political life have been ordered in the chronology attributed to them by the Athenians, regardless of when they were written down.

The episode of Cylon's failed attempted coup and its repercussions is reported by several Greek authors in ways that provide evidence of the combination of religious and political factors in the *aitia* of Athens' religious and civic ideology. Cylon's tale is based on a historical event and various versions of the traditional story have survived. It was mentioned by Herodotus,[23] Thucydides,[24] Plato,[25] by the author of the *Constitution of the Athenians*,[26] Plutarch[27] and Diogenes Laërtius.[28] The versions vary significantly in its dating,[29] in the actions they recount and in its political and religious content, but some significant elements recur throughout most of the versions.

The crisis is expressed as a breakup of the socio-political order of the polis, *stasis*. Two conflicts are at the heart of the episode. One is Cylon's attempt at securing tyranny, a serious crime which is resisted by the polis. The second is the ambiguity of the punishment of Cylon's co-conspirators on the order of the Alcmaeonidae family, on one hand an act of political necessity, on the other a sacrilegious crime committed against the inviolable status of suppliants of the goddess Athena (*hiketeia*). The two-fold nature of the punishment causes the polis to divide into two opposite factions.

The figure of Cylon as a tyrant, who by the late fifth century came to be stereotyped as a rich, impious and lawless enemy of the communality of the polis, is the main tool through which Athenian political thought came to define political equality and democracy. Cylon has some of the characteristics of a conventional tyrant in several versions of the episode. In Herodotus, Cylon is a man who aims for tyranny (ἐπὶ τυραννίδι ἐκόμησε),[30] in Thucydides he is portrayed as an Athenian aristocrat of noble birth who has a position of power in society (εὐγενὴς καὶ δυνατός), a victor at Olympic games, and who had a direct connection with a family of tyrants, having married the daughter of Megacles the tyrant of Megara, a polis which was a traditional enemy of Athens.[31] The attempt of the would-be tyrant to seize power is resisted by Athens' citizens. Thucydides for instance emphasizes the popular opposition to Cylon's attempt, being resisted by all (πανδημεί) the Athenians, including the peasants who came from the Attica countryside to lay siege to the Acropolis that had been seized by Cylon and his band.[32]

In most versions of the episode, the solution to *stasis* is connected with the foundations of Athenian democracy. As a result of the Cylonian affair, Plutarch narrates in *Life of Solon*, the polis of Athens was split between the party of those condemning the Alcmaeonidae archons who had murdered the Cylonian conspirators and those who defended them as opponents of tyranny. *Stasis* reached an acme as the demos became sharply divided (τῆς στάσεως ἀκμὴν λαβούσης μάλιστα καὶ τοῦ δήμου διαστάντος). The anger of the divinities expressed itself by causing panic and divine visions in the polis.[33] A slightly different version of the origin of *stasis* is found in the *Constitution of the Athenians* (2). There the Alcmaeonidae family, considered collectively guilty of impiety, were put on trial and banished, while the Cretan sage Epimenides ritually purified the polis. Afterwards, however, *stasis* erupted between the notables and the mass of the people of Athens and lasted for long time, only to be solved by the common choice by the people of Solon as archon and reconciler, who reformed the constitution and the legal code.

A subject that appears in several versions of the episode as the solution of the polis' crisis is the collective adoption of purification rituals. The concept of *catharsis* is here significantly at the crossroads of civic values, initiation rituals and the development of the polis. In the *Constitution of the Athenians* (1), the figure of the sage Epimenides of Crete is said to have purified the polis (Ἐπιμενίδης δ' ὁ Κρὴς ... ἐκάθηρε τὴν πόλιν) after the trial that had punished the authors of the sacrilege.[34] This theme is expanded in Plato, as he mentions the figure of Epimenides as a figure who incarnates sanctity and religious healing, mystical purification and collective initiation rituals. Addressing an unnamed Athenian, Clinias from Crete briefly describes the coming of Epimenides to Athens. Epimenides was a divine man (ἀνὴρ θεῖος) and a friend of the Athenians, who, ten years before the Persian war, obeyed a prophecy of Apollo, came to Athens and performed certain sacrifices that the god had ordained.[35] What transpires from Plato is the public nature of the sacrifices Epimenides performed, his nature as a man in close contact with divinity, and his acting in support of the collectivity and in conformity with divine prophecies to put into effect the will of Zeus.

In the *Life of Solon*, Plutarch later emphasizes the intertwining of collective rituals of purification and initiation, as well as the Athenian social, constitutional and economic reforms through the figures of Epimenides and of Solon. Despite the decision of the court to send the polluted Alcmaeonidae into exile,[36] diviners declared that the polis was still prey to *miasma*, and in need of ritual purifications (καθαρμοί).[37] As in the *Constitution of the Athenians* and in Plato, the Athenians then called Epimenides of Phaestos to assist them in the organization of purification rituals. Plutarch describes Epimenides as a one of the seven Wise Men, a man loved by the gods (θεοφιλής), learned in divine matters (σοφὸς περὶ τὰ θεῖα), and, using the terms of the mystery cults, learned in divine inspiration and initiation rituals (τὴν ἐνθουσιαστικὴν καὶ τελεστικὴν σοφίαν) (12.4). In Plutarch's version, the ritual purification of the polis is described in terms that point to collective mystical rituals as necessary steps to re-build the harmony of the community *stasis* had destroyed. Epimenides' greatest achievement, Plutarch notes, was to bring the polis to observance of justice and to be better disposed to civic harmony and cohesion (μᾶλλον εὐπειθῆ πρὸς ὁμόνοιαν) (12.5). Plutarch describes the collective purification of the polis of Athens in revealingly religious terms that shed light on the nature of the reunification of the polis. To achieve the goal of purifying the city from Cylon's *miasma* and pacifying the polis (12.1), Epimenides had the Athenians moderate the social conflicts arising from funeral ceremonies that fostered clan conflicts, but above all he had the community initiated, and ritually cleansed it in various rituals to appease the divinity such as purificatory rituals and the construction of new temples (12.5).[38]

Thus, in one of the founding myths of the polis of Athens, it was a holy man who brought Athens back to social and political harmony through religious purification rituals. Evidence of the episode's continuing ideological value in Athens can be found, for instance, in a seated statue of Epimenides that stood by the statue of Triptolemus, opposite the Eleusinium in Athens, noted by Pausanias (1.14.3-4). While the date of the erection of Epimenides' statue is likely to be the fourth century or later,[39] it was a powerful public reminder of the Athenians' belief of the crucial role played by Epimenides and by the mystery cults in a pivotal moment of the early life of the Athenian polis.

We shall observe some elements of the religious and political themes of this episode in *Bacchae* and *Frogs*: the political crisis of the polis; its collective *catharsis* through initiation rituals to eliminate *miasma* and to return to civic cohesion; a defence of the Alcmaeonidae as tyrant fighters, together with a definition of a religious and political *stasis* between the polis of Athens and oligarchic circles supported by the Spartans; and Cylon as a figure of tyrant opposed by the Athenian demos. Each author combined the themes of the episodes in different ways, but their attention to the religious and political themes that emerge from their treatments of the episode is evidence of the importance of these topics in the development of Athenian political consciousness.

In the crucial early period of the Athenian polis, which saw the emergence of an eschatological mystery cult at Eleusis and the composition of the *Homeric Hymn to Demeter*, Solon expressed ethical and political values that shaped Athenian political thought and became particularly associated with the mystery cults. These notions of Solon are worth quoting in some detail, as they are the guiding principles of the ethical and political concerns of Euripides and Aristophanes in *Bacchae* and *Frogs*.

Solon emphasizes the contrast between the rulers of the city, acting in breach of ethics, religion and justice, and the legal and religious order necessary to the polis. The terms he uses echo the expressions we analysed in Plato and Plutarch's characterization of initiates. In fragment 4, the polis' political leaders are beyond laws, act with great hubris, do not know how to restrain their excesses, and do not organize religious festivals in merriment and a spirit of civic harmony (εὐφροσύνας κοσμεῖν δαιτὸς ἐν ἡσυχίῃ) and ignore the sacred foundations of Justice. This behaviour brings about tyranny, *stasis* and war among kinsmen (στάσιν ἔμφυλον πόλεμόν). The idyllic description of the establishment of Justice in Athens through a good rule of law (εὐνομία) would make the polis orderly and perfect (εὔκοσμα καὶ ἄρτια), as εὐνομία punishes those outside the law (τοῖς ἀδίκοις), smooths roughness and quells insolence, dims hubris and shrivels the flowering bud of destruction (ἄτης), stops the deeds of civil strife (ἔργα διχοστασίης), and the anger of grievous conflict (ἀργαλέης ἔριδος χόλον). Then, in the world of men all will be perfect and harmonious (ἄρτια καὶ πινυτά). Do these political goals entail the violent overthrow of the polis' rulers? Solon's solution is peaceful. In fragment 36, Solon defines as the solution of the polis' ills as his having been able to fit together opposite elements, combining equally force with justice (ὁμοῦ βίαν τε καὶ δίκην συναρμόσας), a concept of civic conciliation and equality that is also at the heart of the political message of *Bacchae* and *Frogs*.

6.3 Demeter, Miltiades and Telines

Herodotus' construction of the figure of Miltiades, son of Cimon, and his report on his failed attempt to desecrate Demeter's sanctuary on the island of Paros are evidence of a strand in Greek political thought and Athenian democratic thought in particular: the polarity between the figure of an aristocrat, a wealthy and corrupt would-be tyrant, and its opposite, the mystical and civic connection between mystery cults and the polis, elements that are common the *Bacchae* and *Frogs*.[40]

In his account of the figure of Miltiades, hero of Marathon, Herodotus blends several of the characteristics of an enemy of the polis: like Cylon, he is presented as a member of a rich and powerful family, the Philaïdae, a household wealthy enough to race four-horse chariots at the Olympic games.[41] He is an impious man who imprisoned those who came to him to share his mourning of his dead brother; a man who is the tyrant of the Chersonese under the protection of a personal guard of 500 mercenaries; an Athenian who married the daughter of the king of Thrace and subsequently a Persian woman, a gift from the Persian king Darius. He is above all an ungodly man who attempts to defile the sacred, secret and untouchable sanctuary of Demeter, the most immoral act possible and the ultimate crime that an Athenian could commit. To the Athenians, these were demonstrations of Miltiades' anti-civic immorality: for Athenians acquiring a bodyguard was a blatant tyrannical act, evidence of a tyrant's mistrust and fear of his co-citizens;[42] marrying the daughter of a powerful foreign king of a notoriously bellicose and hostile tribe and accepting gifts from the Persian king, finally, made him a potential enemy of Athens and revealed his ambitions to become an oriental despot.[43]

Herodotus' version of Miltiades' expedition to Paros that followed his victory against the Persians, ostensibly to punish the Parians for their stance during the Persian war but seeking for a personal gain in reality, is one of several accounts of the episode.[44] Herodotus' choice of version allowed him to set the conflict between religion and the sacrilegious would-be tyrant on Paros, an island known for its cult of Demeter.[45] De Polignac notes 'the prestige of Demeter in Paros, where the Thesmophorion contained the sacred objects upon which the safety of the city depended',[46] an opinion shared by Picard.[47]

Miltiades, not succeeding to either obtaining a vast sum of money from the Parians or in breaking through the polis walls, meets Timo, a priestess of the temple of Demeter on Paros. Following her suggestion, he goes to the temple by night, alone, with the intention of moving something that should not be moved (κινήσοντά τι τῶν ἀκινήτων) in the *megaron*.[48] At the door of the goddess' *megaron*, Miltiades, caught by a sudden fearful shudder (φρίκη), runs away. Leaping down from the sanctuary's wall he injures his thigh, a wound that would ultimately cost him his life.[49] Upon his return to Athens he was put on trial on charges of fraud and was fined fifty talents, a fine his son Cimon had to pay after his death. In the meantime, the Parians wished to punish Timo and sent a delegation to Delphi to ask if they should put the priestess to death for assisting the enemy in the capture of the city and for revealing to Miltiades secrets forbidden to males (τὰ ἐς ἔρσενα γόνον ἄρρητα ἱρά). The Pythia in Delphi replied that Timo was in no way responsible, that Miltiades was supposed to end up badly, and something had appeared that had led him to these evils. Timo was therefore left unpunished.

Herodotus' version is centred on the impiousness of Miltiades' attempt to desecrate the sanctuary of Demeter: as Hau comments, 'characters who commit impiety in the *Histories* tend to come to grief'.[50] Scott aptly calls Herodotus' version of the episode an 'urban legend',[51] as it follows the lines of the theme of divine punishment of an impious and rich fraudster. But urban legends also reveal the beliefs of those from which they originate and to whom they are addressed. What was Miltiades trying to achieve in the eyes of Herodotus' audience? The effect that Herodotus wished his passage to have on his readers lies in his description of Miltiades' intention: to move something that must not be moved. Herodotus does not mention explicitly the nature of what were these objects, nor Miltiades' intention, but his readers would have been aware of the wealth contained in the treasure of the temple. What does 'moving what must not be moved' mean? Theft would probably have been described in a different fashion; ἀκίνητα embraces both unmovable, motionless objects and objects that must not be moved, touched or broken into for religious motives.[52] Moving the *hiera* would have desecrated the sanctuary and interrupted the connection between the polis and divinity. This would have endangered the polis' self-identity, cohesion and self-confidence, ensuring that the polis may then become easy prey for the Athenian troops.

The expression used by Herodotus to define the reaction of Miltiades to the unnamed vision he had at the door of the *megaron* is also of significance in decoding Herodotus' religious and moral message: 'he was overwhelmed by shivering fear' (φρίκης αὐτὸν ὑπελθούσης). The term φρίκη suggests the awe and terror that a vision of divinity would inspire in even the bravest of military commanders. What Herodotus may have been suggesting is a theophany of the goddess Demeter, as the Pythia expression is 'an apparition had led him to these evils' (φανῆναί οἱ τῶν κακῶν κατηγεμόνα).[53] The term 'apparition' and Miltiades' reaction to flee in panic suggest the goddess' appearance in the full light of her divinity, a theophany.[54] One may imagine Miltiades facing the goddess as the divine appearance that the *Homeric Hymn to Demeter* describes, beaming light from her skin and flooding the whole house with a glare (276–280). Herodotus' audience would have taken the apparition of the goddess as an intervention in defence of the sacred nature of her cult and of her polis. The hubristic and impious commander of a hostile army had been repulsed and gravely wounded. The Athenian attack had been defeated and the polis of Paros may be imagined having returned to its normal life.

The association between the cohesion of the polis, social and political concord and the figure of the chthonic goddesses and the power of the cult in quelling *stasis* and promoting civic harmony, can also be found in Herodotus 7.153. There the Sicilian colony of Gela had succumbed to *stasis*, and a group of its citizens had been defeated by their opponents and had fled to Mactorium, a nearby inland city. Telines, *hierophant* of the sanctuary of the chthonian goddess in Gela, then went to Mactorium and managed to lead the group back to Gela, assisted only by the power of the *hiera* of the chthonic goddesses, sacred objects like those *hiera* that Miltiades may have attempted to desecrate at Paros. The faction holding Gela was won over and let the exiles return to the polis. Telines' descendants consequently became hereditary *hierophants* of Demeter and Persephone, a post they held for generations. The passage's main significance lies in the role of the cult of Demeter in helping to re-establish civic and religious harmony and cohesion in the polis. As was the case of Miltiades, physical force was to no avail against the goddess, Herodotus implies: Telines, despite being effeminate and physically weak, managed deeds that only a man of brave spirit and manly strength could accomplish. Armed as he was with only the cult's *hiera*, he successfully countered the faction that had prevailed in Gela's *stasis* and persuaded it to re-establish civic peace.

6.4 The Herms' and Eleusinian mysteries' scandal

The complex episode of the scandal of the defacement of the Herms and of the outrage against the Eleusinian mysteries stands out in the narration of Athenian political history in the fifth century, setting the religious and political atmosphere in which Euripides and Aristophanes composed *Bacchae* and *Frogs*. In this section I shall focus on the pivotal role of mystery cults in the development of the Athenian political consciousness at the end of the fifth century.

As Thucydides recounts the episode,[55] during the preparation of the expedition to Sicily, in late spring 415, one day hundreds of the stone statues of Hermes that stood at the corners of streets in Athens were found defaced, their faces destroyed by unknown parties. This gave rise to official enquiries, during which another outrage against Athenian religion came to light, the mock celebration of the Eleusinian mysteries' rituals had taken place in private houses. These celebrations had involved Alcibiades, one of the two leaders of the forthcoming Sicilian expedition. The demos reacted with horror.

The evidence concerning the episode derives from ancient authors who had widely different political views, aims and priorities.[56] On the episode we shall use the account of Thucydides, that of Xenophon, the direct account by Andocides, and that of Plutarch's *Life of Alcibiades,* which was based on contemporary sources.[57] For the episode of Alcibiades' return to Athens in 407 the sources are Xenophon and Plutarch.[58] Despite their diverse ideological approaches, these authors' reports and interpretations suggest that these episodes may be regarded as a turning point in the interrelation between religious sentiments and political thought in the collective imagination of Athenians.

As narrated by Thucydides, the defacement of the Herms was the start of the scandal. In Athens, the Herms were ubiquitous in their apotropaic function, they guarded houses, stood on many street corners and were particularly numerous in places of civic and religious relevance, such as the agora.[59] Whatever its perpetrators and their final intentions, the defacement[60] of the Herms was above all seen by the Athenians as an attack on the political values of the demos as an egalitarian and democratic political body. In their religious and political context, the Herms were a significant iconographic factor in the democratic polis. As Osborne, Furley and Crawley Quinn convincingly argue, the Herms were ubiquitous, powerful reminders of civic and democratic values to passers-by.[61] A group of three Herms had been erected in the area of the agora to commemorate the victors at the siege of Eion that took place in the 470s, a successful campaign headed by Cimon to expel the Persians from Thrace.[62] Aeschines tells the patriotic and democratic implications of the episode.[63] When the victorious generals came back to Athens, the demos gave them the right to set up three stone Herms in the Royal Stoa, a covered portico at the north end of the agora, but on condition that they did not inscribe their names on them as was usual, in order to remind passers-by that the victory belonged to the demos, not to a few generals. As Osborne observes 'a blow struck against the Herms was a blow struck against democracy'.[64]

The mock enactment of the rituals of the Eleusinian mysteries hit deeper into the psychology of the demos than the defacement of the Herms and was an act of grave civic and religious sacrilege. Revealing the details of the rituals to non-initiates was one of the most serious crimes in the Athenian code of unwritten laws and was punishable by death,[65] while mocking the mysteries was a metaphorical act of blasphemous destruction. The fact that mock celebrations of mystical rituals had been performed as a deliberate gesture of civic and religious outrage (ἐφ' ὕβρει) and had been performed for some time in some private houses, made the matter all the more serious. The involvement of Alcibiades, the aristocratic controversial proponent of the Sicilian expedition on one of its two leaders, made the matter highly political and contentious.

Plutarch is explicit in linking the scandal with the sanctity of mystery cults. As he reports in detail,[66] the charges against Alcibiades and his fellow conspirators were extremely serious: committing a crime against the two Eleusinian goddesses (ἀδικεῖν περὶ τὼ θεώ, τὴν Δήμητραν καὶ τὴν Κόρην), mimicking the mystical secret rituals (ἀπομιμούμενον τὰ μυστήρια), enacting them to his companions in his house, wearing the *hierophant*'s robe, calling himself '*hierophant*', his friend Polytion and Theodorus '*dadouchos*' and '*keryx*', and addressing the rest of his companions as '*mystai*' and '*epoptai*' were serious offences against the laws of the Eumolpidae and Kerykes. Whatever the truth about the matter of Alcibiades' involvement, the population felt incensed at the hubristic outrage against the Eleusinian mysteries and supported the measures taken against Alcibiades and his fellow aristocrats. In both Plutarch's and Thucydides' accounts, the response was as determined as the shock had been violent.

How did the Athenians react? Interestingly, Thucydides creates a crescendo in the reactions of the demos to the two affairs. Thucydides stresses the unorganized, massive nature of the support for the enterprise: all Athenians alike fell in love with the expedition (ἔρως ἐνέπεσε τοῖς πᾶσιν ὁμοίως ἐκπλεῦσαι).[67] The terms Thucydides uses emphasize his reservations about the enterprise and the irrational judgement of the crowd. He calls the sentiment of the people passionate desire (ἔρως), a sentiment very far from the civic and mystical term for reason and self-control (σωφροσύνη), and qualifies the people's enthusiasm (ἐπιθυμία) with the term excessive (ἄγαν). The emphasis on the massive support for the expedition moved by greed also defines *in absentia* the smallness of the group who stood in opposition to it, to which the exiled Thucydides and the authors of the sacrilegious outrages may well have belonged.

The immediate reaction of the people to the scandal of the Herms, in Thucydides' narrative, identifies unnamed conspirators as the culprits but is far from being focused on a specific political adversary. The defacement of the statues had initially aroused suspicions of a conspiracy aimed at discouraging the expedition,[68] at introducing into the polis an undefined order of 'newer things' and upset democracy (ξυνωμοσία δήμου καταλύσεως).[69] As Thucydides' readers would have been aware, the wording of the threat to the polis mirrored the wording of the traditional Solonian code of laws inscribed on a stele in the agora that allowed anybody to slay with impunity those holders of a public office after the suppression of democracy. According to Plutarch, fearing the conspirators' intent on a daring, radical venture (ἐπὶ πράγμασι μεγάλοις), the demos reacted to the news in in wrath and fear (ὀργῇ δ' ἅμα καὶ φόβῳ).[70]

It is only after evidence of the blasphemous mockery of the mysteries and the involvement of Alcibiades were brought into the open a few days later, that suspicions became better focused and precise political accusations made. Thucydides describes that the people then became suspicious, developing a belief that the episode was not an isolated act and started considering the conspiracy to disband the demos as part of an oligarchical and tyrannical conspiracy (ξυνωμοσία ὀλιγαρχικῇ καὶ τυραννικῇ).[71] The passage is important. The involvement of the mysteries marked the moment the politically unfocused demos came to define its political stance. The combination of traditional religious and civic sentiments animated the reaction of the people. The demos' traditional anti-tyrannical stance and its devotion to the cult of Demeter helped the development of something akin to a political definition of the adversary of the democratic polis, the oligarchic circles.

The association of oligarchic circles with the sacrilege together with the suspicions of a conspiracy aimed at establishing tyranny in Athens, formed the background of the narration of Alcibiades' return to Athens in 407 in the accounts of Xenophon and Plutarch.[72] Both narrations confirm the central place held by the Eleusinian mystical cult in Athens. After Alcibiades' trial in absentia was concluded by the confiscation of his property and later by the death penalty, all priests and priestesses were requested by decree to publicly curse the name of Alcibiades. They all obeyed except for one priestess, Theanó, who claimed she had become a priestess to pray to the gods, not to curse people.[73] The opposition of the Eleusinian clergy to Alcibiades' return lasted a long time. When Pisander and other envoys from the Athenian fleet at Samos came to Athens in 412 to put forward Alcibiades' plan to allow him back into the city, change the constitution and have the Persians as allies, Thucydides relates how a number of speakers opposed them in defence of democracy, with the Eumolpidae and Kerykes protesting on behalf of the Eleusinian mysteries and calling upon the gods to avert his recall.[74] Hostility to Alcibiades on religious and political grounds continued, despite the growing popularity that led to his recall to Athens in 407. At the initiative of Critias, the charges against him were repealed, the *demos* voted that his property be restored to him, he was crowned and proclaimed general in chief with full authority (ἡγεμὼν αὐτοκράτωρ). The Eumolpidae and Kerykes were asked to revoke the curses they had made at the command of the people, with one exception, that of Theodoros the *hierophant* himself. Xenophon has the *hierophant* significantly link the lifting of the curse to Alcibiades' civic and political behaviour, and has him declare 'No, I invoke no curses on him if he does no wrong to the polis' (εἰ μηδὲν ἀδικεῖ τὴν πόλιν).[75]

The epilogue of the scandal helps shed light on the importance of mystery cults in the polis of Athens at the end of the fifth century. Aware that his political fate in Athens depended on his repairing his religious and civic reputation with regard to mystery cults, Alcibiades, upon his return in 407, decided to wait until after the Eleusinian festival to join the war with the hundred triremes of which he had been given the command.[76] During his absence, the annual land procession to Eleusis had to be discontinued after the Spartans had occupied and fortified the town of Decelea in 413. Decelea was a town high on the slopes of the Parnes mountain range dividing Attica from Boeotia. From there, the Spartans gained an extensive view of a large part of the Attic plain, of the city of Athens, of the harbour of Piraeus and of the land passage between Attica and the north of Greece. From Decelea, the Spartans could attack the Eleusis procession on open grounds. The Spartans' military control over the plain of Attica effectively cut off land communications between Athens and Eleusis. The procession to Eleusis had to be abandoned. While initiands and *epoptai* probably continued their annual voyage to Eleusis by sea,[77] the Eleusinian festival lost the rituals that were open to the public, the procession by land: 'sacrifices, choral dances, and many of the sacred ceremonies usually held on the road, when Iacchus is conducted from Athens to Eleusis, had of necessity been abandoned' notes Plutarch.[78] The procession was a powerful symbol of the cohesion of the polis and of its victory against the

Persians at Salamis, as Herodotus attests:[79] disrupting the procession was an act aimed at the heart of the unity and courage of the Athenians.

In an act of repentance and of allegiance to the polis, Alcibiades then led the renewed annual procession by land to Eleusis, under the protection of his army, as his first public act after his return to Athens in 407.[80] It was a solemn and theatrical act to enhance his holiness in the eyes of the gods and his good reputation in the minds of men (πρὸς θεῶν ὁσιότητα καὶ πρὸς ἀνθρώπων δόξαν).[81] Plutarch describes the scene in detail, emphasizing the religious rituals that Alcibiades had set up. After having secured the way with his army, he led the group of *mystai*, priests and mystagogues to Eleusis, with a large crowd following. The procession marched in an orderly fashion and in silence (ἐν κόσμῳ καὶ μετὰ σιωπῆς), terms that we noted mark the behaviour of the initiates. It was a sacred and devout spectacle (θέαμα σεμνὸν καὶ θεοπρεπές). In the desperate plight of Athens, not able to control the Aegean Sea, banned from her own suburbs, torn by *stasis* (στασιάζουσα), the procession turned the public opinion in Athens to Alcibiades' favour, with some of the Athenians hailing as *hierophant* and *mystagogue* the man they had hitherto considered a sacrilegious criminal.[82]

To summarize, the development and conclusion of the Herms and mysteries affair highlights three major themes intertwined in the perceptions of the Athenians. The first is the strength of the popular veneration for the Eleusinian mysteries; the second is the growing connotation of oligarchic circles as opponents of religion and as threat to democracy; the third is the association, not yet clearly defined, of mystery cults with the polis' democratic and anti-tyrannical ideology of equality.

6.5 Aeschylus, Diagoras and *Asebeia*

The attachment of the Athenians to the sacred nature of the mystery initiation rituals at Eleusis is evidenced by some of the episodes concerning the impiety, *asebeia,* trials that took place in Athens in the fifth century. At this time, charges of *asebeia* and atheism were brought against philosophers such as Anaxagoras, Protagoras, Prodicus, Democritus and famously Socrates, at the very beginning of the fourth century. *Asebeia* was a crime that had no precise definition, as

Aristotle, for example, defined it as a transgression in regard to gods and daemons, or with regard to the departed, or to parents and country, a wide and imprecise definition that was often open to politically motivated charges and interpretations.[83] While the trials have been widely interpreted as the result of a climate of popular hostility against the new sophist-inspired intellectual thought,[84] they also shed light on the association between the demos' religious sense, in particular on its reverence for the mystery cults, and on the polis' political atmosphere.

One such episode concerns Aeschylus the tragedian. A scholiast to Aristotle's *Ethica Nicomachea* 3.2 relates that Heraclides Ponticus, a fourth-century philosopher and disciple of Plato, wrote how Aeschylus once risked being lynched on stage because he seemed to have revealed some of the secrets of the mysteries. He took refuge at the altar of Dionysus, before being brought in front of the court of the Areopagus and acquitted because of the bravery he had shown at the battle of Marathon and the wounds he had received there, where his brother had lost both his hands. It is interesting to note that only his military valour, a pre-eminent civic virtue in Athens, managed to override the religious gravity of his charge of *asebeia*. In a comment on the same episode in his *Ethica Nicomachea*, Aristotle relates that Aeschylus defended himself from the accusation declaring that he was not aware 'that the matter was a secret'.[85] Clement of Alexandria adds that Aristotle defended himself by declaring that he had not been initiated.[86] That Aeschylus had not been aware of the secret nature of the mysteries or that he had never been initiated may have been felt as obviously untrue by contemporary Athenians. Not only was he born in Eleusis, but his *Oresteia* was inspired by mystery initiation rituals. It may be imagined that his trial had encouraged Aeschylus to be less open about the secrets of the mysteries in the *Oresteia* than he may have been in previous plays.[87] If one is to judge public opinion on Aeschylus' relationship with the mysteries by what Aristophanes has him declare in *Frogs,* he was believed not only to be an Eleusinian initiate, but also to have claimed that his whole work was inspired by Demeter.[88]

Ancient references to the case of Diagoras of Melos explicitly mention his *asebeia* in connection with the Eleusinian mysteries and are worth examining in the context of the role played by the polis' judicial bodies in judging religious cases. Diagoras, a contemporary of Socrates and Andocides,[89] was born in

Melos probably in the 460s and lived in Athens, where he was known as an 'atheist' (probably better rendered as 'sceptical in religious matters') poet and philosopher since the 430s.[90] His scepticism of traditional religion was common knowledge in the 420s: Aristophanes alludes to Diagoras in his *Clouds*, the extant second version of which was produced in the early 410s,[91] in *Birds*, produced in 414,[92] and in *Frogs*, produced in 405.[93]

In 415/14,[94] Diagoras was condemned by the ecclesia for his religious views, perhaps in the wake of the religious sentiment arising from the sacrilege against the Eleusinian rituals. Quoting a passage of Craterus, an historian at the end of the fourth century, a scholiast to *Birds* writes that the Athenians had condemned Diagoras for his *asebeia*, where he was accused of revealing the Eleusinian mysteries to all, being disparaging of them and of discouraging those who wished to be initiated. In his absence, the Athenians offered a prize for bringing in Diagoras dead or alive, a decree inscribed on a bronze stele in Athens.[95] The episode is echoed by Diodorus Siculus who recounts that Diagoras, fearing the anger of the demos at the time of the religious troubles of 415, fled from Attica and took refuge in Pallene during the archonship of Charias.[96]

In conclusion, we may be tempted to judge the persecution of so-called 'atheism' in light of the modern sense of toleration for free thinking and the liberty of expression. But the Athenians perceived these episodes in a radically different way: in the fifth century the popular feelings for the cult were very strong, and the actions they took against those who were felt to have breached the fundamental tenets of the Eleusinian cult were severe. The need to have the charges of *asebeia* against Aeschylus judged in the supreme Areopagus court as well as the severity of the alleged judgement against Diagoras are evidence of the demos' association of its religious beliefs with the self-preservation of the polis as a coherent community.

6.6 Religion, the demos and the Arginusae trial

The trial assessing how responsible the generals of the fleet were for the costly outcome of the battle of Arginusae was conducted in the ecclesia in late-summer to autumn 406, a few months before the production of *Bacchae* and

Frogs. Our two sources, Xenophon, a contemporary to the facts, and the first-century historian Diodorus Siculus, give detailed accounts of the battle and the trial of the generals that followed it.[97]

The battle at Arginusae had been the first major victory of the Athenian fleet against the Spartan fleet in the east Aegean, after the Athenian naval defeat at Notium in the early summer of 506. Following that defeat, Alcibiades, widely blamed for his absence from the battle, left Athens for good.[98] The ecclesia replaced him with ten generals. One of them, Conon, at the head of the Athenian fleet, was defeated by the Spartans and came to be blockaded, by sea and by land, on the island of Lesbos.[99] To rescue Conon, despite the lack of resources and of manpower, Athens managed to prepare a 110-ship fleet and manned it with free men and slaves and, Xenophon notes, even knights.[100] The two fleets met off the Arginusae, small islets close to the coast of Asia Minor in front of the island of Lesbos.[101] The Athenians won the battle, but it was a costly victory in terms of loss of ships and men.[102] The battle had been followed by a furious storm, that prevented the fleet from helping the disabled vessels and their crews. Athens lost twenty-five Athenian triremes.[103] In the trial that followed the generals who were present were condemned to death and executed.

What were the generals[104] accused of? Contemporary sources differ on this critical point. Xenophon reports that they were held responsible for not having sailed, as they had been ordered, to the aid of the disabled vessels, therefore not sa123ving the men on board them (ἐπὶ τὰς καταδεδυκυίας ναῦς καὶ τοὺς ἐπ' αὐτῶν ἀνθρώπους);[105] that is, they were responsible for having left the crews of the disabled ships unaided in the gale and the swell (ἄνεμος καὶ χειμών) that followed the battle. In Xenophon, the charge is 'for not picking up the men who won the victory in the naval battle' (οὐκ ἀνελόμενοι τοὺς νικήσαντας ἐν τῇ ναυμαχίᾳ).[106] It was thus for Xenophon a purely military and humanitarian matter.

Diodorus, basing himself largely on the evidence of the contemporary Ephorus and on the author of the 'P' manuscript fragments in the *Hellenica Oxyrhynchia*,[107] tells a markedly different story. In Diodorus, some of the generals believed that the fleet should pick up the dead, not the survivors, after the battle, since they knew that the Athenians would be incensed if the dead went unburied. However, a great storm (χειμὼν μέγας) prevented them from doing so.¹⁰⁸ Diodorus comments on the judgement of the ecclesia, stating that it had condemned to death the victorious generals at Arginusae because they had failed to bury the man who had died in the battle, a charge he emphasizes by recounting the caution of the winning Athenian general Chabrias after the later battle of Naxos in 376, who feared he would be condemned as the generals had at Arginusae because they neglected to bury the dead (ὅτι τοὺς τετελευτηκότας κατὰ τὴν ναυμαχίαν οὐκ ἔθαψαν).¹⁰⁹ This charge against the generals is also confirmed by Plato, who at the time of the affair was in his early twenties and possibly a witness of the trial: in *Menexenos*, he describes the valour of the Athenian crews who had won many battles but who at Arginusae met with undeserved misfortune, since their bodies were not recovered from the sea and were unable to be buried in Athens.¹¹⁰

In normal circumstances, the mention of a violent storm would have probably caused the exculpation of the generals. The order to rescue the living or the dead from the sea was impossible to execute. As any sailor who sailed the Aegean knew then and knows now, northerly gales in the narrow passage between the island of Lesbos and the mainland can be extremely violent in summer, reaching up to force 8 and more on the Beaufort scale, dangerous even to today's large ships. The manoeuvre would have been extremely difficult and perilous as it entailed ships that were undecked and propelled by oars against a gale and swell. Trying to recover the bodies from the water would have potentially sunk the fleet, or otherwise delivered it downwind into the hands of the Spartans at Phocaea and Cyme. Only the heavy losses and the passionate religious beliefs of the people could justify the violence of the reaction against the generals.

Most scholars have followed Xenophon's version, although it makes less sense than Diodorus'.¹¹¹ What moved the ecclesia to condemn the generals collectively to death? As a consequence of following Xenophon's version, the trial has been largely regarded as the result of popular hysteria,¹¹² of the violence and terror inspired by the demos,¹¹³ and a procedure that was 'unjust, much regretted, and probably illegal' as Roberts notes.¹¹⁴ Little discussed by scholars¹¹⁵ (and even found 'surprising' by Andrewes)¹¹⁶ is Diodorus' version, which makes the demos' drastic decision comprehensible and in line with the religious feelings that dominated Athens' political life. Far from being what Andrewes calls a 'disastrous misunderstanding' between two sets of political opponents, the decision of the ecclesia, although extreme, unparalleled and possibly even illegal on procedural grounds, was steeped in Greek religious beliefs.

The sacred duty to bury the dead in religious rituals was fundamental to the self-identity of the polis.[117] The demos mourned the unburied heroes of the battle more than the loss of the men who may have survived the battle, as it was an impious breach of the unwritten law on the burials of fallen warriors that Athenians regarded as divine. The accounts of Xenophon and Diodorus describe vividly the state of mind of the demos in the ecclesia: furious, violent and intolerant. One term Diodorus uses for the wrath of the ecclesia is 'fury', ὀργή,[118] the same term Thucydides uses to describe the state of mind of the demos during the scandal of the Herms;[119] this helps reveal a nuance in the crowd's sentiment, that of pious outrage at a sacrilegious act. Not only was the denial of funerary rituals impious, but it would have caused *miasma* to the whole community. Funeral rituals were a way of purifying the community of the pollution caused by death, and collective purification rituals strengthened civic cohesion and created *homonoia*, as had been the case of the rituals established by Epimenides in the polis of Athens when gripped by *stasis*.[120]

The other significant point of difference between the two accounts regards the depiction of the Apaturia worshippers who joined the ecclesia meeting and of their influence on the ecclesia's decision. The festival lasted three days in the month of Pyanopsium (October) and was one of the longest and most popular in Attica, being the occasion for the ritual expression and enactment of solidarity and bonding between members of the region's phratries, to which all citizens belonged. The Apaturia was a fundamental festival in the life of families, as boys, ephebes and grown men upon their marriage would be accepted by their phratries, the social and religious units of the community that approved access to civic rights and registration of boys into the citizenship/military status. In the festival, girls would offer a sacrifice (*gamelion*) to Athena to officialize their being accepted by the phratria of their husband, a change of civic status that ensured a citizen status for her progenies and her becoming a spouse and mother.[121] Xenophon presents the crowd of the Apaturia festival who attended the meeting at the ecclesia as people whom Theramenes had convinced to pretend to be kinsmen of those who had perished[122] in order to put the ecclesia under pressure. Diodorus instead presents them more credibly as genuine mourners and relatives of the dead, who appeared in the assembly in mourning garments begging the demos to punish those who had allowed valorous men to go unburied.[123] As was the case of the religious motivations of the reaction of the demos to the 415 scandals, Grote may be possibly nearer the mark than most modern historians:

> The men, ... inflamed into preternatural and overwhelming violence by the festival of the Apaturia, where all the religious traditions connected with the ancient family tie, all those associations which imposed upon the relatives of a murdered man the duty of pursuing the murderer, were expanded into detail and worked up by their appropriate renovating solemnity. The garb of mourning and the shaving of the head—phenomena unknown at Athens either in a political assembly or in a religious festival—were symbols of temporary transformation in the internal man. He could think of nothing but his drowning relatives, together with the generals as having abandoned them to death, and his own duty as survivor to ensure to them vengeance and satisfaction for such abandonment.[124]

In Diodorus' account the Arginusae trial shows further evidence of the strong attachment of the demos of Athens to the polis' traditional unwritten laws and to its religious and civic rituals. The trial had also shown how deeply divisive a traditional issue such as the denial of burial rituals could be, and how forceful the reaction of the demos was capable of being when facing an impious violation of rituals, as it had happened in the case of the mysteries scandal in 415.[125] The tension between the demos, openly defending religious principles and asserting its democratic rights above all considerations,[126] and the generals together with those who attempted to defend them, such as Theramenes and Euryptolemus, shows how polarized this debate was.

The conflict at the trial was probably only the visible part of a larger dissatisfaction of the demos with the decision to grant freedom and citizenship to the slaves manning the fleet. Hunt[127] and Asmonti[128] argue that the exceptional steps taken by the Athenians in conferring citizenship on metics as well on any other foreigner who were willing to fight with them, undermined the traditional social and economic order of the polis, and is likely to have caused discontent, particularly in view of the losses caused by the battle. A further motive for the tension may well be linked to the political and constitutional conflict between the generals and the demos regarding the political control of the war and its strategy, well explored by Asmonti. The reaction of the demos therefore had a constitutional *raison d'etre*, that of reaffirming the pre-eminence of the demos in the decisions of the conduit of the war over the autonomy of the generals.

Another factor that may also have played a part in the popular reaction against the generals was the religious and socio/political tension between the demos and those it suspected of oligarchic and anti-religious sympathies. The social status of some of the generals would have provided some grounds for this sentiment. The political figures of the generals Aristocrates, Diomedon, Pericles junior, Erasinides, Thrasyllus and Lysias can be associated with Alcibiades: sworn democrats, but most of them coming from those aristocratic and wealthy families that had been involved in the scandal of the Herms and of the mysteries, a man whose dubious loyalty is well described by the exchange between Dionysus, Euripides and Aeschylus in *Frogs*.

> **Dionysus** What opinion does each of you have about Alcibiades? The polis is in labour about him.
>
> **Aeschylus** Is there an opinion about him?
>
> **Dionysus** Which one? It yearns for him – it hates him – and it wants to have him.
>
> **Euripides** I hate the kind of citizen who'll prove to be slow in assisting his country, swift to harm her greatly, for his good own astute, but of no use for the polis.[129]

Among them, Aristocrates was a man of wealth and influence[130] and had been a member of the Four Hundred;[131] Diomedon was a friend of Alcibiades and Thrasybulus, a group that had democratic credentials but few allies amongst the radical democrats.[132] Pericles junior and Euryptolemus, the man who attempted to defend the generals before the ecclesia, both belonged to one of the richest and most influential families in Athens, the Alcmaeonidae, the family that had been exiled as guilty of sacrilege during Cylon's attempted coup. Erasinides was not a friend of the democrats, and Archedemus had brought him to justice for embezzling public funds he had received while commanding a fleet in the Hellespont.[133] The generals were thus what Asmonti calls 'elite citizens . . . simultaneously a danger to democracy and indispensable to the political decision-making process'[134] to which I would add indispensable to the conduct of the war. The religious background of the condemnation of the generals was therefore also founded on the social and political conflict between the religious demos and those whom the people perceived as impious oligarchs, a tension that found its zenith when the Thirty were brought to power in 404.

6.7 The overthrow of the Thirty and civic reconciliation

As the Spartan Lysander and his fleet blockaded Piraeus after the Athenian defeat at Aegospotami in the autumn of 405, a few months after the performances of *Bacchae* and *Frogs*, the conflict between oligarchs and the demos erupted. Oligarchic circles took advantage of the critical moment and attacked Cleophon, the most influential democratic pro-war leader of the demos,[135] and had him condemned to death by a rigged jury of oligarchs.[136] At some point in the middle part of 404,[137] Athens finally agreed to surrender to the Spartans and the regime of the Thirty was established in the polis. In his detailed narrative of the rise and fall of the regime of the Thirty in *Hellenica*,[138] Xenophon concentrates on the paradigmatic conflict between democratic and religious sentiments of Athenians and the lawlessness, impiety and rapacity of the regime of the Thirty,[139] a theme that is expressed in the subtext of democratic and Eleusinian values that has been mostly unnoticed by scholars. The passage is a further example of the association between Eleusinian mystery values on the one hand and civic and religious reconciliation as a solution to civic strife on the other.

By this logic, the value of Xenophon's account of the regime of the Thirty and its fall is not so much as a writer of 'historical' facts, but as a contribution to the understanding of the Athenian democratic ethic and civic discourse that animates his educational tale, in which he mixes fiction, historical facts and characters into his moral and political discourse.[140] As Dillery puts it, the passage in Xenophon dedicated to the rise and fall of the Thirty is of particular use to historians as it 'reflects the intellectual climate of the day'.[141]

While the connections between Xenophon's depiction of the Thirty as impious oligarchs turning into tyrants, the occurrence of *stasis*, and its solution through Eleusinian values is vital for understanding his account, few scholars have examined it. As Bowden notes, there has been little study of the theme of Xenophon and religion.[142] While Loraux for instance puts the speech of Cleocritus at the centre of her 1997 analysis of the subject of *stasis* and reconciliation as essential components of Athenian politics, she disappointingly fails to focus on the religious aspects of the passage. Some attention to the Eleusinian associations in the passage would have helped in answering her question on the reason why the democrats in Athens chose not to take revenge on their political opponents but embracing instead the values of peace and reconciliation.[143]

Xenophon gradually builds up the characterization of the Thirty as greedy, violent and impious tyrants whose rule inevitably produces civic strife and rebellion, both forms of *stasis*. Xenophon initially presents them as elected by the demos among oligarchic circles in order to draw up the constitutional rules under which the polis would have been organized and ruled;[144] after that, their progression to absolute power and personal rule is described as fast and ruthless. Xenophon shows the progress of the rule and the eventual fall of the Thirty through the conflict between the figures of the tyrant Critias and three characters, Theramenes, Thrasybulus and Cleocritus. The order in which these characters oppose Critias is important, as it reveals Xenophon's religious and political credo. The first opponents of the Thirty is one of their own, Theramenes, whose opposition is not based on the merits of the oligarchic cause but on the excesses of their rule. His character, as well as his death at the hand of Critias, is used by Xenophon to illustrate the futility of opposing the Thirty through constitutional means. Second comes Thrasybulus, a democrat who chose armed struggle to fight against the Thirty, but whose ultimate goal is revenge.[145] Thrasybulus' political stance is thus qualified on ethical grounds: killing in revenge can only cause more killing in revenge, the endless cycle that Athena stopped in Aeschylus' *Eumenides*. The Eleusinian theme of putting an end to *stasis* and of putting into effect a reconciliation of all Athenians is instead at the centre of the speech of the Eleusinian *keryx* Cleocritus, whose speech effectively concludes the conflict in Xenophon's tale and opens an era of civic peace.

Xenophon's choice of Critias as leader of the Thirty and as the arch-villain of the episode is not coincidental. Xenophon had a low opinion of Critias, and he had called Critias the greediest and most violent of the oligarchs.[146] Critias' political past did nothing to contradict Xenophon's opinion. He had been arrested in connection with the affair of the Herms, before being freed on Andocides' evidence.[147] After the fall of the Four Hundred he had posthumously prosecuted for treason Phrynichus, one of the organizers of the Four Hundred coup who had been murdered by political opponents;[148] he was exiled under the democratic regime and returned only after Athens' surrendered to Sparta in order to organize the overthrow of democracy.[149]

Xenophon is careful to lay out a progression towards the Thirty's tyrannical behaviour. Firstly, following the traditional pattern of would-be tyrants in the Athenian imagination, the Thirty called upon a foreign enemy, the Spartans, to send troops to Athens in order to be able to control the polis.[150] Secondly, the long exchange of political speeches by Critias and Theramenes is preceded by a short but revelatory exchange between the two on the subject of tyranny and greed.[151] In Xenophon, Theramenes observes that it was unfair to put a man to death solely because he was honoured by the demos: Critias answers that it would have been foolish for the Thirty, who wished to use their advantage for personal gain not to act as one tyrant.[152] Critias' cynical remark hovers over the rest of the episode. The connection between greed, hubris and lawlessness as features of tyranny was one of the cornerstones of Athenian civic consciousness,[153] and strengthens the depiction of the Thirty as the enemies of the polis. Xenophon then has Critias describe openly the regime of the Thirty as an oligarchy to the *Boule*, the polis supreme court.[154]

In Xenophon, the violence against the Thirty's political adversaries escalated, not only for political reason, but because of personal enmity and in order to rob rich opponents of their wealth.[155] A specific target of the regime' violence for financial gain was the community of metics, to which the speech-writer and orator Lysias' family belonged, an episode that he vividly portrayed in one of his speeches.[156] Standard tyrannical behaviour of the Thirty also included the disarming of people, and the formation of a personal bodyguard that revealed their fear of reprisals.[157] Disregard for religion and committing acts of sacrilege are one of the features of a tyrant. The last act of Critias in Xenophon's account before being killed at the battle of Munichia is to have his men seize Theramenes despite his standing as a suppliant at the altar of the *Bouleuterion*, thus breaching the sacred law on *hiketeia*, the law protecting suppliants.

Here, Xenophon is implying the political limits of what he described as Theramenes' 'lonely fight' against Critias. Theramenes, despite being virtuous, is still an oligarch, ready to accept that the polis should be ruled by oligarchs, the cavalry and hoplites, 'those capable of service with their horses and shields';[158] however, he is opposed to those who believe that a good oligarchy can only be established by the tyranny of a few men. Impious and unjust men cannot be stopped by any individual, even if he is justified and has the agreement of the *Boule*, Xenophon seems to imply,[159] leaving the solution as the Eleusinian reconciliation promoted by Cleocritus. Xenophon describes the end of Theramenes' life in a religious and dramatic way, making Theramenes call to the gods as witnesses to this impious act of the Thirty, the most unjust and impious of men.[160]

Resistance to the Thirty was then led by Thrasybulus of the deme of Steiria, whom Xenophon makes the protagonist of the democratic movement that leads to the fall of the Thirty. Thrasybulus was a good choice for this role, a man whose democratic credentials Thucydides narrates. He had helped the democrats in Samos to beat the oligarchic faction on the island and, together with Thrasyllus, was one of the leaders of the Samos anti-oligarchic revolution in 411.[161] When, some time later, the Samians heard the news of the coup of the Four Hundred in Athens, Thrasybulus and Thrasyllus made all soldiers on the island swear an oath to accept a democratic government, to live in harmony (δημοκρατήσεσθαί τε καὶ ὁμονοήσειν), and to continue the war against Sparta.[162] A valiant general, Thrasybulus is described as fighting against the Spartans together with Alcibiades in the north Aegean. He fought at Cynossema, Abydus, at Cyzicus and Arginusae, major victories of the Athenian fleet.[163] Not mentioned by Xenophon but instead by the author/s of the *Constitution of the Athenians* is an episode concerning Thrasybulus, completing his democratic credentials and giving an insight on the radicality of his views.[164] After the overthrow of the Thirty, Thrasybulus proposed a decree giving full citizens' rights to all those who had supported him as well to other democratic exiles in overthrowing the Thirty and re-instituting the democratic constitution after the 403 amnesty. Thrasybulus' decree was thus strongly egalitarian as among the men who had joined forces with Thrasybulus from Piraeus some were clearly slaves (ἔνιοι φανερῶς ἦσαν δοῦλοι),[165] while other foreigners as well as people of every kind (παντοδαποί),[166] probably numbering 1,000 in all.[167]

Noted briefly by Lysias and Diodorus,[168] is an episode involving the Thirty' violence against the polis of Eleusis which emphasizes Xenophon's Eleusinian discourse on the overthrow of the impious Thirty.[169] Headed by Critias, the Thirty, frightened by the success of Thrasybulus and of his democratic followers in repulsing their attacks on his fortress of Phyle, decided to occupy Eleusis as a possible haven from a democratic revolt. They assembled Eleusis' adult male inhabitants for a military review and had horsemen arrest them. The prisoners were then put to judgement in Athens' Odeum. The judgement was conducted by troops loyal to the Thirty, in the presence of Spartan troops who filled half of the Odeum space. The Eleusinians were condemned and put to death. Xenophon is vague about the number[170] and identity of the executed Eleusinians, but their massacre is designed to horrify the Athenians, for whom Eleusis was the seat of the revered cult of the Two Goddesses and a polis they controlled, a reaction which would be similar to that to the scandal of the mysteries in 415.

The speech that Xenophon has Thrasybulus make before the battle between the Thirty's troops and the democrats on the hillock of Munichia in Piraeus, is explicitly steeped in the terms and sentiments that are simultaneously civic and religious.[171] Addressing explicitly his followers not as warriors, but as citizens of the polis (ἄνδρες πολῖται), Thrasybulus put emphasis on the fact that divinity was now in favour of his party.[172] Xenophon is emphasizing here the divine favour (εὐδαιμονία) Thrasybulus' force enjoys. The gods have assisted us, Thrasybulus says, with a snowstorm,[173] and allowed us victories over superior forces in the past. The gods themselves are openly fighting today with us (οἱ θεοί ... νῦν φανερῶς ἡμῖν συμμαχοῦσι), as the Thirty persecute people who had done nothing against the law. In the finale of the speech, Xenophon has Thrasybulus connect his speech to Eleusinian concepts through several terms connected to the mysteries. Thrasybulus ends his speech to his troops in a solemn *makarismos*, proclaiming as blessed (μακάριοι) those who will win the battle and he who will fall as blessed by the gods (εὐδαίμων). In Thrasybulus' final words, Xenophon emphasizes the contrast between the solidarity of initiates/democrats and the tyrants' hubris. When the propitious moment will come, he, Thrasybulus, will intone the paean and all in accord (πάντες ὁμοθυμαδόν) will bring revenge to those men from whom they have suffered hubristic violence.[174]

Xenophon's emphasis on divinity continues into the ensuing battle. Having foreseen his own death as the price to be paid for victory, the unnamed prophet who was with Thrasybulus led the charge and was killed instantly, after which the attack of the democrats was decisive and victorious.[175] The battle was won and Critias was among the fallen. Following the battle, the survivors in both camps remained mingled together instead of retiring each to his own camp as was usual. But they were all Athenians, many would have had a relative or a friend in the opposite camp, and a discussion started. At this crucial and bizarre moment, where both victors and defeated mixed, Xenophon introduces the apparition of Cleocritus, a fighter in Thrasybulus' army. In Xenophon's account, the figure of Cleocritus embodies the values of mystery cults and his speech to the crowd may have shared some of the characteristics of the speech the *keryx* made to the *mystai* in initiation rituals.[176] Xenophon describes him as herald of the Eleusinian mystery cult and a man of good voice (ὁ τῶν μυστῶν κῆρυξ, μάλ' εὔφωνος ὤν).[177] His figure recalls the massacre of Eleusinian citizens, a survivor of that sacrilegious action, and his sacred role of *keryx* contrasts to the impiousness of the Thirty. In his function as herald, announcing the opening of the Eleusis festivals to the crowd in the agora, Cleocritus would have been a well-known figure to Athenians, and is mentioned twice by Aristophanes, once in connection with mystery cults.[178]

As befits a *keryx* of the *mystai*, Cleocritus first called the crowd to silence, that essential opening address of religious ceremonies. Cleocritus then proceeds to make a speech to troops.[179] It is a plea for peace, a speech of reconciliation, 'a minor masterpiece in a mood of solemn grandeur', as Gray calls it.[180] Xenophon has Cleocritus use the same political address (ἄνδρες πολῖται) as Thrasybulus had used, thus emphasizing from the start the community between victors and vanquished. Cleocritus focuses not on the vengeance that Thrasybulus had promised but instead on the need for the two parties to reconcile their differences.[181] The difference between the political content of the two speeches is of importance, as it marks the transition from violent retribution to peaceful reconciliation as the founding principle of the community of the polis. Here, Xenophon develops his religious and political credo, a concept not based on the concept of divinity supporting the religious democrats as Thrasybulus had done, but instead on the religious ties linking all Athenians as a basis for any form of government that was to rule Athens. The concepts Cleocritus raises are those parallel mystical and civic values that we shall observe in *Bacchae* and *Frogs* as being the core of the message of the choruses/*thiasoi* to the polis.

Cleocritus starts his peroration on a religious tone, in the name of the gods of all Athenian fathers and mothers, ending it on the tears both sides shed for the dead. What is the logic of a civil war, asks Cleocritus, between men who have shared the most solemn religious rituals and sacrificial ceremonies and the finest festivals (ἱερῶν τῶν σεμνοτάτων καὶ θυσιῶν καὶ ἑορτῶν τῶν καλλίστων)? It is a declaration of the primacy of religion over politics, and it comes from the mouth of an Eleusinian high priest and a declared democrat, thus associating the notions of peace to that of the Eleusinian rituals and other religious festivals as experiences common to all the Athenians. Cleocritus' second point emphasizes the other aspects of Athenian life that all Athenians had in common: first their activities in choruses, secondly their school education and thirdly companionship in arms. Both parties, Xenophon has Cleocritus claim, have been companions in choruses, have been schoolfellows and fellow-soldiers (συγχορευταὶ καὶ συμφοιτηταὶ ... καὶ συστρατιῶται), and sharing the same ties of kinship, marriage and fellowship in clubs, *hetairiai* (συγγενείας καὶ κηδεστίας καὶ ἑταιρίας).[182] Cleocritus then asserts the communality of the risks the two parties had run in fighting on land and sea and the communality of their goals; the safety and freedom (σωτηρία καὶ ἐλευθερία) of the polis.

Xenophon, in the powerful finale of Cleocritus' speech, uses solemn religious and ethical terms which express his civic and religious sentiments about *stasis*, the ultimate evil that can befall a polis. The antinomy here is between the state of peace and civic cohesion that would exist between citizens, and the state of civil war the Thirty had brought to the polis. Echoing Theramenes' final exclamation, Cleocritus calls the Thirty the most impious of men, men who have killed their fellow Athenians for the sake of their private gains and brought war between fellow citizens, *stasis*: the most dishonourable, most painful, most ungodly and most hateful thing to gods and men (τὸν πάντων αἴσχιστόν τε καὶ χαλεπώτατον καὶ ἀνοσιώτατον καὶ ἔχθιστον καὶ θεοῖς καὶ ἀνθρώποις πόλεμον ἡμῖν πρὸς ἀλλήλους).

Xenophon brings up some of the same themes in Thrasybulus' speech to the Athenians in the ecclesia, after the fall of the regime of the Thirty.[183] Thrasybulus' speech was delivered after the Spartans had decided to adopt a policy of reconciliation (διάλλαξις) in conquered Athens.[184] The speech of Thrasybulus, addressed to the formal ecclesia of the demos, closes the cycle of the speeches of the episode in an openly political way, and contains a theme absent from his first speech and that of Cleocritus, that of democracy. The speech opens with an address to the men of the city (ἐκ τοῦ ἄστεως ἄνδρες), whom he invites to know themselves, a Delphic moral injunction. To whom was Thrasybulus speaking? In his previous speech he had addressed citizens (ἄνδρες πολῖται), as Cleocritus had done after the battle. Now the definition of 'men of the city' does not mean 'citizens'. Thrasybulus speaks to those who had remained in the city as opposed to those who had followed him to Phyle and Piraeus: the oligarchs and those supporting them, people not worthy of being called citizens.[185] In its literary and philosophical context, the invitation to know oneself is significantly associated by Heraclitus[186] with that virtue at the centre of civic life, self-control, the self-discipline that the oligarchs had been so blatantly unable to muster during the regime of the Thirty. After having warned them to recognize their own arrogance in believing they were more than just the demos, Thrasybulus remarks that the demos, while poorer than the oligarchs, had never done any injustice for the sake of gain, while the oligarchs, richer than anybody else, had been guilty of many disgraceful acts for the sake of it. The only virtues Athenians need are to be true to their oaths and religiously pure (εὔορκοι καὶ ὅσιοι). Do not stir up *stasis* in the city, warns Thrasybulus, and obey our old laws, upon which he dismissed the ecclesia. From that point, writes Xenophon, the two parties live together as free citizens (ὁμοῦ πολιτεύονται).[187] 'Thus ended *stasis* in Athens', Xenophon concludes.[188]

A parallel version to Xenophon's account of the episode and his mystical/civic reading of it can be found in a short passage in Plato's *Menexenos* that strengthens the religious and civic reading of the episode.[189] After the end of the Peloponnesian war, Plato says, tranquillity (ἡσυχία) reigned in Athens, and peace (εἰρήνη) with her neighbours. But then internal war (ὁ οἰκεῖος πόλεμος) erupted, and peace only returned because Athenians from Piraeus and from Athens mixed readily and in a friendly way settled the war with moderation (μετρίως). Plato's use of the term to indicate the absence of tensions in the polis (ἡσυχία), is an expression that Euripides for instance uses in *Bacchae* to describe the cohesion of the polis,[190] while the term for moderate (μέτριος) recalls the theme of rejection of tyranny and anarchy we noted in Aeschylus' *Eumenides* (517–565 and 696–698).

The final agreement between democrats and oligarchs in 403 is defined in the *Constitution of the Athenians* (39.1–6) as the resolutions (αἱ διαλύσεις) of the conflict.[191] The term Xenophon uses for the strategic decision of the Spartans, reconciliation (διάλλαξις),[192] expresses well the political nature of the compromise, in that it granted freedom to those oligarchs who had not been directly responsible for the crimes of the Thirty and provided a democratic constitution for Athenians. Interestingly, it also mainly deals with the religious, impartial, neutral role of the Eleusis sanctuary as a powerful symbol of the general civic and political reconciliation. The oligarchs, fleeing the punishment they expected from the demos, would be allowed to escape to Eleusis and to remain there with full citizen and property rights. They were not, however, allowed back to Athens except for the mysteries' festival. The sanctuary at Eleusis was to be common to both communities, under the care of Kerykes and Eumolpidae in accordance with tradition (κατὰ τὰ πάτρια).[193]

This episode is evidence of the way the Athenians perceived the nature of the crisis of Athens in the last months of the Peloponnesian war. The cults of the mysteries and the egalitarian and democratic ideologies of the Athenians were perceived as closely connected: the orator Isocrates notes that nothing enrages the polis more than violations of the mysteries in matters concerning divinity and, in other matters, attempts to overthrow democracy.[194] The crisis of the polis is seen by Xenophon as essentially a moral and political one, and its solution can only lie in a moral, religious and political reconciliation between all Athenians on terms inspired by the values of mystery cults.

Part Two

The Plays

7

Audiences, Similarities and Scholars' Misapprehension of Pentheus

Some much-debated issues need to be clarified before examining the religious and political content of *Bacchae* and *Frogs*: were the plays intended for the same Athenian public? What is the reason for the similarities between them? How did scholars interpret the plays in the political context of Athens? Why did the majority of scholars miss the categorization of Pentheus as a tyrant?

7.1 *Bacchae* and its audience

I have assumed so far that *Bacchae* was intended for an Athenian audience. Traditionally, however, it has been assumed that Euripides composed *Bacchae* during his stay at the new court of the king of Macedonia, Archelaus, in Pella. Was *Bacchae* originally intended for a Macedonian public? Did Macedonia represent a source of inspiration? This matter has been discussed by scholars at length and has still not been fully resolved.

The main sources on the life of Euripides are the quotations of the peripatetic third-century writer Satyrus in the works of Athenaeus and Diogenes Laërtius, and the fragments of a dialogue by Satyrus on the same subject discovered at Oxyrhynchus in 1911.[1] Satyrus' extant works include details of the author's departure from Athens to the court of Archelaus, as well as details of his death in Macedonia. Written with an educational and hagiographic purpose in a manner far from what we would call a historical biography, the works of Satyrus have had an undue influence on scholarship. Among traditional scholars, Dodds for instance thought that the Macedonian environment was partly responsible for the mystical content of *Bacchae* and felt that 'the renewed contact with nature in the wild country of Macedonia ... had released some spring in the aged poet's mind, re-establishing a contact with hidden sources of power which he had lost in the self-conscious, over-intellectualised environment of late-fifth century Athens'.[2] Roux shares the same vision, with her romantic preconceptions clearly showing as she writes of Euripides' deep religious sentiment in somewhat romantic terms as 'une sorte de frissonnement et un sentiment vague de la divinité'.[3]

Among the most recent scholars' works, those by Revermann,[4] Mills,[5] Hanink[6] and Stewart[7] all accept the tradition of Euripides' stay in Macedonia from about 408 to his death in 407/6 and explore its consequences for the diffusion of the popularity of Euripides in the Macedonian empire. A radically different view has been pioneered by Fairweather, an early doubter of the factual reality in the ancient biographies of poets;[8] he is followed by Lefkowitz who reduced the historical value of Greek poets' biographies[9] and of Satyrus' *Vita*.[10] In 2003, Scullion adopted the same stance, founding his work mainly on the absence of satire on Euripides' exile in Macedonia in *Frogs*.[11] A textual analysis of two passages of *Bacchae*, used by some scholars as evidence of Euripides' stay in Macedonia, hold up relatively weakly: the first is *Bacchae* 409–411, where the chorus reveals that they lead the maenads to lovely Pieria, seat of the Muses, on the sacred slopes of Olympus. In the second passage of *Bacchae*, the chorus invokes Dionysus to put Pentheus to justice, connects Dionysus with the Pieria region in more evocative terms. The chorus wonders where Dionysus is leading his *thiasoi*, and wonders whether it is in the land of the much-wooded coverts of Olympus, where once Orpheus had once played the lyre to trees and wild animals. In a blessing, a *makarismos*, to the region the chorus then calls the region a region of fine horses, enriched by the waters of rivers (568–575).

I do not think that these passages are strong enough evidence to support the conclusion that Euripides' *Bacchae* was composed in Macedonia. Even if one accepts that Euripides may have composed *Bacchae* during his alleged stay there, he had his Athenian public in mind,[12] and it is unlikely that he composed the play for a Macedonian audience. It is, I believe, implausible that such an openly anti-tyrannical play was intended to be performed at the court of a king known for his tyrannical and violent behaviour. Archelaus, Plato for instance comments, is one of those tyrants, kings and potentates who have committed the gravest and most impious offences (μέγιστα καὶ ἀνοσιώτατα ἁμαρτήματα ἁμαρτάνουσι);[13] Aristotle mentions that the assassination of Archelaus had been an act of revenge for the tyrant's hubris.[14] The Athenians' feelings towards tyrants was particularly hostile; if one must find a link between Bacchae and Macedonia, it could well be the figure of its tyrant, Archelaus/Pentheus.

7.2 Similarities between the *Bacchae* and *Frogs*

Scholars have tended to either miss or misapprehend the similarities between the choral odes in the plays, ignoring the extra-textual context of them and treating them as unconnected works in the separate fields of Old Comedy and Tragedy. This has led them to overlook the correlation in their political content and to misunderstand both *Frogs* and *Bacchae*. While the two plays are, in Lada-Richards's words, 'the two most important extant dramatizations of Dionysus in the theatre of the Athenian polis',[15] and the amount of work done by scholars on each play and on the relationship between the cult of Dionysus and theatre is vast, there has been little research and comparative study on the similarity of their religious, ethical and civic content in light of their historical context.

In both plays, the plea for social and political equality, for an end to civic strife, for a return to traditional values and for the re-establishment of peace and civil coexistence through the adoption of mystery cults' values is strikingly similar. While the two plays have been examined and interpreted separately, we shall examine the association between the crisis of the polis, the urgent political content of the plays and the appeal of mystery cults in a city in which mystical initiates formed a substantial section of the community. Only by considering both plays in their historical, cultic, religious and political context can we hope to discard some of our 'modern conceptual hierarchies' and try to 'reconstruct the perceptual filters of the fifth-century Athenian audience'.[16]

Despite the central role of the choral *thiasoi* of Eleusinian initiates in the first part of *Frogs* and of Asian maenads in the whole of *Bacchae*, as well as the similarity of their ritual expressions and of the ethical and political content of their odes, scholarship on the religious and political implications of the chorus has tended to focus separately on each play, as noted for instance by Kowalzig.[17] In the past, some scholars have attributed the use of *Frogs'* choral odes to Aristophanes' knowledge of Euripides' *Bacchae*, with Aristophanes having either seen the play or read the text.[18] *Frogs*, in this interpretation, would essentially be a criticism of *Bacchae*'s treatment of Dionysus' figure and cult; no evidence however exists for this notion.[19]

Among the few scholars who have taken note of the striking similarities between the plays, Segal attributes them to *Frogs* being a reassessment of the Dionysiac cult as too in *Bacchae*, entirely missing the religious Eleusinian content and the impact of *Bacchae* in its historical context. Segal writes:

> There is good reason to believe that Aristophanes knew Euripides' play and may even be alluding to it in several passages. In so far as the *Bacchae* may be regarded as a defence of the divinity of Dionysus and an attempt to return to simpler and more immediate forms of belief, there may be perhaps, paradoxically, some basic similarities with the *Frogs* ... the difference lies precisely in the types of Dionysus presented in the two plays. Against this individualistic, orgiastic god, who manifests himself in subjective illusion, Aristophanes sets the Dionysus of comedy ... There is almost a deliberate attempt to free Dionysus from the dangerous elements that appear in the *Bacchae*.[20]

In his introduction to *Frogs,* Dover, too, notes the coincidence of terms and expressions in the plays, entertaining the possibility that Aristophanes had been aware of the text of *Bacchae* and had made allusions which would have been noticed by drama connoisseurs.[21] In both her studies of *Bacchae*, Foley (1980, 1985) observes the similarities between the language of the early choral odes in *Bacchae* and of the chorus of Eleusinian initiates in *Frogs* but does not pursue the theme further, other than noting the common theme of Dionysus' acceptance by the polis as well as the similarity between the scene mocking the god's costume in *Frogs* (45–46) and that of Pentheus dressing up as a female maenad (821 ff.).[22]

The plays' religious, ethical and political content and the similarity of the two authors' closeness of approach to mystery cults can be clearly perceived by examining the similarities of the two plays, a method that I have followed in the analysis of the texts.

7.3 Politics and scholarship

Bacchae and *Frogs* have attracted much scholarly attention in the course of time, as they have been often considered as the acme of Athenian theatrical productions in its golden era. Most of the commentaries however overlook the plays' political background and content, as well as the relationship between mystery cults and politics in Athens in the second half of the fifth century.

Starting with *Bacchae*, we must begin with its most thorough and influential interpreter, Dodds (1960, original edition 1944). While providing a wide and thorough analysis of the religious context of the play as well as on the place of Bacchae in Euripides' work, Dodds entirely overlooks the civic and political dimension of Dionysiac mystery cults in the polis of Athens at the end of the fifth century, briefly noting 'an Athens crazed by twenty years of increasingly disastrous war'.[23] Dodds focuses on the 'tragic contradiction' of the figure of Dionysus and the conflict generated by the introduction into Greece of what he calls 'the new religions of the orgiastic type... eastern and northern mystery gods, Cybele and Bendis, Attis, Adonis, and Sabazius... probably a result of the social stresses that the Peloponnesian war generated', overlooking on one hand the great antiquity of the cult and on the other the gravity of the domestic political crisis in Athens.[24]

Since Dodds, most scholars have focused on the play's 'paradox', on the Dionysiac cult and have largely avoided its extra-textual context. The earliest work that escaped that focus on 'paradox' was Foley's, who produced a complex and perceptive analysis of the play in 1980, drawn from her 1975 Harvard doctoral dissertation, 'The Masque of Dionysus'; the analysis was followed by her study of 'Poetry and Sacrifice in Euripides' in 1985. Foley reads *Bacchae* as a play that 'emphasizes that both honouring and comprehending the god are essentially theatrical acts, an exploration of the nature of illusion, transformation and symbol',[25] 'a kind of initiation into the mysteries of the divine and the mysteries of the self'.[26] She limits her reading of the play's socio-political context, however, to briefly defining the issues confronting *Bacchae*'s Thebes and *Frogs*' Athens as 'a contradiction between the aim for political equality among citizens and the exclusion of members of the society from full participation'[27] touching an important element of the plays but one that she nevertheless leaves regrettably unexplored. Foley overlooks the direct relevance of the play to the critical political circumstances the city was in, but only very briefly mentions that *Bacchae*'s text 'reflects the precariousness of social and political life in late fifth-century Athens'.[28]

Versnel (1998) also overlooks the implications of the chorus' ethical and civic pleas, disregarding the relevance of the anti-tyrannical stance of the play.[29] In affirming that 'the ancient audience and the modern reader share the same basic qualities for understanding the meaning of the work', Versnel falls into the obvious pitfall of adopting a modern conceptual framework to comprehend such an entirely different reality, to which he somewhat contradictorily adds his 'belief in a historical approach to a work of art'.[30] Versnel adopts Dodds' vision and devotes his essay on the 'Tragic Paradox of *Bacchae*' to show Euripides' aim as 'deliberately presenting Dionysiac religion as one of the new sects that invaded Greece and especially Athens in his time ... converting the eternal Dionysiac ambiguity into a conflict in the actual reality of his time ... [in order] to question the nature of religious convictions in general ... Contemporary authorities condemned the new zealots'.[31] Despite his claim to a historical approach, Versnel entirely ignores the political and the religious content of the play, as well as its historical and political context.

Criticizing Versnel's view of *Bacchae* 's 'tragic paradox' and his vision of Pentheus as defender the polis,[32] Seaford (1996) makes some important contributions to a radical change the way *Bacchae* is to be interpreted, regarding mystery cults and their cultural and political relevance in fifth-century Athens as the play's fundamental context. Yet even he makes only a passing remark about 'the disintegration of the polis ... a constant possibility [that] threatens all its citizens with death or slavery'.[33] Seaford thus correctly connects the play with the crisis of the polis at the end of the Peloponnesian war but surprisingly fails to appreciate the link between the play's religious content and the domestic ethic and political issues the play discusses. In his introduction to his work on *Bacchae*, Stuttard (2016) devotes a chapter to the play's socio/political context. Tempted by associating the play with a conversion from an agnostic religious position to writing the play 'as a warning to non-believers', Stuttard too misses entirely the mystic, civic and political structure of the play, reading the political problems Athens was facing in 405 exclusively from the point of view of the war with Sparta.[34]

Regarding the important political content of *Frogs*, scholars have mostly overlooked the play's egalitarian plea. In his introduction to *Frogs*, Stanford (1958) for instance only dedicates two short paragraphs to the play's historical and political background, noting that '405 [was] no easy time for making Athenians laugh and forget their cares', as they 'must have known that ultimate victory was unlikely', and that the city was suffering greatly from economic decline, from the lack of food, the debasement of the currency and inflation, the ill-effects of the plague and over-crowding. However, he fails to examine the play as a religious and political reaction to the religious and socio-political crisis the polis found itself in.[35]

In his work on the same play Segal (1961), perceptively mentions 'the breakdown of the communal solidarity which the battle of Arginusae and its aftermath exposed',[36] but does not touch the theme of the urgency of the play's religious message in the context of the domestic political crisis of the polis. Segal correctly defines the role of the chorus as 'holy, because they are expressive of the religious unity of the state',[37] and concentrates his attention on Aristophanes' attempt to restore *mousikē* as 'an attempt to re-establish the communal values of literature', as the only way to restore Athens' former greatness. Segal overlooks the role of the chorus in its solemn plea for political equality. Believing however that the play was a response to Euripides' *Bacchae*, he remarks that, in *Frogs*, 'the asocial, orgiastic Dionysus is rejected … as being hostile to this spirit of communal regeneration'.[38] The Dionysiac communal regeneration is in fact not only the focus of *Frogs*, but also of *Bacchae*. In the chapter dedicated to politics in *Frogs*, Dover (1993) identifies the political message of the play as the 'salvation of Athens (that) lies in seeking an end to the war in less intransigent terms', basing himself on a short hint in line 1532, and focusing on the *epirrhema* of the parabasis (687–699) seeing it only as a plea for restoring citizenship-rights to those who had participated in the oligarchic coup of 411.[39]

In his introduction to *Frogs* Sommerstein (1997) extensively describes the military and political situation that the polis was in, but largely ignores the impact of the enactment of Eleusinian rituals on stage on the audiences and the interrelation between mystery cults, theatre representations and politics in a crucial political moment.[40] While Lada-Richards (1999) makes a deep analysis of the play in its wide religious and social context, she refers to the political state of the polis only in the epilogue, as she mentions that the blessings Aeschylus brings to the city are aimed at 'the real-life citizens of the distressed and tormented polis of 405 BC'.[41] Commenting on *Frogs*, Wiles (2011) correctly describes it in the framework of a city living 'in an atmosphere of hysteria and in-fighting, panic and defiance . . . where food was scarce and energy sapped . . . the starving city was on the brink of surrender . . . [threatened by] bitter divisions and differing level of despair,'[42] where 'sharing in collective laughter and fantasising a shared utopia were instrumental in bonding the citizen body'.[43] However, he discusses neither the political relevance of the play's religious content nor the importance of mystery themes in the play's specific political environment.

Griffith's view (2013) of *Frogs*' message accurately connects the mystery content of the play with its 'mood of reunification and community' in its development and in its final scene.[44] His exhaustive work on the political background of the play, however, largely ignores the ethical and political crisis that was dividing the polis, a bitter and violent confrontation that came into the open with the establishment of the regime of the Thirty. Griffith focuses instead on the victory of the figure of Aeschylus as key to the military effectiveness of the polis and to the renewal of the ancient art of theatrical productions. In his review of Griffith's work, Halliwell (2015) is therefore right to point out at a contradiction in Griffith's interpretation of the symbolic nature of Aeschylus in the play, noting 'a glaring comic contradiction . . . [in] the notion that it is Aeschylus, earlier proclaimed the great poet of warlike spirit, who will bring Athens an escape from war.'[45]

7.4 The 'paradox' of *Bacchae*

For a long time scholars have been disconcerted by what they perceive as the play's ambiguity, its 'riddle', as Norwood (1908) for instance calls it,[46] the 'tragic paradox', as Versnel (1998) defines the theme of the play.[47] This sentiment influences their view of the play, giving rise to the widespread perception of a duality in the role of the chorus of maenads, peaceful at first and murderous later, and of an equally double-natured god, friendly and smiling at first but later unnaturally cruel in his punishment of the tyrant and his household. The horror at the scene of the slaying and dismembering of Pentheus has prompted scholars to see Pentheus in a positive light as defending the polis of Thebes, ignoring the evidence of the play on his nature as a tyrant who rules by terror (43, 1310). For this reason, scholars have tended to identify Pentheus with the polis of Thebes, as defender of the city's laws and civic peace, while seeing Dionysus as the god of irrationality and anti-polis destructive violence.

The greatest attention given by scholars to the play's contrasts derives from a notion of the inhuman cruelty and irrationality of the Dionysiac figure and cult, originally expressed by Nietzsche in his *Birth of Tragedy* (1872) and the basis of Rohde's *Psyche* (1898).[48] As Henrichs convincingly argues, the influence of Nietzsche and of Rohde's *Psyche* on scholarship on *Bacchae* and on the Dionysiac cult lasts to this day.[49] These works established some of the tenets that have been the basis of the interpretation of the play adopted by scholars as diverse as Dodds,[50] Winnington-Ingram,[51] Girard,[52] Roux,[53] Oranje,[54] Vernant[55] and Versnel.[56] In his work on the birth of Greek tragedy, inspired by the two men who symbolized the forthcoming German cultural revolution, Wagner and Schopenhauer, a work that he 'never intended to be a work of scholarship',[57] Nietzsche, ignoring entirely the play's historical and cultic background, famously introduces the concept of Dionysus' double nature, as 'cruel barbarised daemon', and of Pentheus as 'a mild, gentle hearted ruler',[58] a theory that has heavily influenced the literary criticism of the play. He also developed concepts such as how tragic performances brought their audiences to 'pitches of Dionysiac frenzy' through a 'horrible "witches' brew"' of sensuality and cruelty',[59] enabling spectators to merge into nature's 'mysterious primordial unity',[60] concepts perhaps vital in the creation of Nietzsche's philosophical system, but extraneous to a modern reading of *Bacchae*. It is curious that Nietzsche's work managed to survive the deservedly scathing criticism of his colleague von Wilamowitz-Moellendorff (1872), producing a vision of the Greek civilization that still influences classical scholars.

By and large, Dodds adheres to the Nietzschean figure of Dionysus as 'the embodiment of tragic contradictions – joy and horror, insight and madness, innocent gaiety and dark cruelty'.[61] Dodds focuses on the contrast between the god and regards Pentheus as 'a conservative Greek aristocrat who despises the new religion ... [and] hates it for its obliteration of sex and class distinctions and fears it as a threat to social order and public morals'.[62] He largely ignores the positive features of the new cult that are expressed in *Bacchae*, as well as the political relevance of representing on stage the killing of a tyrant and of evoking the role of the Dionysiac cult in reconstructing the polis in that particular moment in Athens' life.

Still in the wake of Nietzsche (and probably influenced by the events of the Second World War), Winnington-Ingram (1948) writes that the subject of *Bacchae* is 'the Dionysiac group and its disastrous potentialities ... the drugged peace which alternates with furious violence ... the exclusive and undiscriminating cult of emotions'.[63] Winnington-Ingram focuses exclusively on Euripides' attitude towards religion: 'he is exposing the inadequate conception of divinity' describing 'a religion compounded of beauty and terror ... a religion of unreason'.[64] This peculiar interpretation of the cult of Dionysus as a threat to the cohesiveness of the polis is shared by Segal (1961) who in a passage dedicated to the similarities between *Frogs* and *Bacchae* defines 'the orgiastic Dionysus, [as] essentially asocial, a dangerous god, quick to punish offenses upon his divinity. Defiance of his worship produces individual convulsions that shake the state and negate accepted social values'.[65] In a later, longer work dedicated to *Bacchae*, Segal acknowledges his debt to Nietzsche, calling Dionysus an 'elusive god'. Segal focuses on the god's duality, where 'destruction and creativity coexist ... a culture hero and a threat to civilisation'.[66] While still ignoring both the extra-textual context of the play and the moral and political relevance of its choral odes, Segal limits his remarks noting that 'Euripidean tragedy ... holds a tension between the centrifugal forces it represents – entropy, irrational and inexplicable suffering, chaos, and the centripetal, cohesive forces that lie ... in the creative, ordering unifying energies of the work itself and ... in the mind behind the work'.[67]

Musurillo (1966) too overlooks the play's ethical and political content and emphasizes the cult's unrestrained violence and irrationality. Musurillo defines *Bacchae* as a play of 'tantalizing ambiguity', as 'the promised peace emerges only from orgy and violence'.[68] In his work on violence and the birth of religion as a mean to tame innate human violence Girard (1972) dedicates a few pages to *Bacchae* in a vision that to some extent resembles Dodds': he extends to the whole society the risks inherent in 'the bacchants revel ... a bloodthirsty nightmare ... that spells the disintegration of social institutions and the collapse of the cultural order ... symbolized by the destruction of the royal palace'.⁶⁹ But, unlike Dodds and others, Girard correctly identifies Pentheus' slaughter as a ritual sacrifice, whose 'violent death provided the necessary outlet for the mass anguish, and restored peace ... the rite is directed toward order and tranquillity, not violence' an act that causes 'peace and harmony to return to Thebes';⁷⁰ ignoring, however, the play's relevance to its fifth-century Athenian political crisis.

In his learned analysis of *Bacchae*, Versnel (1998) falls into the same trap, that of perceiving the play as a paradox and of ignoring the political aspects of the play. As such, Versnel focuses on a largely artificial reading of the play as a paradox, a conflict between Pentheus as prosecutor in an impiety, *asebeia* trial in the first part of the play and an *asebeia* defendant in the last part.⁷¹ There is no hint at the figure of Pentheus as tyrant and no attention to the political and religious situation of the polis of Thebes as a transparent model of post-411 Athens, while emphasizing the traditional reading of the figure of Dionysus as a paradoxical and ambiguous deity.⁷²

8

Politics in the Plays

Euripides' *Bacchae* and Aristophanes' *Frogs* share a broadly common political content, the context of which is the political situation that developed in Athens after the scandal of the Herms and of the Eleusinian mysteries in 415, which was when the plays were being composed.

The political polarization of Athens had gained grounds since the scandal. What may have been a gesture of scorn and spite by a number of young aristocrats opposing the Sicilian expedition and the radicalization of the war, had become explicit goals of the oligarchic circles: to seize power, to abolish the democratic constitution and institute a new one that would keep the demos out of power. The first attempt took place in the summer of 411.[1] In Thucydides' narration, the continuing hostility between the oligarchic circles, favouring an oligarchic regime and a cessation of the war, and the democratic demos, which favoured a form of radical democracy and the continuation of the war, came into the open in the seizure of power by a large group of oligarchs, the Four Hundred. The episode in Thucydides is marked by the systematic manner in which the oligarchic circles organized themselves. Bands of young aristocrats organized themselves and created an atmosphere of terror. The members of the oligarchic circles were well organized in military fashion: those who were members of the army remained at their posts waiting to be summoned to fight against opponents while the other soldiers withdrew for the night; the Four Hundred and some 120 young men entered the *Boule* carrying weapons, ready to slay any member of the *Boule* who would oppose them.[2] Assassination became a tool in political conflict, as it had last happened with the murder of Ephialtes in the 460s. Among the first victims in the preparation of the coup in 411 had been Androcles and others hostile to the conspirators.[3] The murder of Hyperbolus, one of the leaders of the democrats, and Phrynichus, a moderate among the Four Hundred, soon followed.[4]

Tensions in the city remained high in the period between the fall of the Four Hundred in the autumn of 411 and the seizure of power by the Thirty in 404. The public opinion was polarized as the oligarchic circles continued the organization of a plot to deprive the democratic ecclesia of its powers and to sign a peace treaty with Sparta. On the democratic side, the reaction to the heightened activity of the opponents became radical, evidenced for instance by the decree of Demophantus of 410 that requested all citizens to swear his allegiance to the democratic constitution and his willingness to slay anybody attempting to overturn it.[5] Open political violence was endemic. When Alcibiades returned to Piraeus on the wake of his success to free the Hellespont in 407, despite the popularity of his recall that called a vast crowd of people to Piraeus, he feared he may have been assassinated once on land.[6] Only when he saw a crowd of his friends and political allies, among which was his cousin, assembled in the crowd, did he dare to go ashore.[7] In 405, a few months after the performances of *Bacchae* and *Frogs*, in preparation of the seizure of power of the Thirty, the oligarchs put Cleophon, leader of the democrats, on trial on trumped-up charges and had him to death.[8] The high state of tension between the two political factions made the fracture of the polis a frighteningly concrete prospect against which we must interpret the political content of *Bacchae* and *Frogs*.

The economic and military situation was in 405 certainly precarious. Despite the traditional notion that the Athenians' military power depended on their control of the sea, as Themistocles and Pericles had recommended, the loss of control over the largest part of Attica was a grave matter. What would have been the consequence of additionally losing control over the Dardanelles, through which flowed the corn that fed the city, would have been clear to the Athenians of 405. Athens would have found itself with no bread, no allies, no money and no ships, being besieged by land and sea, as Xenophon later noted.[9] A defeated Athens could expect to be treated the same way the Athenians had treated other poleis during the war, such as the Melians, of whom they had killed all the men and enslaved the women, Thucydides warns.[10] Surprisingly, however, the demos was still largely in favour of continuing the war, and even after the decisive Spartan defeat at Cyzicus (410), the democratic leader Cleophon convinced the ecclesia not to accept the Spartan peace offer. His support for the war continued in the war's final months, as mentioned in *Frogs* (679, 1504, 1532), up until his death.

With rare exceptions, the scholars who, with hindsight, interpreted the plays in their historical context have put them against the background of the war against Sparta that Athens was in the process of losing and on its effects on the Athenian population. Yet, there is no mention of a war in *Bacchae* apart from Pentheus' bellicose stance against the maenads, and in *Frogs* the main reference is the exclamation of the slave Xanthias, who wishes to have fought with the navy, which would have allowed him to be disfranchised as a slave so as not to obey Dionysus' order to carry the duo's baggage.[11] The second instance is mentioned by Charon, who does not accept slaves in his boat, except those who fought in the life-or-death naval battle (190–191). The third is in the parodos, where the chorus excludes from its dancing rituals those who betray a fort or the fleet, allow contraband or help in financing the Persian fleet (362–365) and a comment in the parabasis on the need to give full citizenship to those who fight in the fleet (693–702).

Euripides' and Aristophanes' exclusive focus on domestic political and religious matters seems perhaps paradoxical to a modern reader, who would tend to assume, with the insight of what was to happen in 404, that the preeminent thoughts of Athenians would be focused on Athens' precarious military position. In fact, as it had happened in 415, the Athenians' concerns focused primarily on domestic religious and ethical matters.

8.1 The polis and *stasis*

The central political issue that *Frogs* and *Bacchae* have in common is the division and conflict, commonly defined as *stasis*, in the polis, an issue mostly unnoticed by scholars. The two authors emphasize the domestic, moral and political nature of the polis' crisis: in *Bacchae*, the conflict between the divinity of Dionysus, the community of mystery initiates and the polis' tyrant causes a division that threatens the survival of the polis. In *Frogs*, a similar conflict exists in the first part of the play between the *thiasos* of initiates and the political leaders ruling the ecclesia and, in the second part, that between the symbolic figures of Aeschylus, defender of the polis' traditions and its future saviour, and Euripides, its corruptor.

Running against the grain of the majority of scholars, I argue that the political theme of the crisis of the polis is at the very core of the two plays. In the plays, the term polis is mostly used in the sense of 'people', 'political and religious community', 'body politic', 'state', rather than a physical place where people live (in *Bacchae* the physical place would be χθών, as in 1, 15, 48 etc. or γῆ, as in 23, 213, 312, 664) and recurs some twelve times in *Bacchae* and eleven times in *Frogs*.[12] In *Bacchae*, 'polis' is a term that Euripides uses repeatedly to express the opposition of the community of Thebans to the way its tyrant refuses to recognize Dionysiac rituals and the god's divine status.

In *Bacchae*, as Dionysus declares, Thebes is the first polis in Hellas (20) that must learn what it is to be uninitiated in his mysteries (ἀτέλεστος) (39); Thebes is the first Greek polis in which the god will establish his initiation rituals (ἐμὰς τελετάς) (22) and its people will be able to 'see' his divinity (610). Before the tyrant and the deity, the polis is united, with no distinctions: as Pentheus rejoices at the crowd at the gates of the polis magnifying his name, Dionysus would delight at being honoured by the community in the same way (320). The association of Dionysus with the welfare of the polis is reiterated by Tiresias a few lines later as he encourages Cadmus to entreat the god on behalf of the polis; and the polis to do nothing evil (κἀξαιτώμεθα ὑπέρ τε τούτου καίπερ ὄντος ἀγρίου ὑπέρ τε πόλεως τὸν θεὸν μηδὲν νέον δρᾶν) (362). The religous link between the community of citizens and Dionysus is emphasized when the first messenger recommends Pentheus to receive the god into the polis for the good of its citizens (770). After the death of Pentheus, the relationship between Pentheus, the polis and Dionysus is clearly expressed by Cadmus in his dialogue with Agave and in his eulogy of Pentheus. 'You were mad (ἐμάνητε), and the whole polis was in a bacchic frenzy', Cadmus says to Agave who wonders how and why she had gone to the Cithaeron (1295). Addressing the corpse of the dead Pentheus, Cadmus observes 'you were a terror to the polis, o child' (1310), summarizing the conflictual relationship between the community and its ruler.

Euripides' religious and political thought is rendered in *Bacchae* in terms that are both radical and extreme. Early in *Bacchae*, the crisis is the worst the Athenians could imagine: the division of the polis is unimaginably total, as the gender-divided community has ceased to function. The secession of women, struck by divine frenzy (32–33), deprives the community of its future and of elements vital to its day-to-day existence.[13] In *Bacchae*'s Thebes, women have ceased weaving, a highly symbolic image that Euripides stresses three times

(118, 514, 1236) to mark the end of the domestic, feminine industrial activity in the polis. The essential elements of the unity of the polis, its religion, communality and solidarity of equals, are in the hands of the maenads on Mount Cithaeron, while the royal palace lies in ruins and the male population stands in fear of its tyrant. The polis of Thebes has emphatically ceased to exist: the male population who remains in the city is an appendix of its ruler: Pentheus first remark to Thebes' males is his order to destroy Tiresias' mantic shrine and to capture Dionysus, addressed with a generic 'let someone go with great speed' (στειχέτω τις ὡς τάχος) (346). No longer under the control of the polis and of male authority, the city's women exercise the communal values of the *thiasos*: they are now a body as strong and cohesive as the city's soldiers, they successfully oppose armed villagers with their *thyrsoi* (761–764) and show great joy, unity and cohesion throughout the play (157–159, 743–745, 1090–1110, 1024–1152 etc.). Throughout their choral odes the Asian women powerfully express the religious and civic values along which the polis may be reconstructed, once the tyrant and his family have been disposed of.

Yet, despite their fear of the tyrant (1310), the men in Thebes do not share the tyrant's rejection of the god: the whole polis is in effect on the side of Dionysus, as Cadmus later tells Agave (1295). Euripides construes the expression of the readiness of the male side of the polis to accept the divinity of Dionysus in a subtle crescendo in the description of off-scene action by three messengers: a servant (434–450), and two servants, the first a herdsman (660–777), and the second a servant of Pentheus (1043–1152).

The first report received from the mountain to Pentheus is delivered by a servant of the tyrant. Euripides emphasizes the weight of the servant's report and warning by the final sentence in the first stasimon that immediately precedes it: 'Whatever the mass, the ordinary people, have taken as normal and practice this I would accept' (τὸ πλῆθος ὅ τι/τὸ φαυλότερον ἐνόμισε χρῆ-/ταί τε, τόδ' ἂν δεχοίμαν) (430–432). The servant, one of the mass of people, while reporting the capture of the stranger (Dionysus who is under disguise), lets slip his dissent with Pentheus' hostility to the stranger and his own sympathy with him, by revealing to have confessed to stranger that he acted in shame (441–442) as he was only following his duty. What the servant says makes clear the silent conflict between the male elements of the polis and the tyrant. For the tyrant, the god is merely a stranger, a sorcerer, an enchanter, an effeminate man with fragrant hair and light-coloured locks and the grace of Aphrodite in his eyes (ξένος, γόης ἐπῳδὸς ... ξανθοῖσι βοστρύχοισιν εὐοσμῶν κόμην ... ὅσσοις χάριτας Ἀφροδίτης ἔχων), bent on having sex with young girls under the pretence of in joyous initiation rituals (κεὐφρόνας συγγίγνεται τελετὰς προτείνων εὐίους νεάνισιν) (233–238). But the wild beast the servant had been sent to chase, the prey (τήνδ᾿ ἄγραν ... ὁ θὴρ) reveals himself to the servant to be a gentle creature, who laughed as he let himself to be tied and led off offering no resistance (433–440). His *thiasos* of maenads has escaped its prison, their chains and the bolts on the doors broken by no human hand, the servant adds ominously. 'This man has come here to Thebes full of many wonders, the rest is your concern' (πολλῶν δ᾿ ὅδ᾿ ἀνὴρ θαυμάτων ἥκει πλέως ἐς τάσδε Θήβας. σοὶ δὲ τἄλλα χρὴ μέλειν) (449–450), warns the servant as he finishes his report to Pentheus.

The first messenger's report to the tyrant (660–777) is delivered after Dionysus' freeing himself from his prison, his reunion with the Asian thiasos and the destruction of Pentheus' palace. It contains a description of the behaviour of the maenads on Mount Cithaeron, which confirms and amplifies the miracles performed by the 'man of wonders': 'extraordinary acts greater than miracles' (δεινὰ δρῶσι θαυμάτων τε κρείσσονα) (667). The intuition and allusion of the servant are here reality. While revealing his fear of Pentheus' sharp temper and excessive authoritarian rule (τὸ βασιλικὸν λίαν) (671) that tempers his speech, the messenger's report to the ruler and to the polis, on the magical, superhuman behaviour of the maenads on the mountain is long and detailed. The maenads are explicitly introduced at the beginning of the report as 'queenly maenads' (βάκχαι ποτνιάδαι) (664). They are described as asleep in the wilderness in total relaxation, not drunk and neither involved in sexual games as Pentheus had surmised. They give their milk to young deer and wolf cubs while snakes lick their cheeks, the very earth opens up at the touch of their *thyrsoi* and water, wine and milk start to flow. An idyllic picture. But, when provoked by the servant and his companions, a group capable of great fury: with their bare hands they dismember the herd the servant and his companions had with them, they attacked the villages on the plain and beat the armed villagers with their *thyrsoi*. Openly acknowledging the divinity of the maenads' daemon (769), the messenger pleads for Pentheus to receive him into the city for two reasons: he gave mortals the grape vine that stops suffering, and that, without wine and the joy of sex, all mankind's pleasures would cease (τὴν παυσίλυπον ἄμπελον δοῦναι βροτοῖς./ οἴνου δὲ μηκέτ' ὄντος οὐκ ἔστιν Κύπρις / οὐδ' ἄλλο τερπνὸν οὐδὲν ἀνθρώποις ἔτι) (772–774).

Despite his fear of his master, the messenger closes his speech with a direct warning: by nature, Dionysus is inferior to no other divinity (Διόνυσος ἥσσων οὐδενὸς θεῶν ἔφυ) (775–777). These last lines are of primary importance in the interpretation of the attitude towards the cult of the male side of the polis. They are usually attributed to the Lydian maenads' chorus. The only exception, as far as I know, is Norwood, who noted 'the strangely submissive tone of the chorus ... a belated timidity ... essentially inconsistent [with the report of Dionysus' might]' but attributes them not to the messenger but to an anonymous Theban,[14] a hypothesis correctly rejected by Dodds.[15]

I argue that these lines are the logical conclusion of the first messenger's report for several reasons. Firstly, just before it, the chorus of Lydian maenads manifests great exultation at being reunified with Dionysus. The chorus is finally free to worship its god and exults at Pentheus' defeat. The royal palace is in ruins, Dionysus has freed himself from his chains, Pentheus clearly shows his powerlessness against the god and the insolence of a murderous man (φονίου δ' ἀνδρὸς ὕβρις) (555) is approaching its end. It is unseemly, therefore, for the chorus to be suddenly submissive in front of Pentheus, particularly at the end of the messenger's report on the maenads' miracles on the mountain.

Secondly, the messenger had expressed his fear of speaking freely to the tyrant before delivering his report (668–671), a remark that it would be natural to repeat before stating that the stranger should be accepted into the polis as a god.

Thirdly, the servant uses a term for his fear (τάρβος) to talk freely to his king, the same term used by Cadmus to describe Pentheus as terror to the polis (1310). The link between the two expressions emphasizes the only sentiment of the male side of the community versus its tyrant: not respect or reverence but fear. Finally, the first messenger's final remark on the divinity of the god matches the tone and content of the final warning of the second messenger to the polis (1150–1152) and serves as an introduction to the civic and religious warning to the polis the second messenger brings.

After the death of Pentheus, the mood of the polis changes further, as the second messenger, a slave (1027), gives the Theban community a warning at the end of his report on Pentheus' death. He starts by saying that the crazed Agave is coming to the city holding the severed head of Pentheus, thinking that she is holding a lion's head as a victory-prize (1147). The messenger then openly reiterates Tiresias' warnings as well as the choral ethical and religious appeals. The wisest (σοφώτατος) possessions of men are moderation (τὸ σωφρονεῖν) and veneration (σέβειν) for the things of the gods (1150–1152). The tyrant is dead, the threat to the polis is overcome. The second messenger's short speech opens the way for the play's decisive exodos. The polis can now regain its gender composition, its communality and cohesion, as it now can freely accept the divinity of Dionysus and the tenets and rituals of his cult.

In Aristophanes' *Frogs*, the polis of Athens is in grave decline and is described as gravely disjointed. The crisis is not due to the war; instead, it is an ethical, religious and political crisis. Aristophanes has recourse to dramatic marine metaphors to define the crisis of the polis, as other authors did before him.[16] In *Frogs*, the polis is described as struggling in heavy seas (πόλις χειμαζομένη) (361), in the arms of the waves (κυμάτων ἐν ἀγκάλαις) (704). The polis is having labour pains (ἡ πόλις γὰρ δυστοκεῖ) (1423) and the chorus advises and teaches the whole community what is good for it (686). The term 'polis' is used again in a crescendo in 732, 1049, 1083, and emphasized three times in Dionysus' explanation of his mission to preserve the polis: 'I came down here for a poet; and why? So that the polis may survive and go on holding its choral festivals. So, whichever of you (*Euripides and Aeschylus*) is going to give good advice to the polis, he is the one whom I will take back with me (1418–1421). A few lines later, Dionysus asks the two poets to reveal their opinion of the polis and their plans to save it (ἀλλ᾽ ἔτι μίαν γνώμην ἑκάτερος εἴπατον / περὶ τῆς πόλεως ἥντιν᾽ ἔχετον σωτηρίαν) (1435–1436). In 1457, Aeschylus comments on the people the polis uses as officers: 'is it the honest?' (πότερα τοῖς χρηστοῖς;). To Dionysus' negative answer Aeschylus exclaims: how can one save a polis that does not accept either a smart cloak or a goatskin mantle? (πῶς οὖν τις ἂν σώσειε τοιαύτην πόλιν, / ἣ μήτε χλαῖνα μήτε σισύρα συμφέρει;) (1458–1459). In 1501, it marks Pluto's welcoming of Aeschylus' victory in the *agon*, and in the last verses that conclude the play it marks the chorus' sanctioning of his mission to give 'great ideas to the polis that will bring great and good things' (τῇ πόλει μεγάλων ἀγαθῶν ἀγαθὰς ἐπινοίας) (1530).

Stasis is presented in *Frogs* through the contrast between Athens' past and present, between the old moral and civic values that made the city rich, powerful and well-ordered, and the present decay, where the polis is torn between two sets of values in both parts of the play: those of the choral *thiasos* and those of the polis' current leaders in the first part, and those symbolized by Aeschylus on one side and by Euripides on the other in the second part. Aristophanes' first mention of domestic strife, the hateful *stasis* (στάσις ἐχθρὰ) as enemy of the polis is significantly contained at the beginning of the chorus' parodos (359). Coming immediately after the religious interdiction to the impure and uninitiated to participate in the sacred dances, the appeal to exclude 'those who do not try to resolve *stasis* but stir it up and fan its flames' (ἢ στάσιν ἐχθρὰν μὴ καταλύει… ἀλλ' ἀνεγείρει καὶ ῥιπίζει) (360) is greatly emphasized. The polis' leadership is as debased as its currency (717–737), the polis' gymnasia have ceased their role of educating the youth: 'the polis is run by bureaucrats and buffooning monkeys of politicians who deceive the public and no one is capable anymore of carrying the torch at the city festivals, as gymnasia are left empty' (κᾆτ' ἐκ τούτων ἡ πόλις ἡμῶν / ὑπογραμματέων ἀνεμεστώθη / καὶ βωμολόχων δημοπιθήκων / ἐξαπατώντων τὸν δῆμον ἀεί, / λαμπάδα δ' οὐδεὶς οἷός τε φέρειν / ὑπ' ἀγυμνασίας ἔτι νυνί) (1083–1088). People in Athens 'have cast aside their proper artistic education and the art of tragedy' (ἀποβαλόντα μουσικὴν / τά τε μέγιστα παραλιπόντα / τῆς τραγῳδικῆς τέχνης), spending instead their time sitting idly in senseless chatter with Socrates the philosopher (1491–1499). The polis has been weakened by the collapse of discipline in the army as even the crew of the *Paralos*, the official Athenian military messenger ship, feels free to discuss orders with their officers (1071) and the traditional financial funding of the fleet is now impossible as wealthy men have ceased to finance the navy on the pretence of poverty (1065).

The two sides are separated by class, education, ethics and attitude toward religion. On one side are Athens' military and political leaders whom Aristophanes describes in scathing terms that emphasize the bitter tones of Athens' political division, tones mirroring those of *Knights*.[17] The ruling class is composed of Thracian redheads, probably an allusion to the democratic leader Cleophon: these people are as debased as the newly introduced bronze currency, as worthless as their forefathers, so low in class that they could not even be chosen as ritual scapegoats, (who were usually chosen among the destitute) (730-733).[18] The polis is full of miserable and impious thieves of sacred offerings, of charlatan mob-monkeys, of lowly under-clerks who constantly cheat the demos (1083-1086). The communities of the dead in Hades and of the living in Athens share in *Frogs* the same division. There is trouble in Hades, Aeacus warns Dionysus and Xanthias, as the community of the dead is divided by a most formidable *stasis* (πρᾶγμα πρᾶγμα μέγα κεκίνηται μέγα / ἐν τοῖς νεκροῖσι καὶ στάσις πολλὴ πάνυ) (759-760). Hades is no better than Athens, being populated by clothes-thieves and pickpockets, father-beaters and burglars, all of whom are Euripides' supporters (772-774).

On the opposite side in *Frogs* are those who were formerly the leaders of the ecclesia, people Aristophanes defines as the good and virtuous, *kaloi kai agathoi* (727-729).[19] They are people who share the same aristocratic birth, aptitude for self-control, moral and civic education as citizens through athletics, membership of choruses, practice of *mousike* (τῶν πολιτῶν θ' οὓς μὲν ἴσμεν εὐγενεῖς καὶ σώφρονας/ἄνδρας ὄντας καὶ ικαίους καὶ καλούς τε κἀγαθοὺς/καὶ τραφέντας ἐν παλαίστραις καὶ χοροῖς καὶ μουσικῇ) (727-729). They are the people among whom the polis should chose its rulers, people who share the play's chorus' values. In *Frogs*, the polis' weakness comes from being torn by domestic quarrels, embodied in the second part of the play in the opposition between two of its tragic poets, as the character of Euripides in the play personifies the new and corrupt ways of the city and that of Aeschylus its glorious and prosperous past to which the polis must return.

Aristophanes emphasizes the core point of his political stance by significantly putting at its core the role of choral festivals in the cohesion of the polis. The polis must be preserved (ἡ πόλις σωθεῖσα), in order that it could continue the performances of its Dionysiac choral festivals, Dionysus declares (1419), a concept that defines well the essence of the city's spirit that the god and the Eleusinian chorus have in common: the polis exists as a community because its members organize and share the god's festivals, participating in and watching dithyrambs and plays in the god's theatre. In *Frogs*, the crisis is not inevitable, and the city may still find a solution to its weakness. The city is suffering but does so as one in the process of delivering a child (ἡ πόλις δυστοκεῖ) (1423).

To summarize, the two authors refer to the same Athenian political division but in a different way. Euripides makes the division a nearly abstract, extreme philosophical concept pushed to the limit, perhaps also because of his distance from Athens in his days in Macedonia. Aristophanes instead is engrossed in Athens' day-to-day political fight between the aristocrats and the demos. Still, both cities need saving.

8.2 The polis and tyranny

Pentheus the tyrant is the dominant figure in *Bacchae*, together with his opponent, Dionysus. In this section, I shall focus on defining the figure of the tyrant as a political and moral symbol in fifth-century Athens, a figure of popular fear and hatred.

Fifth-century literature, particularly Greek tragedy, is rich in depictions of figures of tyrants who stand in to against the polis.[20] Despite the dissimilarity of the authors' approaches, the figure of tyrants (and the would-be tyrants) share several morally negative characteristics: isolation, wealth and greed, ungodliness, hubris, self-indulgence, spite for others, violence. The collective view of the evils of tyranny played, in Raaflaub's words, 'a perhaps indispensable role' as an object of popular hatred, useful as a tool for the polis in defining its democratic self-identity and its civic and moral values.[21] As Mitchell puts it, 'Athenian democracy defined itself against autocracy'.[22] In Old Comedy, 'the concept of tyranny played a significant role in creating the ideology and enforcing the regime of radical democracy', as Henderson writes.[23]

In the middle of the agora stood the visual embodiment of the polis anti-tyrannical ideology, the tyrannicides statuary group.[24] The statues of Harmodius and Aristogiton, slayers of the tyrant Hipparchus, would serve as a daily reminder for all Athenians of the hero status of the two men, being embodiments of the anti-tyrannical ideology in Athens. The statues had been originally sculpted by Antenor some time after 511, pillaged by the Persians in 480, rebuilt in 477/6, and commented on by Pausanias in the first century AD.[25] The statue group stood in a highly symbolic place, in the heart of Athenian religious and civic symbology and expressed a 'conflict flagrantly displayed as an integral dimension of the democratic political experience', and of the democratic consensus versus oligarchic *stasis*.[26]

The religious cult of Dionysus and the anti-tyrannical and anti-oligarchic democratic stance of the polis came together in a highly symbolic occurrence. After the fall of the Four Hundred in 411, the ecclesia bound all the citizens of the polis to a new radical collective political institution: the decree of Demophantus in 410 requested all Athenian citizens to swear a democratic oath in public. As befits Athenian constitutional matters, the law establishing the oath was presented as a revision of an old law attributed to Solon, as Andocides reports.[27] The 'Solonian' law,[28] inscribed on a stele in front of the *Bouleuterion*, stated that anybody who held any public office after the overthrow of democracy (δημοκρατίας καταλυθείση), may be slain with impunity, no taint shall rest upon his slayer (ὅσιον εἶναι) and he shall possess the goods of the slain.[29] The same law is referred to in the *Constitution of the Athenians* as θέσμια πάτρια, confirming its legendary ancestral status.[30] The new law made it compulsory for all Athenian citizens to swear the oath composed by Demophantus.[31] The oath significantly committed all citizens to take justice in their hands and slay the enemies of democracy with legal and religious impunity (ὁ ἀποκτείνας... ὅσιος ἔστω καὶ εὐαγής). It also identified the new enemies of democracy in addition to those holding any public office after a tyrannic coup: anyone who suppresses democracy in Athens, anyone who attempts to become a tyrant, or supports one, and oligarchs. It also notably calls him a non-citizen, a war enemy of the polis (πολέμιος). The oath establishes an explicit connection with the powerful symbol of anti-tyrannical democratic ideology, as each Athenian citizen committed himself to materially support any tyrant-slayer and his children, just as Aristogeiton and Harmodius and their children had been supported. It is also evidence of the urge to establish a radical form of democracy to oppose the continuing threats from would-be tyrants and oligarchs. As Lycurgus later observed, the oath is what keeps democracy together (τὸ συνέχον τὴν δημοκρατίαν ὅρκος ἐστί).[32]

Andocides writes that each year all Athenian citizens, organized militarily by tribes and demes, were called to pronounce the oath of Demophantus before the start of the City Dionysia festival (πρὸ Διονυσίων).[33] Mostly unnoticed by scholars, but convincingly reconstructed by Shear, the place and timing of the collective oath ceremony was highly significant because of its associations with the Dionysiac cult.[34] Shear compellingly argues that the ritual took place on 9th Elaphebolion, a day after the presentation of the plays to the public, the *Proagon*,[35] and a day before the beginning of the Dionysia festival. The date indicates a close connection with the Dionysia and the festival's religious and civic associations, such as the display of the allies' tribute, the libation of the ten generals and the parading of the war orphans.

In view of the significance of the civic ceremony involving all citizens, the civic and religious associations of the oath site are of importance. Where did it take place? In the absence of direct evidence scholars have made different assumptions. The size of the crowd in attendance would impose great restrictions on possible venues. In the period we examine, Andocides' 'all citizens'may have meant a crowd of some 30,000 people.[36] Shear plausibly argues that the site where each deme would swear the oath in turn was the *lithos*, the oath-stone that stood in front of the Stoa Basileios in the north-western corner of the agora, where the polis' nine archons annually swore to abide by the laws.[37] In the open space of the agora, the meeting place where the oath ceremony would have been performed was a site on which several monuments stood, the visual embodiment of Athenian democracy and of the Dionysiac cult, as Sourvinou-Inwood and Seaford argue.[38] Bisected by the Panathenaic way and the starting point of the road to Eleusis, the site was filled by religious and civic monuments. To its western side were the Stoa of Zeus Eleutherius and the Old *Bouleterion* building in front of which stood the stele with the text of the old 'Solonian' law. The statues of Aristogiton and Harmodius stood some one hundred metres to the east, while to the north stood another democratic symbol, the group of the three Herms dedicated to the Athenians led by Cimon who had expelled the Persians from Thrace.[39] At the centre of the area stood the oath stone. Beside the oath stone stood the ground hearth altar, the *eschara*, the hearth of the polis as a family community, and the Altar to the Twelve Gods, the focal point of the agora,[40] a sanctuary to the Olympian divinities where suppliants would seek the asylum of the gods and of the polis,[41] and the site from which distances from the city were measured.[42]

The area had significant Dionysiac associations[43] and in particular with the god's ritual reception by the polis, the *xenismos*, which was the reason for the Dionysia festival. The procession that started the Dionysia festival brought the archaic statue of the god from its sanctuary underneath the Acropolis to the theatre of Dionysus, stopping at the *eschara* where the god who came from outside, the *xenos* god, would be symbolically received by the polis' basileus in the Stoa Basileios. Around the *eschara* the participants of the procession would perform sacrifices, sing hymns and dance.[44] The Dionysiac nature of the performances at the site is suggested by Pindar, who wrote a Dionysiac dithyramb for the Athenians that may well have been sung and danced on the occasion. In it, the poet symbolically invites the twelve Olympian gods to join the chorus dancing and singing around the altar, the crowded, incense-fragrant navel of the city of Athens and to honour Zeus and the ivy crowned god whom people call Loud-Roarer and Loud-Shouter (τὸν Βρόμιον, τὸν Ἐριβόαν), two of Dionysus' appellations, with dances and the music of *auloi*.[45] These associations are strong: the dithyramb, Dionysus, the Altar, dancing, singing and music, associations that mark the fusion of civic and mystical sentiments in a high moment in the life of the polis of Athens.

8.3 Euripides and tyranny

The intermingling of Dionysian and civic themes and visual symbols in the oath ceremony provides an important visual and cultic background for Euripides' treatment of the same themes in *Bacchae*. This section is dedicated to examining Euripides' characterization of the figure of Pentheus as a tyrant, who stands in opposition to the god Dionysus and his *thiasoi*. With rare exceptions, this definition of the figure of Pentheus as tyrant and of Dionysus as a preserver of the polis is controversial among scholars.

Euripides' political thought evolved over time. One of its major themes was based on the negative figure of the tyrant. I shall focus first on Euripides' evolution of thoughts on the subject in his *Supplices* (produced at some date between 424 and 420),[46] and then in *Bacchae* (composed probably between 411 and 407/6). Euripides' treatment of the theme of tyranny, of the Eleusinian cult, and of democracy in *Supplices* is a good base from which we can interpret the figure of Pentheus in *Bacchae*. Comparing the two plays sheds some light on the continuity of the political implications of the mystery cults in Athens and their antithesis to tyranny.

The choice of Thebes as Athens' antagonist is significant in both Euripides' plays, *Supplices* and *Bacchae*, as it is a city that the Athenians traditionally connected with the excesses of tyranny. As Morwood notes, the massacre of war prisoners by Thebans and Spartans after their victory in 427 over the city of Plataea, traditional ally of Athens, helped Athenians to make Thebes a symbol of what they believed Athens was not: impious, brutal, and ruled by tyrants.[47] In *Supplices*, the antinomy between Athens' democratic and religious values and those of the tyrant Creon is vividly illustrated. As in Sophocles' *Antigone*, the conflict arises from an impious breach by Creon, ruler of Thebes, of one of the ancestral laws, the *patrioi nomoi*, which prevents the community of pious mothers of Argive warriors, fallen in battle before Thebes' walls, to bury their dead, in itself a marking of an autocrat's ungodliness and disregard for the law preserving the poleis of Greece (311–312). The women are headed by Aethra, queen mother of Theseus, and the chorus of the children of the fallen is headed by Adrastus, king of defeated Argos. As is the case in *Bacchae*, the play's anti-tyrannical stance embodies the complex religious and civic process of the political self-definition of Athenians. In the play, the contrast is between the benevolent and democratic champion of Athens, Theseus, who comes to the Argive mothers' aid in support of Athens' traditional value of religious piety command, and the arrogance of Creon's messenger in his defence of Creon's decision not to allow the ritual burial of the fallen Argives. The antinomy between the impiousness of the Thebans, including their tyrant Creon and the figures of the Athenians, Theseus and his mother Aethra, is what drives the play.

Lawlessness and ungodliness are not the only criteria that condemn the autocrat: his one-man rule jeopardizes the survival of the polis. In *Supplices*, in his first entry on the stage, Theseus defines Creon as the haughty tyrant (σεμνὸς τύραννος) of Thebes (384). Athens, unlike Thebes, is not ruled by one man, affirms Theseus in his reply to the Theban herald. The polis is free: it is the demos who is the lord (δῆμος ἀνάσσει), magistrates take yearly turns in ruling it, and the poor have the same political power as the rich (403–408). Unaided by counsel, an autocrat is inevitably prone to being rash and overambitious (508). Nothing is more hostile to a polis than a tyrant (οὐδὲν τυράννου δυσμενέστερον πόλει), Theseus famously declares, as under tyranny there are no laws common to all, and there is no equality (429–432). Ethics define politics: the conflict between Theseus and Creon animates the political polarity between the democratic and generous Athens and the violent tyrannical

Thebes (308). The Thebans disregard divine laws (νόμιμ' ἀτίζοντες θεῶν) (19) and human laws (ἄνομοι) (45), a feature that is emphasized throughout the play (123, 311); this contrasts the religious principles, generosity and piety of Theseus and the Athenians (189, 335–345, 365–380 etc.).

Although mystery cults do not have an open role in Euripides' *Supplices*, the place where the play is set is significant as it emphasizes the visible and constant presence of the Eleusinian cult. Instead of taking place in Thebes or Athens as would have been natural, the play takes place in Eleusis opposite the temple of the goddesses. The continuous visual presence of the Eleusinian cult would have been an integral element of the impact of the play on the audience, and a powerful reminder of the opposition between mystery cults and the reverence towards divinity, *eusebeia* on one hand, and ungodliness, tyranny and *asebeia* on the other. This strong visual element is accompanied by several Eleusinian motifs throughout the play. The first word of the prologos that sets the mystical tone of the play is Aethra's prayer to the goddess and her invocation to 'Demeter, guardian of this land of Eleusis'. It is to the holy hearth of the Two Goddesses that Aethra declares to have come in solidarity with the women of Argos (33–34). The day on which the play takes place has also a high significance in its religious Eleusinian implications, as Aethra is in Eleusis to perform sacrificial rituals on behalf of the land's crops (28–29). It is the day of the *Proerosia*, the rites performed in the autumn 'before ploughing', the Eleusinian festival that commemorates the beginning of agriculture, founded when, according to the Parian Marble, Demeter came to Athens to instruct Triptolemus on the art of agriculture.[48] The figure of Demeter and her initiation rituals permeate the play: her mysteries are touched on (173), Demeter is defined as the fire-bearing goddess (260); Demeter and Persephone are invoked by the chorus as witnesses to the failure of the women's supplications (261 and 271); Theseus warns his mother not to cry beside the holy hearth of the goddesses (290); Theseus describes his army ready to march to Thebes as it camps in Demeter's holy grounds (392); and Evadne declares her wish to join her dead husband in the bridal chambers of Persephone (1022).

The play's setting also emphasizes the powerful connection between death rituals and the Eleusinian assurance of a blessed afterlife, as expressed in the *Homeric Hymn to Demeter*, and as noted by Sourvinou-Inwood.[49] The immortality of ritually buried initiates is hinted at by Theseus who warns

Creon's messenger to maintain the laws of all Greeks by allowing the bodies of the dead to return to the earth so their souls can go to heaven (πνεῦμα μὲν πρὸς αἰθέρα,/τὸ σῶμα δ' ἐς γῆν) (533–534), a significant remark as it is made on Persephone's holy grounds, from which the chorus earlier warned Adrastos to rise (271).

8.4 Pentheus the tyrant

The figure of Pentheus, tyrant of Thebes, dominates *Bacchae*. In the play, Euripides pushes the religious and political themes found in *Supplices* to the extreme. The mystery cult theme in *Supplices* is a powerful but largely silent background to a treatment of the values of *eusebeia*, of political equality and of the vices of tyranny. In *Bacchae*, mystery cults are openly on stage in the person of the protagonist Dionysus and of the Asian and Theban women who compose the god's *thiasoi*. The tyrant, who in *Supplices* is absent from the stage, in *Bacchae* is antagonist and expresses openly the evil and violent nature of a tyrant. The tyrant in *Supplices* leads his army to defeat but survives, while in *Bacchae* Euripides emphasizes the evilness of the tyrant, adopting the traditional mythological theme of how the god has the tyrant opposing him ritually dismembered. The solidarity in *Supplices* between women, the mothers from Argos and Aethra, develops into the mystical cohesion of the female *thiasoi* in *Bacchae*.

Euripides' construction of the figure of Pentheus as tyrant is markedly more complex and more extreme than his treatment of tyranny in *Supplices*. Far from being the incarnation of the polis' civic virtues as many scholars would have him, Euripides develops the concept of tyranny as the enemy of the polis that he had explored in *Supplices*. In *Bacchae*, Euripides introduces the figure of Pentheus early in the play in Dionysus' prologos. From the start, he defines Pentheus' two main political features: his absolute political power and his reckless fight against divinity. The polis' founder and ruler, Cadmus, gave his grandson the 'powers of tyranny' (γέρας καὶ τυραννίδα) as a gift, but now his grandson fights against deity in his treatment of Dionysus' cult (43–45). Euripides could have used the term 'power', *kratos* or 'kingly authority', *basileia*, had he wished to imply the legality of Pentheus' power, but he used the term *tyrannis* instead. The notion of tyranny as the one-man rule, absolute power, the reverse of political equality and the rule of law, echoes its definition we noted in Aeschylus' *Eumenides* (696) and in Euripides' *Supplices* as the main enemy of the polis. The description of Pentheus' power is an openly political one, announcing the antagonism between the tyrant and the polis that stands at the core of the play.

Several features characterize Pentheus as a tyrant. Firstly, there is the tyrant's isolation, emphasizing his remoteness as ruler in his unfettered and uncontrolled absolute power. Since the departure of his mother and aunts, who led the Theban *thiasos* to the mountain, Pentheus is alone in both his family and in his polis in his opposition to Dionysus. His own grandfather, Cadmus, founder of the city, is a worshipper of Dionysus, making a sacred enclosure of the ruins of Semele's house (10–11), and openly sharing the cult of the god with the prophet Tiresias (195–196). The men of Thebes are ready to accept the new god despite their fear of the tyrant: however, Pentheus is alone and proud of his isolation. 'Alone among Theban men I dare to do this', Pentheus exclaims when asking Dionysus to guide him to the *thiasos* on the mountain. The term 'alone' is twice repeated in emphasis by Dionysus in his ambiguous reply, 'Alone you are toiling for this polis, alone' (962–963). Isolation and boundless self-confidence mark the tyrant. Being alone entails having the sole responsibility of the exercise of power: unlike for Homeric kings, no council of elders advises Pentheus, who constantly refuses to heed the advice of his grandfather Cadmus, of Tiresias, of Dionysus and of the messengers.

The second feature is how Pentheus rules by force. Cadmus himself remarks of Pentheus that he was the man to whom he had given power (κράτος), over the land (213). The first messenger uses the same term as he comes to the presence of Pentheus to report what he had seen on Cithaeron. He addresses Pentheus formally as ruler (κρατύνων) of this land of Thebes (660), and later as lord (ἄναξ) (670). The term κράτος implies force, possession and power by might.[50] The archaic term ἄναξ 'lord, master' (LSJ) is mostly used to address deities and is far from any definition of power limited by laws. Pentheus thinks, plans and acts outside the laws that define the communality of the polis: 'Dwell with us, not outside the laws', Cadmus admonishes him (331). But might alone does not create power (δύναμιν), Tiresias warns Pentheus (310). Pentheus only believes in his own power: believing Dionysus to be human, he declares that he is more powerful (κυριώτερος) than Dionysus in chains (505), a claim that would have sounded impious and hubristic to the audience that is aware of the divine nature of the prisoner. As Segal notes, the power of Pentheus over the polis is constantly defined in terms that indicate constraint, binding and enclosing, terms that emphasize that the only relationship he has with the citizens of Thebes is one of command.[51] Pentheus sees his polis not in terms of the community living in it, but as a site locked by towers (653); a fine-towered city (1202): a fortress that defends him from the maenads outside and is a prison for those inside it.

As he enters on stage, Pentheus announces that many maenads have been caught and imprisoned, guarded by wardens, while he will hunt the rest of the *thiasos* from the mountain like wild animals (228), even threatening Tiresias himself to be chained with the maenads (ἐν βάκχαισι δέσμιος μέσαις) (259). Chain (δεσμός) is a term Euripides uses nearly obsessively eleven times in the play (226, 444, 447, 518, 615, 616, 634, 644, 648, 755, 1035). Despite having been told the magical way the imprisoned maenads freed themselves from their chains, Pentheus' interrogation of Dionysus ends with his instructions to his attendants to shut the god in the stables of the horses, so that all he can see is a gloomy darkness (ὡς ἂν σκότιον εἰσορᾷ κνέφας) (509–514), an image that suggests a prison in Erebus. But force alone cannot keep the polis together.

The third aspect of Pentheus is his behaviour as a military leader in his feverish but powerless hostility towards the cult of Dionysus. He wages war not on an army of enemies but on a group of unarmed women, the epitome of ridicule for a real army leader. The maenads are not even human to Pentheus; they are wild animals, unworthy of being beaten in battle (226–268, 434, 436, 451), and which are to be sacrificed (796). As the audience would have realized, Pentheus' desire to slaughter the maenads (780–785), who represent the whole female side of the polis of Thebes, is the ultimate expression of the hubris of absolute power and an ultimately self-destroying threat. Pentheus' enemy cannot be defeated by human hands. Frenzy inspired by Dionysus (μανία), Tiresias had warned in 302–305, can scatter even an army deployed for battle in panic. In his instructions to his soldiers after the capture of Dionysus, Pentheus does not mention the maenads in the passage except with a disparaging 'those women'; he decides they will be sold as slaves or kept as household slaves at the looms (514). This vividly describes the paradox of the tyrant's absolute power but total inability to rule his polis: as slaves who would have been sold abroad, women would leave the polis childless; if they remained in Thebes, they would not be able to take up either the full role of the female community as slaves at the loom.

The fourth element of Pentheus' portrait is his mental state, making him unfit to rule and unable to perceive the cult's reality. At his entry onto the stage in the first episode he is depicted by Tiresias as 'in a flutter' (ὡς ἐπτόηται) (214), setting the tone of Pentheus' inability either to grasp what is happening in Thebes or to control it. Coming after the lyrical and mystical parodos that sings the praise of the god and the happiness of his *thiasos*, the initial speech of the tyrant confirms Tiresias' description, as the audience would have perceived it as an obsessed tirade full of fantastic and prurient notions on what the maenads actually do on Mount Cithaeron. In response, Tiresias defines Pentheus repeatedly as a madman (269, 312), crazy in a most painful way (326), and observes that a man with a good tongue but no brains cannot be a good citizen (271), nor a man who lacks self-control (σωφροσύνη), the essential quality of a member of the community (504). But a tyrant does not need self-control: as the first messenger timidly remarks to the tyrant, Pentheus is dominated by a wild temper and an excessive use of his autocratic power (670–671).

The fifth mark of the tyrant Pentheus is his being the opposite to the interrelated concepts that define the polis' civic and religious values. In reply to Pentheus' entry speech, the chorus exclaims its horror at the tyrant's ungodliness (δυσσεβεία) and his lack of respect for divinity (263). Pentheus is the enemy of all the gods, of laws and of justice (ἄθεος, ἄνομος, ἄδικος) (995, 1015), a powerful expression of three alpha privative adjectives the chorus uses as it invokes Dionysus, defining Pentheus again as impious, ἀσεβής (490, 502). He is the very antithesis of those moral and civic virtues, self-control and veneration for divinity (τὸ σωφρονεῖν καὶ σέβειν τὰ τῶν θεῶν) that the second messenger recommends to the polis (1150–1152). In the words of the chorus as it moves to the tyrant's sacrifice, Pentheus' sentiments are criminal; he is moved by an uncontrolled rage, a man whose mind is mad, and whose spirit is frenzied (997–1000). A crucial component of how the Athenians perceived a tyrant's character in *Bacchae* is hubris, that ultimate offence that threatens the cohesion and order of the polis in Greek traditional thought. It is the moral vice that Heraclitus for instance defines as more dangerous to the polis than a blazing fire,⁵² the pitfall that Aeschylus urges the polis to avoid in *Eumenides* (517–565) and the accusation that was moved against Alcibiades.⁵³ As Sophocles remarks, hubris and tyranny are intimately connected (ὕβρις φυτεύει τύραννον).⁵⁴ After Pentheus' initial tirade against Dionysus, the chorus defines this hubris against Dionysus as unholy (375), and later as a feature of a murderer (555).

Autocratic, violent and impious: these are the characteristics of Pentheus the tyrant in public. Pentheus, however, behaves humanly within the royal family, as befits the traditional image of an autocrat in the archaic pre-democratic polis days. In his speech on the dead body of Pentheus, Cadmus fondly recalls Pentheus' loyalty and kindness to himself and his punishment of those who wronged and dishonoured him (1308–1322). The royal family versus the polis, tyranny as an obstacle to the development of the community: this is the central religious and political conflict in *Bacchae*.

8.5 The adversaries of the chorus in *Frogs*

In contrast with Euripides' philosophical approach and in line with the style of Old Comedy, Aristophanes' politics in *Frogs* are closer to the Athenian reality his audience lived in, a political reality dominated by the new class of political leaders who held sway in the ecclesia,⁵⁵ a different class of leaders after the death of Pericles in 429. The leaders who succeeded him, writes Thucydides (whose aristocratic political opinions were not far from those of Aristophanes), because of private ambitions and private desire for monetary gains (κατὰ τὰς ἰδίας φιλοτιμίας καὶ ἴδια κέρδη), occupied themselves with private quarrels and introduced civil discord at home. They were, writes Thucydides, responsible for the disaster of the Sicilian expedition, for stasis in the polis, for Athens' allies abandoning the alliance and for the Persians giving support to the Spartans, the sum of Athenian ills at the end of the fifth century.⁵⁶

Aristophanes identifies the leaders of the demos in 405 in a similar tone of ethical and political condemnation. Aristophanes expresses the nature of Athens' cultural and political division in religious terms through the voice of the chorus of mystery initiates. In the second part of the parodos (354–368),

Aristophanes voices the strongest religious act of condemnation of the enemies of the polis and of its civic, cultural and religious rules.[57] Aristophanes' direct political plea is expressed as a *prorrhesis*, the formula that was delivered by the two chief priests, the Eumolpidae and Kerykes, at the beginning of the Eleusinian festival that excluded non-Greek speakers and murderers from the rituals.[58] The tone is that of a *prorrhesis*, but the content is openly political. After an opening appeal to keep religious silence, *euphemia*, the list of the political enemies of the chorus who are targeted in the religious exclusion is detailed and extensive, being ordered by the gravity of the crime.

The list starts with the religiously impure and those with no experience of mystical rituals, as well as those who had never watched, danced or sung on the secret initiation rituals (ὄργια) of the Muses, nor been initiated in the Bacchic mysteries, thus showing Aristophanes' emphasis on the pre-eminence of mystery values in his political valuations. As was the case with *Thesmophoriazusai* 331–351, the chorus then turns to Athens' politics with comical sounding but severe denunciations, marking first those who utter words of buffoonery at the wrong time (358), a note probably directed at war hardliners in the ecclesia, such as Cleophon.[59] The list continues with those who provoke *stasis* for private monetary gain, *kerdos*, and are not at peace with their fellow citizens, a passage which emphasizes the contrast and tension between the collective values of the polis versus the destructive self-interest of the individual.

The list of those excluded from the chorus' sacred dances include different sorts of enemies of the cult and of the polis. First of all, there are the traitors: corrupt office holders, those who betray forts and fleets to the enemy, the tax collectors who use their office to smuggle fleet supplies to the enemy, as well as those who provide funds to the Persian navy. Then the list only half-comically extends to soloists of dithyrambs who soil the altar of Hekate and politicians who nibble away at the fees of comedy writers, having been ridiculed by them in the theatre's ancestral rituals of Dionysus. This last is an appeal, only partly comical, that stresses the educational and opinion-forming role of theatre in the life of the polis beyond its seemingly jocular tone, a fundamental civic role that Aristophanes solemnly states twice in *Frogs* (686–687 and 1008–1010). Following the ritual exclusion, *Frogs*' political message is made stronger and more formal by the closing verses, also probably belonging to the formula of the rituals: 'to these I proclaim, and again I proclaim the ban, and again a third time I proclaim the ban that they stand out of the way of the initiates' dances' (369). The list continues in the *agon*: the polis is led by bureaucrats, oafish democratic apes always cheating the people (1084–1086), runaway citizens, loafers, rascals and miscreants (1014–1015).

8.6 The polis and money

An issue mostly neglected by scholars, the introduction of money in the form of gold and silver coinage was a crucial factor in the development of the polis.[60] Initially used by the polis of Miletus at the beginning of the seventh century, it spread rapidly through the Greek world. Athens started using it at the time of Solon. The polis was then able to use the silver mined in Laurion and the gold from Thracian mines to mint silver and gold coins. This transformed the rate of Athens' economic growth from one which followed the slow growth of population to a faster one fuelled by the use of money in international trade, allowing the polis to import the goods it lacked and to export the goods it produced. Money transformed Athens' society as it allowed people to exchange goods as well as to balance debts and credits outside 'the ancient principles of solidarity through kinship and reciprocity'.[61] Money thus depersonalized economic exchanges and dematerialized wealth. Its effect on Athenian society at large was to increase the polarization between the haves and the have-nots, radicalizing socio-political tensions.

The term Athenians used to define a monetary gain and the greed for money was *kerdos*. The term *kerdos* implies the unfairness of a personal gain in contrast with a communal use of wealth.[62] In Homer for instance, it implies the unfair advantage held by those who are able to perceive before others the occasion of a gain,[63] while in *Antigone* (222) Sophocles notes that the greed for gain, *kerdos*, often destroys people associating the figure of the tyrant with Creon's sordid greed for money (αἰσχροκέρδειαν) (1056). In Athenian political and religious consciousness, the craving for wealth is associated with the polis' lawless political leaders and with *stasis*: as we noted in 6.1, Solon makes them responsible for the 'inescapably festering wound their greed for wealth inflicts on the polis arousing civil strife'.[64] A craving for wealth for its own sake is one of the traits of character of the traditional tyrant. Money made it possible, for instance, for an individual to amass liquid monetary resources in a way that was impossible in the non-monetary economy. An individual, often a tyrant, could thus, for instance, raise a private army without having to have recourse to family and tribe allegiances. Tyrants would use private armies to defend themselves from the demos, a practice we observed for instance in Herodotos' account of Miltiades' hiring 500 mercenaries (6.39.2). To the egalitarian polis, a private army is the opposite of what an army was for the polis, namely the embodiment of its well-ordered egalitarian cohesion; a private army is a manifest declaration of the tyrant's alienation, of his mistrust and fear of his co-citizens.

The greed for money is one of the elements defining political leaders in *Frogs*, as it defines one of the traits of the tyrant in *Bacchae*. In *Bacchae*, Euripides contrasts the nature of gold for the mystic *thiasoi* with what gold represents in Pentheus' mind. For the maenads, gold is free for all, a gift of Dionysus: Mount Tmolos is rich in golden streams, exclaims Dionysus to his *thiasos* (153), golden are the wings of Purity (373) and golden is the god's *thyrsus* (553). Instead, for Pentheus, gold is his own possession, its quantity measurable and exchangeable, gold is the unmeasurable price (μυρίον χρυσοῦ σταθμόν) Pentheus is ready to pay to assuage his mad desire to watch the maenads on the mountain (812–813); money is the irrelevant price of a whim. In *Frogs*, the theme of the greed for money as the cause of the corruption of the polis looms large. Aristophanes connects the greed of monetary gain, *kerdos*, with the phenomenon of civic unrest, *stasis*. In the play's parodos, some of the citizens are guilty of encouraging *stasis* in order to gain a profit, *kerdos*, using the term in a manner similar to Thucydides' definition of post-Periclean political leaders. In the plays, the theme of money helps emphasizing the division of the polis: tyrant and the wealthy on one hand, the demos and the Demetrian and Dionysiac initiates on the other.

9

Mystery Cults and the Choruses

9.1 Dionysus and Demeter, mystery deities

In *Bacchae* and *Frogs*, the connection between religion and the polis is put into effect by setting the cults of Dionysus and Demeter, two of the main religious cults of the polis of Athens, at the plays' core. In no other extant tragedies or comedies is religion as pervasive as it is in these plays: the two playwrights intend to impact the polis powerfully through its most important religious beliefs, cultic rituals and religious symbols. The association between these two deities in the plays as well as its tradition is the focus of this chapter.

In *Bacchae*, although the setting and development of the play is apparently Dionysiac, the pairing of the two divinities is explicit from the start, in Dionysus' prologos. Although not mentioned explicitly, the Eleusinian goddess is shown through in her association with deities that had the role of earth mother: Rhea and Cybele.[1] This association is evidence of Euripides' knowledge of, and interest in the Orphic cult and lore, a cult that became a component of the Dionysiac cult in the fifth century. In the prologos, Dionysus addresses his *thiasos*/chorus of Lydian maenads as his assistants and travel companions (πάρεδροι καὶ ξυνέμποροι ἐμοί), mentioning the remote legendary Mount Tmolos and describing mystery ritual dancing and the rousing Phrygian rhythm of the drums (τύμπανα) sacred to the mother of gods, that Dionysus had invented together with mother Rhea (55–63).[2] Immediately afterwards, in the first lines of the parodos, Euripides emphasizes again the association between the chorus, Dionysus, Cybele and Rhea devoting the second strophe of the parodos to a blessing, a *makarismos* of the initiate who celebrates the mysteries of great mother Cybele (78–79). In the fifth strophe, the chorus invokes the Cretan Corybantes who created the tympanum, mixed it with the sound of Phrygian *auloi* and gave it to mother Rhea to beat the rhythm of the

Dionysiac dances (120–134): a complex image of the birth of Dionysiac musical instruments and his dances that is echoed for instance in Plato's observation on the music of Corybantic rituals we mentioned earlier.

> For all the good epic poets utter all those fine poems not from art, but as inspired and possessed, and the good lyric poets likewise; just as the Corybantian worshippers do not dance when in their senses, so the lyric poets do not indite those fine songs in their senses, but when they have started on the melody and rhythm they begin to be frantic, and it is under possession – as the bacchants are possessed, and not in their senses, when they draw honey and milk from the rivers – that the soul of the lyric poets does the same thing, by their own report.[3]

A few lines later, Demeter is mentioned by Tiresias in a solemn context. Answering Pentheus' accusations against Dionysus and his cult, Tiresias warns him that 'there are two first things among humans: Demeter, who feeds the human race, and Dionysus, who introduced wine to mankind, the only remedy against human suffering' (274–280). The two deities are significantly coupled in their gift-giving nature, having given the legendary gifts that make life possible and bearable and freed mankind from the fear of death: food, wine and the (unmentioned, but well-known) initiation rituals. The connection between the choruses, Demeter and Dionysus is strong in both plays. Iacchus/Dionysus is in both plays called a travel companion (συνέμπορος) of the choral procession in both plays – a Dionysiac in *Bacchae* and a Demetrian in *Frogs* (*Bacchae* 57; *Frogs* 396).

In *Frogs*, the chorus is explicitly composed of Eleusinian initiates, but its parodos starts with an invocation to Iacchus to join the sacred parade, as happened in reality during the yearly procession to Eleusis.[4] The god is invited to join the Demetrian choral dance that is 'holy and sacred to the blessed initiates' (ἀγνάν, ἱερὰν,/ ὁσίοις μύσταις χορείαν) (335–336). Dancing is then emphasized as the joyful ritual activity of the Eleusinian chorus, but Dionysiac images of torches and nocturnal initiations are used to invoke the god Iacchus, 'brilliant star of choral nocturnal initiation rituals' (νυκτέρου τελετῆς φωσφόρος ἀστήρ) (343). Demeter is only invoked after Iacchus, and Aristophanes identifies the goddess with qualities that connect her cult to the city's prosperity: as goddess of the fertility of the land, and queen of the choral initiation rituals (ἁγνῶν ὀργίων ἄνασσα) (386–387). Demeter is then openly paired with Iacchus, as the chorus again invites Iacchus to join them to meet the goddess (399–400). The second powerful reference to Demeter in *Frogs* is made by the soon-to-be demi-god Aeschylus, Eleusis-born, future saviour of Athens, who, before entering the *agon*, solemnly invokes the goddess, nurturer of his mind (ἡ θρέψασα τὴν ἐμὴν φρένα), to make him worthy of her mysteries (886–887). Set at the very beginning of the *agon* between Aeschylus and Euripides in the second part of the play, the exclamation sets the religious background of the rest of the play under the aegis of the goddess and of Dionysus, the judge of the *agon*.

The two cults need to be put in context to appreciate the maze of associations that would have been known by the public of the plays. In Hesiodic mythology the two deities were separate, with no special links. Dionysus is not mentioned in *Theogony*, while he is referred to briefly in both Hesiod's *Shield of Heracles* (398 ff.) and in *Works and Days* (609 ff.), solely as deity of wine. Demeter on the other hand is mentioned frequently in Hesiod's works, for instance in *Theogony* 454 as daughter of Cronus and Rhea and in *Theogony* 912 as bed-companion of Zeus and mother of Persephone; however, she is never mentioned in conjunction with Dionysus. The presence of Dionysus is evoked in the *Homeric Hymn to Demeter* through an allusion to his companions, the maenads, when, in the description of Demeter running joyfully towards Hermes and Persephone down a thick wooded mountain, her behaviour is likened to that of a maenad (386).

In what may be called the Orphic tradition on the other hand, the connection between the worship of Dionysus and that of Demeter/Persephone was close. As Iles-Johnston convincingly argues, the Greeks started recomposing and elaborating the theological world of Homer and Hesiod into new myths and cults at the end of the sixth century, using some of the existing deities such as Demeter and Dionysus to create their mystical theological system. The figure of Orpheus then took on the attribute of founder of both the Eleusinian and the Dionysiac mysteries, symbolizing the gradual merger of the two cults. In the first or second-century AD work attributed to Apollodorus, Orpheus is mentioned as discoverer of the Dionysiac mysteries; in Diodorus he is a Dionysiac initiate and importer of Dionysiac rituals from Egypt (1.23, 6.7, 1.96, 4.25 etc.). A similar information is provided by Theodoret (Kern 103), who quotes Plutarch fragment 43 (212 Loeb) which relates that the Eleusinian mysteries were imported by Orpheus from Egypt, with him transplanting the ritual of Isis and Osiris into the ceremonies of Deo (Demeter) and Dionysus into Greece. This development had the effect of increasing the similarities between the two deities, particularly in making Dionysus into a chthonian god of eschatological initiation to parallel Demeter's cult at Eleusis.[5]

In the same period the figure of Demeter also started being assimilated into other ancient deities and assumed new roles. The tradition of the association between Rhea and Dionysus may have been ancient, as poetry composed in the late seventh or early-sixth century and attributed to Eumelos[6] attests that Dionysus had received purification from Rhea at Mount Cybele in Phrygia, had been taught the initiation rites and roamed over the world dancing and celebrating the rites.[7] Some other evidence of the pairing of the two gods as chthonian, eschatological deities is for instance in the Bacchic gold tablets. In a tablet from Pherae, the initiate asks to be sent to the *thiasoi* of the *mystai* as he possesses the rituals of Bacchus and those of Demeter Chthonia and of the Mountain Mother.[8]

In fifth-century tragedy and poetry, the pairing of the deities was common. Pindar for example calls Dionysus the 'companion', πάρεδρος of Demeter, the same term used by Euripides in *Bacchae*.[9] The chorus in Sophocles' *Antigone* invokes Dionysus as 'lord of the hollows of Demeter of Eleusis', evidence of Dionysus' role in the rituals.[10] In the third stasimon of Euripides' *Ion*, the chorus sings of Dionysus as he observes the torch procession and the dances of the starry sky, the moon and the fifty daughters of Nereus beside the spring of the lovely dances (παρὰ καλλιχόροισι παγαῖς) that celebrate Demeter and Persephone (1074–1089), a clear reference to the reituals at Eleusis.

In Euripides' *Helen*, the chorus recounts the myth of Demeter, whose fury and sorrow at the loss of Kore is only relieved by Aphrodite playing Dionysiac musical instruments; this event prompts Demeter to join the Dionysiac music by taking up Dionysus' musical instrument, the deep sounding *aulos*, and delighting in its loud voice (1301–1368). Callimachus equally notes the common ritual framework of the two deities: 'whatever vexes Demeter, vexes also Dionysus.'[11] Strabo notes that the Greeks attributed all orgiastic, Bacchic, choral ceremonies and mystical initiations to Demeter, and that they gave the name of 'Iacchus' not only to Dionysus, but also to the leader (ἀρχηγέτης) of the mysteries, Demeter's own daemon, the personal deity of the goddess. Strabo also notes that certain aspects of the rituals were common to both cults, as the Greeks associated everything of an orgiastic, Bacchic or choral nature, as well as the mystical initiation rituals, to Dionysus, Apollo, Hecate, the Muses, and above all to Demeter.[12]

Archaeological evidence points to 'the coexistence of the great Attic cults of Dionysus and the Two Goddesses on the hill of Eleusis',[13] and there exist multiple references to a sanctuary of Dionysus in the town of Eleusis that belonged to the demos of Eleusis, an important sanctuary where theatrical performances were held, and public decrees were set up.[14] Archaeological remains point to the presence of Iacchus/Dionysus at the mystery ritual of Eleusis since at least the sixth century BC, as Versnel points out,[15] basing himself on a black-figured amphora of the mid-late sixth century attributed to the Priam Painter which depicts Dionysus in a two-wheeled chariot of Triptolemus.[16] Further hard evidence of an early dual cult of Dionysus and Demeter outside Attica and its existence in the first half of the fifth century was found in the ruins of the sanctuary of Persephone at Locri Epizephyrii on the Ionian coast of Calabria. In this sanctuary, a number of votive *pinakes*, clay relief plaques, have been found. On one of the *pinakes*, Persephone is seated holding a cockerel in her right hand and sheaves of corn in the other, while Dionysus stands in front of her, offering Persephone a *kantharos* of wine and carrying a vine branch on his shoulders.[17]

The association between the two gods, if one follows Carpenter's identification of the deities in the east side of the Parthenon frieze, was popular in Athens in the age of Pericles.[18] Demeter and Dionysus are depicted sitting in a pose that suggests a particularly intimate association between the two deities.[19] Dionysus, wearing a mantle over the lower part of his body, is seated in the opposite direction of the other gods who are present in this part of the frieze, resting his right arm on Hermes' shoulders. His pose suggests a divine figure who has different characteristics from Olympian deities. The reason for his posture is Demeter, who leans forward towards Dionysus, her knees between his, holding a torch in her left hand, with her right hand raised to her face, perhaps in grief at the loss of her daughter. The two deities form a small close group in the formal and solemn festivities for Athena, as if sharing a particular form of familiarity.

Clinton finds their simultaneous induction into the Eleusinian rituals as evidence, at least for the fifth century, for the overlapping of the two cults we shall encounter in *Bacchae* and *Frogs*.[20] Clinton concludes cautiously that 'evidence seems to reflect, on a local level, the coexistence of the great Attic cults of Dionysus and of the two goddesses on the hill of Eleusis'. The existence of the cult in the fourth century is supported by Pausanias' report that in the temple of Demeter in Athens there were three statues by Praxiteles, a sculptor active in 370–330 BC: they represented Demeter, Persephone and Iacchus.[21] Significantly, the paired deities of Demeter and Dionysus were also the gods celebrated at the women-only Haloa festival in the fourth century.[22]

The two deities share some defining characteristics. First, both are described in myth as coming to Attica from abroad as outsiders, strangers, *xenoi*. In Athens, the legendary advent of the two deities was celebrated with *xenismoi*, public rituals of welcome and entertainment of the 'foreign' gods, according to Plutarch.[23] In myth, the two deities came to Attica from abroad as *xenoi* at the same time, while Pandion was Athens' king, according to Apollodorus. Celeus received Demeter and Icarius received Dionysus.[24] In Greek myth the arrival of a *xenos* god, often Dionysus, and his impact on the community provides a solution to the community's internal strife imposing civilized civic practices by founding his cult.[25] In the *Homeric Hymn* dedicated to her, Demeter comes to Eleusis from Olympus after roaming over dry land and sea (43), describing herself to the girls at the well as coming to Eleusis from Crete via Thoricus having crossed Attica from its eastern to its western border (123–126). Dionysus in *Bacchae*, on the other hand, comes to Thebes not only from the fabulous world of 'the lands of the Lydians and Phrygians, [through] the plains of the Persians, and the Bactrian walls, and the land of the Medes, and ... Arabia, and the whole of Asia', but also from the Greek-speaking world of the cities on the coast of Asia Minor, 'full of Greeks and barbarians' (13–19).[26] One of the founding myths of the Dionysiac cult for Athenians was the image of Dionysus 'Eleuthereus' that had been brought to Athens by Pegasus 'probably a missionary of the cult'[27] from the town of Eleutherae, on the border between Boeotia and Attica on the east side of Mount Cithaeron, a place as liminal as Eleusis. It was an event that Athenians had celebrated since the earliest days of the festival of the Great Dionysia.[28]

Both *xenoi* gods brought gifts to humankind, gifts whose acceptance cause a deep transformation of social structures, after the initial and often violent disorder created by the arrival of the 'new'. For the Greeks, the gift was an essential component of personal and communal reciprocity, the basis on which rested the Homeric cohesion of the community;[29] in the case of a divine gift, its grateful acceptance was essential in ensuring humankind's role in the cosmic order. The gift of wine by Dionysus as *xenos* is described in several similar myths. In his study of Dionysiac *xenia*, Massenzio[30] argues persuasively that myths related to Dionysus' gift of the art of winemaking created a new phase of cultural organization. This point marked a decisive change in Greek civilization, from one where political power is in the hands of a king and the main economic activity is domestic animal farming handled by individuals or families, to one based on economic activities, such as vine and grain-growing and winemaking, which are only economically viable as a collective and organized activity of a cohesive community. The simultaneous arrival of Demeter and Dionysus was thus meant to mark the aetiology of the polis through its adoption of agricultural techniques in Attica. Not only do the *xenoi* deities transform the economy, they also revolutionize culture and social organization down to its fundamental element: family life. Other myths related to the figure of Dionysus connect the figure of the deity to his role in liberating women from patriarchal authority. Several of Dionysus' myths (Oenotropae, Icarius, Staphylus, Oenopion etc.) focus on the arrival of the *xenos* that allows women to escape their fathers' authority,[31] transforming a closed household structure into one that is at least partially open, a myth that Euripides elaborates and expands in *Bacchae*.

As we noted, equally revolutionary are the gifts of Demeter in the *Homeric Hymn*. In the *Hymn*, the goddess describes herself to the girls drawing water at the well as the Giver (Δωσώ) (122), and, as she later proclaims her divinity to the women in the palace, she defines the nature of her gift: 'I am Demeter, the greatest source of help and joy to mortals and immortals' (269). Her gift not only grants the fertility of the soil[32] but also marks the foundation of those rituals that give mortals an abundance of spiritual and physical goods (ὄλβος) during life and in the afterlife, the equivalent of immortality (475–482).[33] In a similar way to *Bacchae*, the *Homeric Hymn* suggests a radical social change, as the heads of the ruling families of Thebes become the priests of the new cult and the whole people (271) shows its communal solidarity in building the temple and participating in the goddess mysteries.

Farming, grain-harvesting and winemaking are by their nature collective endeavours, their success dependent on a communal organized effort, social cohesion and the favour of divinity. As purveyor of food to mankind, Demeter is thus also goddess of social peace and communal unity. These implications of the cult of the goddess are made clear for instance in the finale of Callimachus' *Hymn to Demeter*, a third-century hymn written in honour of the sacred basket-carrying procession established by Ptolemy Philadelphus and imitating a similar ceremony held in Athens, as a scholiast notes.[34] In the *Hymn*, Demeter is closely associated with Eleusis (13–16, 28–30), being defined as preserver of the polis' in harmony and prosperity (ἔν θ' ὁμονοίαι ἔν τ' εὐηπελίαι) and as provider of food in abundance, as preserver of herds, of harvests, and of peace, so that he who ploughs may also reap.[35]

The two deities were also paired in Eleusinian rituals. Demeter and Iacchus/Dionysus famously appear in Herodotus as saviours of the Athenians during the Persian invasion of 480 in a scene that was reported to him by Dicaeus, an Athenian exile who had accompanied the Persian army in its invasion of Greece.[36] From afar, Dicaeus and his companion observed a cloud of dust, as 30,000 people would produce marching in procession,[37] floating from Eleusis through the plain, and heard the loud, ritual cry of 'Iacchus!' that traditionally accompanied the mysteries' procession to Eleusis. As the cloud floated towards Salamis where the Athenian fleet was waiting for the arrival of the Persians, Dicaeus observed that, since Attica had been abandoned by its inhabitants, the cry was surely divine (θεῖον τὸ φθεγγόμενον) and that it came from Eleusis to assist Athens. He thus predicted the disaster that would befall the Persian fleet and the defeat of the Persian invasion. Interestingly, Herodotus comments on the nature of the Eleusinian initiation rituals as being open to any Athenian or other Greek who wished to be initiated (ὁ βουλόμενος μυεῖται). The allusion to the personal wish of the initiand is important as Herodotus thus stresses the voluntary and individual nature of adhesion to the rituals, as well as their panhellenic inclusiveness.

The emphasis given by Euripides and Aristophanes to the two Athenian mystery initiation deities is thus significant, as it associates the call for a renewal of the polis with two of its religious foundation myths.

9.2 Mystery cults' spaces

In *Bacchae* and *Frogs*, Euripides and Aristophanes recreate the atmosphere of Dionysiac and Eleusinian initiation rituals through similar vivid visual imagery, using some of the descriptions of the heavenly world and religious rituals that, as we noticed in chapter 2, were traditionally associated with mystery cults. We shall start by examining the location of the religious action of the plays, the meadows of the goddess Demeter in Hades in *Frogs* and the Dionysiac wilderness of Mount Cithaeron in *Bacchae*. Both playwrights use the similar traditional idyllic images of wild nature to describe mental and physical places that may be termed as 'liminal', space-time 'pods' distant from the polis both geographically and psychologically, outside the normal functioning of society and the polis' social structure, places where the mystical initiation rituals could be enacted in freedom from normal human social behaviour.[38]

In *Frogs*, as Heracles describes Hades to Dionysus and Xanthias (154–157), rituals take place in verdant fields rich with myrtle groves (μυρρινῶνας) where the *thiasoi* of the god-blessed initiates women and men dance, play the *aulos* and clap their hands. 'Myrtle' refers to the adornments of initiates in Eleusinian mystical rituals, a term that also defines Iacchus' crown (329–330). In the parodos of the play, the chorus of Eleusinian initiates invites Iacchus to join the dances in the meadows (λειμῶνα) (326), the dwelling place of the Muses (1300). Mentioned by Sommerstein only in a brief note,[39] and unnoticed by Lada-Richards, the term 'meadow' (λειμών, ἄλσος) is used in *Frogs*' parodos several times and emphasizes the idyllic nature of the spaces of Demeter's rituals. Colours and lights abound in Hades and are often linked to meadows and greenery: the goddess' meadow is in flames (φλογὶ φέγγεται λειμών) (344), the chorus of initiates advances in procession towards the goddess' flowery meadows (ἐς τοὺς εὐανθεῖς κόλπους/λειμώνων) (373–374), light and torches illuminate a nocturnal procession to Demeter's flowery grove (ἀνθοφόρον ἄλσος) where women and girls dance and sing all night in the goddess' flowery meadows, blooming with roses (ἐς πολυρρόδους/λειμῶνας ἀνθεμώδεις) (445–450).

Similar mystery-related images of thriving nature can be found in *Bacchae*. In the play, the Dionysiac mystical spaces on Mount Cithaeron are set in contrast with the city of Thebes, defined by the emphasis on its military aspect, a feature we saw associated with the rule of the tyrant Pentheus. In the play, the maenads' lush and heavenly surroundings far from the city are emphasized several times. In the mystical spaces that are Dionysus' realm, nature is a friend: the *thiasos* of Theban women does not need shelter from the weather as it sits on the mountain under green firs on roofless rocks (33–39). In contrast to the walled city of Thebes (653), the dwelling of the maenads on the mountain is a blissful place: the maenads relax in the glens (πρὸς ὀργάδας) (445), sleep peacefully in the open (683), are like fawns playing in the verdant pleasures of the meadow (ὡς νεβρὸς χλοεραῖς ἐμπαί-/ ζουσα λείμακος ἡδοναῖς) (866–867), and rejoice in the wilderness in the shady-leaved forest (875–876). The second messenger, who accompanies Pentheus to the mountain, watches maenads singing and crowning *thyrsoi* hidden in a grassy valley in the shade of pine trees, surrounded by cliffs, crossed by a stream, (1051–1052). Through a valley with a runnning stream, swollen by melted snow and broken boulders, the maenads run as fast as doves fly to catch Pentheus (1093–1094).

On the god's mountain, the laws of nature are superseded by the deity's powers, a feature Euripides emphasizes almost obsessively in the play by using the term 'mountain' (ὄρος) some eighteen times. Mountains reverse the normal order of things: on Mount Tmolos the gold flows (154); eternal snow covers Cithaeron (662), but herds of cattle graze on it (677); there, nature offers maenads goods that are normally produced by humans and used in religious ceremonies: milk, wine and honey (144–145, 704–711). On the mountain, the maenads feed roe deer and wolf-cubs with the milk they have denied their own children (699–700) while snakes lick their cheeks (698, 767–768). The maenads live in peaceful harmony with wild beasts but react furiously against men and herds violating their territory (734–745), a gory scene that seems to confirm the violent clash between the Dionysiac collective community and a pastoral economic structure in mythology.

To summarize, the vivid evocation of the visual aspects of the magical, heavenly surroundings of mystical cults in both *Bacchae* and *Frogs* emphasizes the religious, political and moral tensions of the polis. On one hand, the world of initiates outside Thebes' walls is at peace, joyful, enjoying the bliss of dancing and singing in their rituals in honour of Demeter and Dionysus; on the other, a male-only group obeys a tyrant in terror (in *Bacchae*) and a decaying Athens is prey to greedy and corrupt rulers and officials (in *Frogs*).

9.3 Lights in the night, fire and torches

As we observed in 2.5, the visual features related to lights in darkness characterize the imagery of mystery initiation rituals and structure the mystery subtext of the *Homeric Hymn to Demeter* (5.1) and Aeschylus' *Oresteia* (5.2). Torches, fire and mystical divine light in darkness illuminate *Bacchae* and *Frogs*, helping to emphasize the religious content of the choral odes and create a powerful background atmosphere for the enactment of mystery rituals on stage.

The visual element of light in darkness dominates some of the key passages of the plays as it did the Eleusinian and Dionysiac rituals. The environment of the rituals in *Bacchae* is the night, as befits Dionysiac cults: in their first encounter Dionysus remarks to Pentheus, who has prurient suspicions on the behaviour of women in the dark, 'darkness possesses solemnity' (σεμνότ' ἔχει σκότος) (486), where the term σεμνότης, 'gravity, solemnity', is often used to define the divinity of mystery rituals, as for instance in Euripides' *Hyppolitus* (25).[40]

Among extant tragedies, the association of Dionysus with the night, stars and torches is not unusual. It is mentioned for instance in Sophocles' *Antigone* (1147–1148) where the chorus invokes Dionysus and calls him 'leader of the chorus of stars whose breath is fire, overseer of the voices in the night'. Similarly, Euripides in *Ion* (1074 ff.) describes Dionysus as sleepless in the night, watching the torch procession marching to Eleusis, and dancing beside the spring of the wonderful dances in the company of the star-like Zeus, the moon and the fifty daughters of Nereus. In the later *Orphic Hymns*, Dionysus is repeatedly associated with fire, being defined as 'born from fire' (πυρίσπορε) and 'fire-blazing' (πυριφεγγές)'.[41]

In ancient Greece, fires and torches were tools of ritual purification, emanating light in darkness and symbols of unalterable purity which 'had powerful sacral associations'.[42] Divinities are often portrayed with torches in their hands in iconography, particularly deities associated with the underworld and mysteries such as Demeter, Hecate and Persephone. Torches were used in rituals in both the Eleusinian and Dionysiac mysteries. In *Bacchae*, the torch is the blazing symbol of Dionysus' mystical light, marking the appearance of the divine light in the darkness of the human condition. The god appears in the parodos of *Bacchae* carrying the burning flame of the pine torch (πυρσώδη φλόγα πεύκας) as he rushes around the mountain (146), an image echoed by Tiresias as he describes the god leaping on the Delphic rocks with pine-torches (σὺν πεύκαισι) in his hands (307). Torches, sacred fire and divine light are also powerful mystical elements in the central scene of the god's reunion with the *thiasos* of Asian women, the destruction of Pentheus' palace and the tyrant's vain fight against the god that marks the start of Pentheus' Dionysiac initiation and punishment (576–641).[43] While the palace begins crumbling, Dionysus instructs the chorus to light the gleaming lightning torch (ἅπτε κεραύνιον αἴθοπα λαμπάδα) and burn the palace (594). The thread that connects the scene is the fire of Zeus' lightning that the chorus observes is still burning on Semele's tomb (596–599), the god's own birthplace, the fire that illuminates the scene, a fire that Dionysus re-ignites (623–624).

The mystical, pure and marvellous light we noted in 2.3 and 2.5 in Plutarch's experience of initiation and in Plato's *Phaedrus*, appears once more in the scene of Pentheus' slaughter. As Dionysus' voice resounds from inside the palace, the chorus exults and calls the god 'our light, greatest of Bacchic rituals' (608). The same light, lit by the god in the courtyard of the palace,[44] illuminates the palace in the scene's acme that marks the end of Pentheus' power and the beginning of his initiation and sacrifice/punishment (630). It is again a sacred light and fire that marks the high point of *Bacchae*, as the voice of Dionysus from heaven guides the *thiasos* to Pentheus to perform the human sacrifice that kills the tyrant. As the forest falls silent a light of holy fire (φῶς σεμνοῦ πυρός), suddenly illuminates the space between heaven and earth for the duration of the sacrificial ritual (1083).

Frogs' analogous action is in the darkness of Hades, with the appearance of a mystical light coinciding with the vision of the *thiasos* of initiates. In the dialogue between Heracles, Dionysus and Xanthias (136–157), Heracles describes what Dionysus and Xanthias will meet in Hades: at the end of their initiatory journey, they will see the most beautiful of lights (φῶς κάλλιστον) that illuminates the *thiasoi* of men and women blessed by the gods clapping their hands (155–157). Images of flames are used almost obsessively in *Frogs*: the entry of the chorus of initiates is announced by the most mystical whiff of torches (δᾴδων αὔρα) (312–314); flaming torches are in the hands of Dionysus, that brilliant star of nocturnal initiation rituals (341–343); sun and divine light shine bright on the initiates in *Frogs* and on them alone (454–455); and the meadow where the chorus of initiates dances and sings is lit up with flame (351–353). A sacred torch (φέγγος ἱερόν) is carried by the chorus of initiates as they dance in honour of Demeter (448). In *Frogs*, the return of Aeschylus to the light of the upper world, thereby saving the polis of Athens and closing the play, is similarly illuminated by torches and choral dancing and singing (1524–1527). Bright lights illuminate the play's final scene, when Pluto orders the escort to shine sacred torches (λαμπάδας ἱεράς) to accompany Aeschylus back to the light (ἐς φάος) (1525–1529), an image that probably deliberately echoes the finale of Aeschylus' *Eumenides* (1002–1047), where torches, and a sacred light (φῶς ἱερόν) (1005) accompany the procession accompanying the *Semnai Theai* to their temple with a torch devoured by fire (ξὺν πυριδάπτῳ λαμπάδι) (1041).

9.4 The choruses/*thiasoi*

In this section I shall explore the role of the choruses in *Bacchae* and *Frogs*. The choruses of these plays are unique in extant tragedy and comedy as *thiasoi* composed of mystery initiates: Asian Dionysiac maenads in *Bacchae* and Eleusinian initiates in *Frogs*. In the two plays, what Calame calls 'the authority of the choral voice' blurs the differences between the choruses' reality and their dramatic role.[45] In the plays, the chorus members interpret the fiction represented on the stage as well as performing a ritual role as worshippers of Dionysus Eleuthereus in the real-life Great Dionysia festival. They thus impersonate a mythological character in the fiction while simultaneously interacting with the actual Athenian audience as a part of a mystery ritual. As Henrichs puts it,

> the boundaries between the realm of the imagination and the realm of the polis were more fluid than we might think. The Athenian audience was better equipped than we are to move easily without qualms between the two realms. Much of the polis of the here and now was a construct of the imagination, composed of the fictional fragments of the past, and conversely, the mythical past was perceived as a primordial image of the polis. Tragedy functioned as one of the most effective mediators between the two realms, at least in Athens.[46]

From a political point of view, the behaviour of the choruses in the plays is marked by the cohesiveness, organization and authority of the *thiasoi* of initiates. The choruses create a moment of religious, ethical and political collective reflection and prefigure the cohesion, order and unity of the polis-to-be. In the plays, the choruses introduce and define themselves in the parodoi and they do so in a similar way, evidence of the intention of the authors 'to communicate the ritual to the audience in a more immediate and captivating form', as Ferrari notes in his work on *Bacchae*'s parodos.[47] As soon as they march into the orchestra (*Bacchae* 64–169; *Frogs* 323–459), the choruses declare their sacred and ritual nature, a statement that characterizes their similar ethical and religiously authoritative interventions in the rest of the plays.

The metres and musical modes suggest that both Euripides and Aristophanes felt the need to give great immediacy and emotional impact to the message of the choruses. Significantly, both parodoi use extensively the rarely used Ionic metre, a metre connected to dithyrambs and Dionysiac worship. The Ionic metre sets the tone of much of *Bacchae*'s choral songs, a metre used for instance in the choral strophe on milk, wine and honey flowing from the ground (144–153), in the first two strophes of the first stasimon on Purity (370–401), and in the whole second stasimon (519–575).[48] The music that accompanies the chorus, at least in *Bacchae*'s parodos, would have been expressed musically in the Phrygian mode, as the chorus declares (86, 126–127, 158). The Phrygian mode, as we noted in 4.2, was a heavily rhythmic mode sung and danced to the music of the *aulos*, an exciting and passionate mode that stimulated the chorus and the audience into a state of ecstasy. Similarly, in *Frogs*' parodos Aristophanes uses the Ionic metre in the choral invocation to Iacchus (324–353), while the choral political plea in 354–371 is in anapaests, the customary metre for the chorus.[49]

The similar structure and formulaic expressions of the two parodoi suggests that they may have been an enactment of a part of the Eleusinian public rituals.[50] At their entry into the orchestra, the two choruses mention the joy of performing for Dionysus: in *Bacchae,* a sweet pain, a delightful labour (66–67, 1053); in *Frogs*, Dionysus is the deity who shows the chorus how to travel a long way without pain(402–403), a notion associated with the bliss felt by worshippers in preparing and performing Dionysiac rituals.[51] After the parallel ritual invocation of Iacchus/Dionysus to lead the chorus (in *Frogs*) and a brief proclamation of its own nature as a *thiasos* of Dionysus' worshippers (in *Bacchae*), the choruses use in a remarkably similar way the traditional *euphemia*, the ritual warning to the public not to use inauspicious language. Its use is destined to impart a great religious solemnity to the song of the choruses, as for instance it does in Aeschylus' *Eumenides* 1035, 1038. The tone of the two songs is set in the same ritual tones, destined to praise and please the god and to 'suggest a well-disposed deity, a pious community, and a favourable outcome'.[52] In *Bacchae*, the chorus exclaims 'let everybody by keeping sacred silence (στόμα εὔφημον) make himself pure' (70), while in *Frogs* the chorus pronounces a nearly identical formula (354-5), 'let all speak fair' (εὐφημεῖν χρή).[53]

Far from being an empty formula, the ritual *euphemia* warning sets the tone for the choral odes in the plays, making their moral and political pleas all the more religiously authoritative and collective as well as having a powerful effect on the plays' audiences. The power of spoken words addressed to deities in religious rituals such as processions, sacrifices or the pronunciation of oaths was great, and their acceptance by the divinity, was thought to shape future reality.[54] In both parodoi the choruses use similar ritual invitation formulae, often accompanied by double cries that 'may reflect the actual practice of ritual'.[55] In *Bacchae*'s double choral role, the pressing invitation to the people of Thebes to join the mystical procession implies one addressed to the play's audience to join the festivities and rituals of the god: 'Who is on the road? Who is on the road? ... Who is in the palace? Let him come out! Let everybody make himself pure by keeping sacred silence!' (68-69). Again, 'Onwards bacchantes! Onwards bacchantes!' the chorus exclaims as it addresses the Thebans to join the choral dance escorting Dionysus to the mountain (83-84, 165). 'To the mountain! To the mountain!' the chorus exhorts the Thebans as it presses them to become bacchants and wear the cult's garb (116). Similarly, in *Frogs*, despite the relative lesser weight of the chorus in the play, the first words spoken by the chorus of initiates are an invocation to the god: 'Iacchus, O Iacchus! Iacchus, O Iacchus!" (316-317), repeated in 325 and 342, and exclamation of reciprocal encouragement such as 'come now!' (ἄγ' εἶα) in 396, 'dance!' (χωρεῖτε) in 444, cries that may also be taken as appeals to the audience.

The use of the ritual exhortation emphasises the sacred solemnity of what follows: in *Bacchae* a frenzied, highly lyrical prayer to Dionysus in honour of his divine nature, powers and cult, ending with the theophany of Dionysus leading his *thiasos* on the heights of Cithaeron, a sweet vision (ἡδὺς ἐν ὄρεσιν)

(135). The second part of the parodos of *Frogs* (354–368) is a religious and civic condemnation and exclusion from the choral dances and religious rituals of political opponents of the chorus mingled with invocations to Demeter and Iacchus,[56] a religious/civic public proclamation (πρόρρησις).[57]

In *Frogs*, the end of the *agon* between the two poets and Aeschylus' victory is marked by a *makarismos* (1482–1499) pronounced by the chorus. As noted in our analysis of the *Homeric Hymn to Demeter*, the *makarismos* was probably a collective chant performed by the mass of initiates saluting the newly initiated in Eleusis, a chant that pointedly plays an important part in *Bacchae* and *Frogs*.[58] In *Frogs*, the chorus defines the reason for Aeschylus' victory, and simultaneously describes the qualities of the ideal civic man, the poet himself. 'Blessed is the man (μακάριός ... ἀνήρ) who has an intelligent and precise mind (ξύνεσιν ἠκριβωμένην) ... is judged to have good sense (εὖ φρονεῖν), an intelligent man (συνετός) ... who will bring blessings to his fellow citizens and blessings to his own friends and relations because he is an intelligent man (διὰ τὸ συνετὸς εἶναι)' (1482–1490). The emphasis on the term 'intelligence' (συνετός) reveals in fact one of the qualities of Aeschylus, his being a mystery initiate. The term, while generally meaning 'intelligence, sagacity, knowledge', also denotes someone who has the sacred knowledge that is gained by initiation, as Bernabé argues.[59] The passage should be compared with the *makarismos* in the finale of the crucial third stasimon in *Bacchae* (902–912). There Euripides calls hallowed (μακαρίζω) a man who spends his day-to-day life blessed by divinity (εὐδαίμων). This association of the two *makarismoi* strengthens the religious content common to *Bacchae* and *Frogs*.

Both authors emphasize the freedom, civic and religious piety, communality and joy of the initiates through their descriptions and enactment on stage of the choral dances, songs and music. In *Bacchae*, the noun and verb 'dance' (χορός, χορεύω) are used some eighteen times, in *Frogs* some fifteen times. Terms connected with choral dancing and singing are remarkably similar in the plays and highlight the similarity of Dionysiac and Eleusinian choral rituals in *Bacchae* and *Frogs*. The choruses dance and sing to the tune of Dionysus' musical instruments, the reed pipe (αὐλός), in *Frogs* 154, 212, 312, 513, 1302 and in *Bacchae* 128, 160, 380. Both plays introduce the instrument with a similar expression: (αὐλῶν πνεῦμα) in *Bacchae* 128, and (αὐλῶν πνοή) in *Frogs* 154. The ritual movements of the dances are also parallel in the plays:

the stomping of feet in the dance (*Frogs* 331, 375; *Bacchae* 863–864), shaking heads in the air (*Frogs* 328; *Bacchae* 150, 240–241, 865).

A further element that characterizes the choruses in the plays is their joy: dancing, joy and laughter had a particular cathartic role in mystical rituals. Plato for instance notes, with regard to the Corybantes preparing the initiand to his ritual initiation in the *thronosis* ceremony, that in those rituals there are dances and the playing of games and sporting matches (ἐκεῖ χορεία τίς ἐστι καὶ παιδιά),[60] as gods are lovers of games (φιλοπαίσμοι).[61] With regard to the Eleusinian rituals, the aetiology of the liberating role of laughter is in the *Homeric Hymn to Demeter*. There, at the house of Celeus, it is the servant Iambe (her name is a clear Dionysiac allusion), who with her jokes moves the unsmiling, *agelastos,* goddess to smile, laugh and cheer her heart, thus ceasing her mourning for her daughter (200–205). The use of obscenities and laughter were part of religious rituals, as it is attested in other festivals such as the Demetrian Haloa, the Thesmophoria, the Demetrian/Dionysiac procession to Eleusis,[62] and in Dionysiac processions.[63] In *Bacchae,* the chorus' joy is recurrently stressed with words such as 'sweet, pleasurable' (ἡδύς) in 66 and 135; the chorus laughs with the pipes (μετά τ' αὐλοῦ γελάσαι) (380); Dionysus is the laughing god in 439 and 1020 and the verb 'rejoice' (χαίρω) is used in 134, 423, 1006, 1033, 1040 and in *Frogs* 244. In *Frogs,* the term most frequently used to define the chorus activity is 'play' (παίζω): used in 230, 319, 334, 375, 388, 392, 407, 411, 414, 523.

To summarize, central to the plays is the joy, cohesion, communality and religious and cultic observance of the choruses in a critical moment for the cohesion of the Athenian polis. These sentiments would have struck an emotional and political chord with the spectators, most having been partners in choral activities that were an essential part of Athenian religious and civic education. The audiences would thus be drawn into identifying themselves with the chorus and its political and religious message, the subject of the next section.

9.5 Religious, moral and political values

Ethical concepts associated with mystery cults such as 'wisdom/cleverness' (τὸ σοφόν), 'knowledge' (σοφία), 'blessing by the gods' (εὐδαιμονία), 'reverence towards divinity' (εὐσέβεια), 'calm' (ἡσυχία), 'self-control'(σωφροσύνη) and 'orderly behaviour' (εὐκοσμία), play an essential role in *Bacchae* and *Frogs* in defining mystery cults' beliefs and ethics. In contrast with the human and evil nature of hubris, of tyrants and of *stasis*, these terms describing wisdom, the favour of the gods, civic harmony, self-control and collective cohesion are simultaneously religious and political.

The nature of wisdom, /τὸ σοφόν/σοφία, terms that appear some twenty-five times in *Bacchae*, is central to the philosophical, religious and political content of the play. The interpretation of the passages where τὸ σοφόν is defined in *Bacchae* has caused great controversy amongst scholars, giving rise to opposite visions of the play, of Euripides' depiction of Dionysus, of his cult and of the play's philosophical and political significance. The concept of wisdom and the use of the cognate terms σοφός/τὸ σοφόν/σοφία etc. is in *Bacchae* complex and sometimes ambiguous. Euripides uses the whole range of the meanings of these terms in the play in a manner that would have been probably clear to his audience, but less so to us. The modern clear distinction between different meanings such as 'skilled thinking', 'intellectual trickery', 'bit of wisdom', 'cleverness', 'knowledge' and 'mystical wisdom' may not have been as clear in fifth-century Athens, where the positive and negative aspects of the concepts may have overlapped, and their meaning would only have been clear in their context. Scholars have attempted to define precisely the use of the terms that express in *Bacchae* the notion of 'sophistic reasoning', 'cleverness' versus 'knowledge', 'wisdom', often coming to opposing conclusions.[64] Leinieks for instance believes that τὸ σοφόν means 'wisdom', while σοφία means 'cleverness';[65] Arthur, on the other hand, comes to the opposite conclusion.[66] To evaluate the concept of wisdom in *Bacchae* it is worthwhile to follow the thread of its development throughout the play.[67]

I would argue that Euripides associates the concept of σοφός with the knowledge acquired in mystical initiation, in opposition to Pentheus' lack of such knowledge. In *Bacchae,* the association of the concept of σοφός with mystery cults is established early and developed gradually. Euripides introduces the term σοφός in the opening lines of the dialogue between the two old friends, Tiresias and Cadmus, in the first episode. Tiresias introduces himself by saying that he has come to the royal house to join the rituals in honour of Dionysus together with his old friend Cadmus (170–177). As Cadmus comes out of the palace to welcome Tiresias, he declares he recognized the wise voice of a wise man, a concept emphasized through the use of a repetition of the term σοφός (178-179), which Cadmus uses again a few lines later to address his friend Tiresias (186). Cadmus then connects wisdom with the participation in mystical cult rituals: it consists of glorifying Dionysus with all one's energy, wearing the cult's garb, striking the ground with the *thyrsus* and joining the communal dances in his honour (180-188). The adherence to the cult makes the two old men not only wise, but the only men in Thebes in their senses (εὖ φρονοῦμεν) (195), a term that merges the notion of sound judgement and common sense into that of mystical wisdom, a theme accompanying the development of the notion of civic/mystical ethical themes in the play.

Immediately after, Tiresias emphasises the divine and eternal nature of ancestral traditions, of which the Dionysiac cult is one, in contrast to the limited nature of τὸ σοφόν that human reason can hope to achieve (200-209). Accepting the admittedly problematic and controversial transmitted text,[68] the passage develops the choral declaration in the first strophe of the parodos on the ancestral and eternal nature of the Dionysiac cult (71-72). In the passage Tiresias declares that human reasoning (λόγος) fails to overthrow ancestral traditions that are as eternal as time (παραδοχάι ... ὁμήλικαι χρόνῳ), even when human thinking manages to reach wisdom through the highest levels of intellectual power (δι' ἄκρων τὸ σοφὸν ηὕρηται φρενῶν). I argue that not only does this passage proclaim that timeless traditions cannot be overturned, but it also suggests that divinity cannot be fully comprehended by human reason alone, thus anticipating the theme of the exchange between Dionysus and Pentheus in the second episode (434-518) and the theme of the third stasimon.

The notion of σοφός as marking initiates is again asserted by Dionysus in his first dialogue with Pentheus on the subject of mystical knowledge gained through initiation rituals (τελεταί, ὄργια) in the second episode. Pentheus' scepticism on the cult perfects his characterization: throughout the dialogue between Pentheus, Tiresias and Cadmus, Pentheus perceives as riddles the tenets of Dionysiac rituals, while for Dionysus they are only comprehensible to initiates: it does not make any sense (οὐκ εὖ φρονεῖν) to speak of wise things to a non-initiate (465-490).

After the allusions to the concept of wisdom and of ancestral traditions made by Cadmus and Tiresias in the first episode, the concept becomes more precise in its civic, religious and Dionysiac connotations in *Bacchae*'s first stasimon (370-433). Its central place in the stasimon emphasises its importance in the play, as the stasimon is dedicated firstly to magnifying the figure of the god Dionysus, the deity of banquets, of dances, of laughter and of wine that brings an end to human cares, and secondly to defining the moral and civic virtues of Dionysus' cult. In the first antistrophe the nature of wisdom is further defined through the association between calm life and good sense (ὁ τᾶς ἡσυχίας βίοτος καὶ τὸ φρονεῖν) and its contrast with unbridled mouths and lawless folly. The term ἡσυχία is multifaceted: it means generally 'rest, quiet, peace', but also denotes the serene and silent state of initiates,[69] and the state of calm of a community that lives in harmony and *homonoia*.

In contrast to some interpretations of the passage, I argue that Euripides expresses the notion that (mystical) wisdom (τὸ σοφόν) is not cleverness (σοφία)[70] and that trying to exercise one's intelligence to understand matters that are not within the human sphere only shortens one's life.[71] This concept is clearly linked to Tiresias declaration on the limits of human reason (200-209). This is the real wisdom for mankind: to acknowledge the limits of human reason in dealing with divinity and to recognize the essence of wisdom for men: internal peace, absence of conflicts and prudence in one's life and thinking. The stasimon powerfully ends in emphasizing Dionysus as lover of Peace, bringer of prosperity (ὀλβοδότειρα Εἰρήνα), who is the goddess who feeds the young (κουροτρόφα θεά) and the simplicity of the creed of common people: to live a happy life and to keep one's mind wise (σοφὰν φρένα) and far from extremists (417-432).[72]

In the exchange between a triumphant Dionysus and the defeated but defiant Pentheus in the third episode, the term σοφός appears three times in two lines, in a variety of tones: sarcastic in the mouth of Pentheus: 'Clever, clever you are, except in which you should be clever' (σοφὸς σοφὸς σύ, πλὴν ἃ δεῖ σ' εἶναι σοφόν); in full possession of his divinity is Dionysus' reply: 'Where it is needed, I am clever by nature' (ἃ δεῖ μάλιστα, ταῦτ' ἔγωγ' ἔφυν σοφός) (655-656).

The play's third stasimon (862-911) develops further the mystical definition of τὸ σοφόν and its implications for mankind. Before examining the controversy surrounding the interpretation of this crucial choral ode, I shall examine its connections with other passages in the play to make its context clear. The chorus sings the third stasimon after Pentheus' surrender to Dionysus and the god's declaration that Pentheus will be given justice by dying (θανὼν δώσει δίκην) at the hands of the Theban *thiasos* (847). The first part of the choral ode is a choral self-description as a maenad dancing joyfully in all-night dances (ἐν παννυχίοις χοροῖς) like a fawn playing in the verdant pleasures of a meadow, rejoicing in solitude in its liberation from its hunter Pentheus. This idyllic picture of the joy of a maenad in the wilderness is deliberately linked with the end of the first stasimon, which similarly describes a maenad moving her swift-footed limbs as she leaps like a foal (165–166). Then the chorus meditatively asks twice in a refrain the same rhetorical question (877–881; 897–901):

> What is wisdom (τί τὸ σοφόν)? Or what is the finer gift from the gods among mortals (ἢ τί τὸ κάλλιον/παρὰ θεῶν γέρας ἐν βροτοῖς)? Is it to hold the hand over the head of your enemies (ἢ χεῖρ' ὑπὲρ κορυφᾶς/τῶν ἐχθρῶν κρείσσω κατέχειν)? (No, for) what is fine is dear always (ὅ τι καλὸν φίλον ἀεί).[73]

In the first antistrophe (882–896), a reply to the question raised, Euripides emphasizes the concept of divine power (τὸ θεῖον σθένος) as the only power mankind can trust, as it punishes the impious who in his folly does not honour divinity.

> The divine power is slow to stir, but nevertheless trustworthy (ὁρμᾶται μόλις, ἀλλ' ὅμως / πιστόν <τι> τὸ θεῖον / σθένος). It brings into account those mortals who, with mad judgement, honour arrogance and do not glorify divinity (ἀπευθύνει δὲ βροτῶν / τούς τ' ἀγνωμοσύναν τιμῶν / -τας καὶ μὴ τὰ θεῶν αὔξον- / τας σὺν μαινομένᾳ δόξᾳ). The gods ... hunt down the impious one (θηρῶσιν τὸν ἄσεπτον). For never should one think and act above the laws. It does not cost much to believe that whatever that is divine (ὅ τι ποτ' ἄρα τὸ δαιμόνιον) and what is tradition over a long period is eternal by its nature and inborn with it (τό τ' ἐν χρόνῳ μακρῷ νόμιμον / ἀεὶ φύσει τε πεφυκός).

These seem to me clear references to Pentheus, the tyrant who believes in power and violence, the man from whom the maenad has successfully escaped. Up to this point Euripides depicted the figure of Pentheus through his violent declarations against the cult, the maenads and Dionysus (226 ff., 241, 246, 345 ff., 355–356, 509 ff., 780 ff., 796–797, etc.). He is the man who honours arrogance, the man of hubris, the impious man, two characteristics of the tyrant the chorus charged Pentheus with after Pentheus' initial tirade against Dionysus: hubris against Dionysus is unholy (οὐχ ὁσία / ὕβρις) (375), hubris is a feature of a murderer (φονίου δ' ἀνδρὸς ὕβρις) (555). The use of the term 'eternal' (ἀεί) is also significant, as it directly connects the strophe with those ancestral traditions that the chorus invokes in referring to Dionysiac rituals (τὰ νομισθέντα γὰρ αἰεὶ / Διόνυσον ὑμνήσω) (71–72) and which Tiresias declares cannot be overruled as they are as old as time (πατρίους παραδοχάς, ἅς θ' ὁμήλικας χρόνῳ / κεκτήμεθ') (200–209). The implicit answer is clear: only divinity is eternal, as are mystery rituals; Pentheus is deluded in thinking he can overcome with violence the infinite and eternal power of divinity and of traditional customs.

We shall now turn to the concept of the happiness of initiates blessed by the divinity (εὐδαιμονία).[74] In the epode of the third stasimon (902–912), a religious formulaic blessing, a *makarismos,* closes the stasimon, and associates the wise gift of the gods with the rituals and values of the mystery cults. At the centre of the *makarismos* in the epode is εὐδαιμονία, defined as that divine-given favour that causes an abundance of goods, mystical bliss and fullness of joy in day-to-day life, a state that wealth or power cannot create. The passage completes and emphasizes the theme of εὐδαιμονία sung by the chorus in the parodos (72–82). There, the chorus blesses as similar to a god (μάκαρ), he who enjoys divine favour (εὐδαίμων), in having witnessed the divine initiation rituals, keeps his life pure (βιοτὰν ἁγιστεύει), joins the *thiasos* and performs Bacchic rituals. In the epode of the third stasimon, a passage that has 'a liturgical ring,'[75] the key word εὐδαίμων amplifies the theme of the parodos and is repeated in a crescendo, three times in eleven verses. The epode gives three definition of εὐδαιμονία. εὐδαίμων is the happy man who has saved his life from a storm at sea and has reached the harbour (902–903); εὐδαίμων is he who has overcome human suffering (εὐδαίμων δ' ὃς ὕπερθε μόχθων / ἐγένεθ') (904–905); he who lives far from human ambitions and is εὐδαίμων on a daily basis, him I call blessed (τὸ δὲ κατ' ἦμαρ ὅτῳ βίοτος / εὐδαίμων, μακαρίζω) (905–911).

In the first definition, the contrast between the calm waters of the harbour and the stormy sea evokes the concept of quiet (ἡσυχία), a term that in political terms refers to civic harmony as opposed to hubris and *stasis* and is the term that the chorus uses in the first stasimon of the play. There the chorus declares that a life in peace and good sense remain untossed (ὁ δὲ τᾶς ἡσυχίας / βίοτος καὶ τὸ φρονεῖν / ἀσάλευτόν τε μένει), ἡσυχία being the virtue that holds the polis together (389–392).[76] In the second definition, the notion of mystery initiation being able to overcome human suffering is akin to that 'deliverance from evil' (ἀπαλλαγὴ πόνων) we noted in the prologos of Aeschylus' *Agamemnon* (1) as the state of rest, calm and concord the watchman wishes for himself and for the polis of Argos. The third definition completes the *makarismos*. After observing the competition between men to reach wealth and power, where some succeed and some do not, the chorus concisely notes: 'he whose day-to-day life is blessed by divinity, him I call blessed' (910–911), repeating the makarismos in the parodos (73 ff.).

The religious, ethical and political polarity that animates *Bacchae* comes into the open in the fourth stasimon (977–1023). On one side the nature of the tyrant is powerfully summarized. The *thiasos* of Theban women is called to punish the 'man dressed as a woman' (ἐν γυναικομίμῳ στολᾷ), 'the frenzied spy' (λυσσώδη κατάσκοπον) (977–981). Pentheus, son of the Theban dragon, is a 'godless and criminal outlaw, a mere mortal' (ἄθεος, ἄνομος, ἄδικος, Ἐχίονος / γόνον γηγενῆ) (995–996). The tyrant is only a man, his opponents are deities. The women of Thebes are described as divinities exerting justice, as they are called 'fast hounds of Lyssa' (θοαὶ Λύσσας κύνες). The goddess Lyssa ('raging frenzy'), is a deity akin to the Erinyes, and here is associated with manifest justice (δίκα φανερός), daughter of Zeus.

In the second strophe (997–1010), a difficult and debated passage, 'full of textual uncertainties',[77] the chorus affirms its moral credo which echoes and completes the ethical and religious threads of the play.

> To whom tries to fight the invincible mystery rituals with raging violence, death is an unhesitating teacher of moderation for opinions with regard to religion (τὰ θεῶν): to behave like a mortal means a life free of grief (βροτείως τ' ἔχειν ἄλυπος βίος). I do not envy wisdom (τὸ σοφόν): I rejoice in hunting those things that are great and manifest (χαίρω θηρεύουσα / τὰ δ' ἕτερα μεγάλα φανερά τῶν ἀεί) – they lead life towards the good – † to be pure and reverent by day and night, to honour the gods casting out the customs that are outside justice (ἦμαρ ἐς νύκτα τ' εὐ-/ αγοῦντ' εὐσεβεῖν, τὰ δ' ἔξω νόμιμα / δίκας ἐκβαλόντα τιμᾶν θεούς).

The ethical thoughts of the chorus are echoed concisely by the second messenger as he closes his report on the slaying of Pentheus to the polis before the imminent arrival of Agave that we analysed (1150–1152). The passage links τὸ σοφόν in its mystical sense to τὸ σωφρονεῖν and τὸ καλόν, concluding the construction of the theme. Moderation and self-control (τὸ σωφρονεῖν), the messenger warns the polis now free from its tyrant, and veneration for divinity (σέβειν τὰ τῶν θεῶν) are the finest and wisest possessions of mankind (κάλλιστον ... καὶ σοφώτατον κτῆμα). This statement significantly prepares what follows, namely the choral cry of victory over Pentheus, the exodos that witnesses the return of the crazed Agave to the city, the theophany of Dionysus as a deity that reassembles the community, the foundation of the Dionysiac cult in the city and the exile of Cadmus and his family.

A significant moral and civic concept we noted in *Bacchae* is 'self-control', 'soundness of mind', 'moderation' (σωφροσύνη). It is a concept that we noted Plato associates with the sense of justice (δικαιοσύνη) and the favour of the gods (εὐδαιμονία).[78] As we examined in Aeschylus' *Eumenides*, a work that can be considered an example of the aetiological myth of the formation of the polis of Athens, σωφροσύνη is the civic virtue that the converted Eumenides declare the Athenians have finally acquired, the value that makes it possible for the collective life of the polis to exist (1000). In *Bacchae*, σωφροσύνη and τὸ φρονεῖν are often used as cognate terms of τὸ σοφόν. The values expressed by the term σωφροσύνη include prudence, mastery of oneself, the avoidance of hubris, that individualistic violence that is the biggest threat to the community.[79] Σωφροσύνη is thus a virtue made necessary by communal coexistence and simultaneously an ethical tenet of the Dionysiac cult.

The term σωφροσύνη is a central feature of Euripides' definition of the wisdom of initiates, of the communality and cohesion of the cult, in contrast with Pentheus' lack of self-control and lack of wisdom.[80] Euripides frequently uses the term σωφροσύνη in *Bacchae*: he uses it twice to define the sexual self-control of the maenads involved in bacchanals against Pentheus' prurient suggestions (316, 318); he uses to define Dionysus' calmness and control of the dialogue with Pentheus, who 'is not in control and has no sense' (σωφρονῶν οὐ σώφροσιν) (504, 1341); as 'the self-controlled gentleness of temper' (σώφρον' εὐοργησία) of 'the wise man' (σοφὸς ἀνήρ) (641); as the orderly behaviour of the maenads on the mountain (940) whose religious rituals show good sense (329); and as the way Tiresias defines Cadmus and himself, as being the only men of good sense in Thebes (196). Opposed to the powerful force threatening the cohesion of the community, as we noted for Euripides a calm life and good sense (ὁ δὲ τᾶς ἡσυχίας/βίοτος καὶ τὸ φρονεῖν) hold households together (389–392). The expression links a socio-political dimension with one deriving from the mystery cults: ἡσυχία is the serene state of initiates,[81] the peaceful state of the *thiasos* in 683–686, and simultaneously it is a sentiment that ensures a situation of civil concord where the community's cohesiveness of households is preserved. This definition of civic cohesion thus prefigures the polis-to-be that will gather all the inhabitants of Thebes and that will be founded on good sense and self-restraint, values that the community will adopt from the *thiasoi*.

A concept vital in understanding the political message of *Bacchae*, and a term closely connected to σωφροσύνη, is 'orderly behaviour' (εὐκοσμία). We analysed this term in Solon as one of the terms defining a well-ordered and harmonious polis, in Plato's description of the chorus following Zeus in his ascent and in Plutarch' accounts of the behaviour of initiates in 2.3–4, and in Plutarch description of the procession of initiates to Eleusis under the escort of Alcibiades' army in 6.4. It is a feature of the thiasos/chorus' behaviour that prefigures the collective good conduct, order and organization of the ideal polis-to-be. The maenads on the mountain are introduced as three well-ordered *thiasoi* of Theban women asleep in the early morning, resting on foliage in a serene and composed way, σωφρόνως (683–686), contrasting with Pentheus' prurient image of the maenads as drunken women in the grip of lust (221–225) and inebriated women hunting for sex in the woods (687–688). The passage in which the messenger describes the maenads' awakening emphasizes the collective nature of the maenads' organization, using terms that recall the coordinated and self-controlled order of a military body preparing for action (689–698). In fact, Euripides' audience would have associated the term κόσμος, 'order' with the notion of military order, self-control and discipline. The semantic universe of the term encompasses several fields of collective organized behaviour: the military order as in Homer,[82] discipline and order in a military sense in Aeschylus' *Persians* 399–400, and in Solon fr. 3.33 the term is paired with *eunomia*. In the speech Thucydides put in the mouth of the Spartan Archidamos for instance, Archidamos praises the Spartans for being both warlike and wise through their sense of order (διὰ τὸ εὔκοσμον) and self-control (σωφροσύνη).[83]

Upon Agave's war cry all the maenads, both young, old women and young girls, rise in an organized way, marvellous to watch (θαῦμ' ἰδεῖν εὐκοσμία): all make together the same gestures of dressing up in their ritual garb, a ritual Euripides describes vividly (695–711). The military tone of the passage is emphasized by its composition, echoing the scenes of Patroclus and Achilles dressing for battle in the *Iliad*.[84] The maenads let their hair hang loose over their shoulders, a gesture that marks their freedom from their domestic customs, adjust their fawnskin garments, deck themselves with crowns of ivy, oak and bryony. Upon Agave raising the war cry, all maenads take their *thyrsoi*, shout in unison (725) and assault the herd of cattle that the messenger and his companions were leading to the mountain. The image expresses the immense force of the thousand hands of the coordinated *thiasos* that force to the ground the aggressive bulls (743–745). It is as disciplined soldiers (ὥστε πολέμιοι), that the maenads fall upon the cattle and the towns below Cithaeron (752).

The prefiguration of the polis-to-be as a well-organized and cohesive community of equals is emphasized again by Euripides in the scene of the hunt and the slaying of Pentheus by the *thiasos* of Theban women (1024–1152). This is the aspect that Euripides stresses, an aspect largely ignored by scholars who have focused their attention on the savagery of the act of tearing up their live victim, *sparagmos*. In their hunt for the tyrant the maenads act in the same organized collective cohesion they had in the third episode, leaping over streams and cliffs, and use the collective force of 'innumerable hands' (μυρίαν χέρα) to uproot the tree where Pentheus is hiding (1090–1110). The images of the maenads' communal coordination and collective power in the hunt suggest a well organized group of soldiers successfully attacking an enemy position, an impression strengthened by their joint war-cry of triumph (ἀλαλάζω), normally used by soldiers and almost never by women (1133). Seaford's note on the term's usage may be expanded:[85] not only does it mark the divinely inspired abilities of the maenads who have been gifted with manly military virtues, but it also associates the organized behaviour of the *thiasos* to a military formation in battle.

In this light, the short fifth stasimon (1153–1164) honouring Dionysus and praising the punishment of Pentheus as a triumph in the maenads' fight against the tyrant, would appear far from Dodds' 'song of vengeance',[86] and from being the 'transition from a shout of triumph to a cry of grief'.[87] It is instead a hymn of triumph, a civic and religious call, a shout of victory against the tyrant, associating the death of the tyrant with the Dionysiac initiation rituals that are about to be instituted in Thebes. It ends with a sarcastic reference to the conviction of Agave and of her *thiasos* to have won a prime prey, a young wild animal instead of Agave's child, Pentheus. 'Fine indeed is the contest to put the hand to drip in the blood of a child' (καλὸς ἀγών, χέρ' αἵματι στάζουσαν / εριβαλεῖν τέκνου) (1163–1164).

Similarly, in the Athens of *Frogs*', similar values animate the choral opposition to the people holding sway in the ecclesia, and also define the values of the Athens of yesteryear associated with the figure of Aeschylus, the poet whom Dionysus sends to Athens to save its community through his mystery-inspired teachings. The play describes the contrast between the values of mystery cults and those of the men holding sway in the ecclesia, similar to the contrast in *Bacchae* between the polis, the member of the cult and the polis' tyrant.

Let us begin by exploring the choral values. In *Frogs*, Aristophanes characterizes the initiates' *thiasos*/chorus in a similar way to the way Euripides does in *Bacchae*. The term εὐδαιμονία used by Euripides, is also used in Heracles' introduction to Hades' initiates in *Frogs*, describing the nature of the chorus as "happy *thiasoi*, blessed by divinity' (θίασοι εὐδαίμονες) (156–157). The collective cohesion of the *thiasos*/chorus of initiates that we noted in *Bacchae* is also the leitmotiv of the parodos of *Frogs*. There, the chorus marches onto the stage in a Bacchic parade, singing and dancing in unison under the guidance of its leader. The chorus invokes Dionysus to join the *thiasos*' 'pure dance among the pious initiates' nabe (330–336), an expression that powerfully define cults. One should imagine the chorus' dancing steps to the rhythmic tune of the *aulos* being well-rehearsed and synchronous: a stage projection of its organization and unity, as the chorus delivers its first political warning to the polis.

In *Frogs*, Aristophanes uses several of the terms expressing religious and civic values we have remarked on in *Bacchae*. For instance, the same double meaning of the term 'wise/mystery initiate' (σοφός) we noted in *Bacchae*, may also be discerned in *Frogs*, a term which Aristophanes' uses some fourteen times in the play. In the parabasis, Aristophanes defines the two dramatists in the *agon*, Euripides and Aeschylus, as 'the two wisest of men' (σοφοῖν ἀνδροῖν) (894), and later Aeschylus as a wise man (ὁ σοφὸς Αἰσχύλος) (1154). The term echoes and strengthens Aeschylus' mystical exclamation at the beginning of the *agon* as he invokes Demeter, nourisher of his inspiration, and wishes to be worthy of her mysteries (886–887), confirming the poet's status of initiate into the mysteries. The nature of Aeschylus' mystical wisdom is defined in the choral *makarismos* that closes the *agon*. Dionysus there calls Aeschylus wise, having not only an astute and precise mind (συνετός), but also having that proven good sense (εὖ φρονεῖν) by which he can teach Athenians much (1482–90). As Bernabé argues, the term συνετός also defines those who have received the sacred knowledge of initiation.[88] This definition of the term can also be found in Pindar *Olympian 2* (83–85) where Pindar describes his target audience of mystery initiates in the close of his ode. 'I have many swift arrows in the quiver under my arm, arrows that speak to the initiated [συνετοῖσιν]. But the masses need interpreters.'

The multi-faceted nature of the term σοφός continues throughout the whole of *Frogs*. Aristophanes calls the Athenians 'the wisest by nature' (σοφώτατοι φύσει) (700), laments 'the lack of wise sophisticated men' (σοφῶν ἀνδρῶν ἀπορίαν) in Hades (807). 'Thousands of wise men compose' (σοφίαι μυρίαι κάθηνται) the Athenian audiences (677); 'serious and wise thinking' (φρονεῖν) is a quality of spectators (962). These are men who oppose *stasis*; 'men peaceable towards other citizens' (εὔκολοί πολῖται) (359). In the parabasis of *Frogs*, Aristophanes uses several interrelated terms to define the 'good' citizens (719–730) whom the polis should cease to ignore: they are men of good birth, self-controlled (εὐγενεῖς καὶ σωφρόνοι); just, good and virtuous men (καλοὶ κἀγαθοί); and men of traditional education in athletics, in participation in public choruses and in artistic endeavours; men with great military experience (ἐστρατευμένοι); men who read books and understand the finest points of literature (τὰ δεξιά). The spectators of theatre works are the best of men, so sophisticated (ὡς ὄντων σοφῶν) that they are in a position to follow whichever theme tragedians show them (1113–1117).

To summarize, both playwrights stress similar aspects of the moral and civic values on the basis of which the cohesion of the polis will be restored in

Thebes and Athens. These values are emphatically religious and civic, merging mystical wisdom and veneration for the divine with the civic primacy of self-control, organization and order. In *Bacchae* and *Frogs*, the political objective is the reconciliation of the people and the overcoming of their division, the reconciliation that is at the heart of Xenophon's interpretation of the fall of the Thirty.

9.6 Interpreting *Bacchae*'s stasima

Most commentators have either misread entirely or given little importance to the ethical and political content that marks the choral odes in *Bacchae*. With regard to the strong egalitarian characteristic of the Dionysiac cult in the first stasimon (370–433) several scholars miss the point. By putting the irrational fury and violence of the *thiasoi* at the centre of his interpretation, Winnington-Ingram for instance entirely misses the political content of the play's first stasimon, defining the chorus' aspiration to 'contentment' as a 'negligible ideal', the gift of wine a 'Lethean source of oblivion' and dismisses the egalitarian reference to the common man, as he can be 'courageous, loyal, cruel and treacherous, violent, patient and crassly stupid'.[89] Dodds, in contrast, puts the passage's egalitarian note in the context of Euripides' 'deeper kinship with the intuitive wisdom of the people than with the arid cleverness of the individuals', but unfortunately does not pursue his note on the nature of Dionysus as an egalitarian god whose worship 'probably made its original appeal to people who had no citizen rights and were excluded from the older cults associated with the great families'.[90]

While Musurillo relegates the political relevance of the stasimon to noting that the social equality is 'suggestive of the equality of nature', he follows Winnington-Ingram in emphasizing the alleged ambiguous nature of the play and in contrasting the passage's 'peaceful acceptance of the god who brings laughter and dancing to the wail of flutes' to the finale of the play, 'where there is a touch of the malign'.[91] Among commentators, to the best of my knowledge only Seaford[92] and Di Benedetto[93] point out that the expression implies the egalitarian nature of the polis. In his commentary, Di Benedetto correctly notes that, in the last antistrophe of the first stasimon, the Dionysiac cult comes close to a political vision: the basic values of the cult are those of the well-ordered polis, and correctly puts *Bacchae* in the context of the restoration of democracy after the coup of 411.

The passage where the discrepancy of scholarly interpretations and translations of choral odes is clearer is *Bacchae*'s pivotal third stasimon we examined earlier. Despite the clarity and coherence of the progression in defining the moral and religious creed of the Dionysiac cult in *Bacchae* that we have followed, the controversy over the interpretation of the chorus' question in 877–881 and 897–901 has divided scholars. The traditional reading of the passage,[94] exemplified for instance by Murray (1904), translates the refrain rather freely as

> What else is Wisdom? What of man's endeavour
> or God's high grace, so lovely and so great?
> To stand from fear set free, to breathe and wait;
> to hold a hand uplifted over Hate;
> and shall not Loveliness be loved for ever?

In his 1944 translation Dodds has it as

> What is wisdom? Or what god-given right
> is more honourable in the sight of men
> than to keep the hand of mastery over the head of a foe?
> Honour is precious: that is always true.[95]

Dodds' interpretation, probably influenced by the Nietzschean notions of the chorus personifying an irrational violence reverses not only the role of the chorus at that key moment of the play, but also the ethical and political relevance of Euripides' message in *Bacchae*. Surprisingly, Dodds' view is still adopted by most commentators and translators, being followed by scholars as diverse as Nagy,[96] Vellacott,[97] Kovacs,[98] Di Benedetto[99] and Mills.[100] In his 1948 interpretation Winnington-Ingram has the refrain as

> What is wisdom? Or what gift from the gods
> is fairer in the sight of men
> than to hold the hand of mastery over the head of enemies?
> That which is fair is ever dear.[101]

This interpretation leads Winnington-Ingram to put the question in a context of violence and power, and to conclude that the 'fundamental pattern of the play is that the religion of Dionysus is shown first as the source of peace and joy then of violence and cruelty'.[102] In my view, this interpretation requires not only altering the transmitted text but stands in opposition to Euripides' whole construction of the mystery cults' religious, moral and civic creed, of its faith in the virtues of moderation and peace, the cult's love of laughter, dancing and singing, its veneration for divinity, and destroys Euripides' complex composition of the notion of mystical wisdom.

It should be noted that several scholars oppose to the traditional reading of the passage in *Bacchae* 877–881 and 897–901. Observing the inconsequentiality of the passage in its traditional interpretation, Blake (1933), in his early perceptive work on the refrain, compares Euripides' use of the particles ἢ and ἤ, coming to the conclusion that the second ἢ should be read as ἤ, and that an interrogation mark was needed after ἢ χεῖρ'. In contrast with Murray, Blake thus translates the refrain as

> Quid id quod sapiens? Vel quid pulchrius a deis munus inter mortales? An manum super caput hostium praestantiorem retinere? Id quod vere pulchrum et honestum est, semper est gratum.[103]

After Blake, Roux (1972) correctly reintegrates the transmitted text of the crucial chorus refrain and translates it thus:

> Qu'est-ce que l'humaine science [τὸ σοφόν]? Quel est le don des dieux le meilleur ici-bas? Est-ce d'appesantir de sa main dominatrice sur la tête des ennemis? [Non, car] le Bien nous est ami, toujours![104]

Roux thus convincingly rectifies the interpretation that equates wisdom and the good, Blake's *pulchrum et honestum* (καλόν), with force and violence. Other commentators, such as Leinieks,[105] and Seaford[106] have developed an interpretation that fits better with the religious, moral and political content of the play. Seaford for instance has it as

> What is the wise [gift], or what is the finer gift from the gods among mortals? Is it to hold the hand powerful over the head of your enemies? [No, for] What is fine is dear always.

noting that the opposition between permanent mystical happiness and the temporary nature of power and wealth is a traditional topic in Greek literature.[107] However, I would be inclined to disagree with both Roux and Seaford on the interpretation of τὸ σοφόν. On the one hand Roux connects τὸ σοφόν with the human knowledge gained by reason, which stands in contrast with Euripides' previous use of the term τὸ σοφόν; on the other hand, by connecting wisdom with the gods' gift, Seaford disconnects the remark from its close connection with that in the first stasimon: (mystical) wisdom (τὸ σοφόν) is not cleverness (σοφία) (395).

The question-and-answer passage in the third stasimon concludes the gradual approach to the concepts of wisdom and self-control Euripides has been carefully building up since the encounter of Cadmus and Tiresias in the first episode. In the third stasimon, the sense of the term τὸ σοφόν is the same as it was in Tiresias' and Cadmus' definition, that is 'mystical wisdom' (395). The conclusion of this theme is also in the second messenger's final words we examined, as he advises the polis that the wisest possession of people consists of self-restraint and veneration for divinity (τὸ σωφρονεῖν δὲ καὶ σέβειν τὰ τῶν θεῶν), those virtues associated with the mystery cults (1150–1152). The definition of power over the enemy as wisdom and as the good that is dear forever (φίλον ἀεί), seems thus logically questionable. Regarding Euripides' use of the word τὸ σοφόν, as we have examined, it is difficult to associate the chorus' alleged power of revenge over Pentheus with any form of wisdom, whether in its 'cleverness' or 'mystical wisdom' sense.

Secondly, what was the mood of the Asian chorus at the end of the third episode (576–861)? Was it one of raging fury, as the Dodds' approach would have it? The royal palace has been destroyed by an earthquake and is in flames, the chorus is now freed from its chains and blissfully reunited with Dionysus who has freed himself from his prison, Pentheus is defeated and exhausted and a messenger has brought news of the awesome behaviour of the maenads on Mount Cithaeron. Under the magic spell of the god, Pentheus cross-dresses as a woman, takes up the accoutrement of the cult and follows Dionysus to the mountain, signalling his submission to the god and his metamorphosis into one about to be initiated, an initiand. The speech of Dionysus to the maenads at this point declares Pentheus' divinely pronounced death sentence at the hands of his own mother (847–861). Pentheus the initiand is now also a sacrificial victim. The notion that the Asian chorus expresses at this moment its violent desire for revenge on Pentheus is thus inconsistent: the tyrant has been defeated and Dionysus has taken the semblance and powers of his divine self. The fight is over, divinity prevailed, the chorus wish for Justice to be established has been fulfilled.

Third, the tone of the Asian *thiasos* in the play is never violent, a prominent feature in contrast to the tyrant Pentheus. In the parodos there is no hint of violence in the idyllic visions of the mystical *thiasos* on the mountain in the company of Dionysus; in the first stasimon the chorus extols Purity (370–373), ἡσυχία and τὸ φρονεῖν (389–390), mystical wisdom and humility before the divine, and peace and acceptance of the beliefs of ordinary people, sentiments that are the opposite of violence and revenge. In the second stasimon the chorus invokes Dionysus to restrain the tyrant's hubris (555), as a threat to the religious beliefs and the harmony of the polis. The question of the wisdom of holding one's subduing hand on the head of the enemy is thus, I argue, a direct reference to the folly of Pentheus who believes that violence is a mean of ruling the polis.

10

Political Implications

In this section, we shall focus on how Euripides and Aristophanes similarly develop the political theme of mystery cults as the religious and political paradigm that solves the polis' internal political divisions, granting its reconstruction through moral and religious purity and political harmony, in *Bacchae* and *Frogs*. Both authors had well-known political positions: Euripides may be considered a democrat, and so he was called, for instance, in *Frogs* 954, while Aristophanes had aristocratic views, evidenced for instance by his mockery of the figure of the warmongering democrat, Cleophon, in *Frogs*.[1] Despite their different political outlooks, the political solution to the crises in Thebes and Athens in the plays largely coincides, evidence of the process of amalgamation of egalitarian and democratic sentiments with the values of mystery cults during the last part of the fifth century.

The political/religious outlook of the two plays about Dionysus, the divinity who leads the polis towards reconciliation and harmony is similar in *Bacchae* and *Frogs*. The choice of this deity, as well as that of the nature of the *thiasoi* and of the rituals that belonged to two mystical cults, emphasizes the mystical cults as a source of political ideals and action. The notion of Dionysus as saviour of the polis, common to both plays, was not new: in Sophocles' *Antigone* (1140–1145), Dionysus is invoked by the chorus to 'come with purifying feet over steep Parnassus [1145] or over the groaning straits' (μολεῖν καθαρσίῳ ποδὶ Παρνασίαν ὑπὲρ κλιτὺν / ἢ στονόεντα πορθμόν) in order to save polis of Thebes from the plague. In Sophocles' *Oedipus Tyrannus*, as it enters the orchestra, the chorus invokes the gods to save the polis from the plague (209–215). After praying to Apollo, Ares and Zeus, the chorus invokes Dionysus, Thebes' scion, 'to draw near with the blaze of his shining torch, our ally against the god unhonoured among the gods' (πελασθῆναι φλέγοντ᾽ / ἀγλαῶπι ‾ ˘ ‾ / πεύκᾳ 'πὶ τὸν ἀπότιμον ἐν θεοῖς θεόν) (213–215).

The intervention the Thebans were invoking in Sophocles is, in *Bacchae* and *Frogs*, described in its actual happening. The fundamental value of mystery cults, equality, is central to the plays.

10.1 Equality in *Bacchae* and *Frogs*

Mystery cults transcend social, gender and age differences. The inclusiveness and equality of mystical cults as values for the polis to adopt and cherish in opposition to the rule of one man, is a theme we have explored in the *Homeric Hymn to Demeter,* where the Demetrian cult is created by the entire population (πᾶς δῆμος) (271) and is open to all who wish to be initiated (480). We have also observed similar egalitarian notes in Aeschylus' *Eumenides,* as the goddess Athena declares that a host of men and women will honour the *Semnai Theai* (856) and that she has chosen the judges of Orestes' trial out of all the Athenian citizens (487).

In *Bacchae,* Euripides' political thoughts on the cult's inclusiveness pervade the whole play. Great emphasis is given to the theme by its early appearance in the prologos. Here Dionysus declares that his cult allows non-Greeks, *barbaroi*, to join the cult, as the god declares to have instituted his dances and initiation rituals in the cities of Asia, where Greeks and barbarians are mixed together (18–19).[2] All barbarians have already been initiated (482), Dionysus declares to Pentheus later, as they have good sense (484). The notion of non-Greeks mixing with Greeks and adopting the cult has been ignored by scholars such as Dodds, but it contains an important indication of how the cult defined its socio-political nature. Not only does this passage suggest the context that allowed in Asian cities the syncretism between the Dionysiac cult and foreign cults in Asian cities,[3] but implies that the rituals are open to that vast underprivileged class of non-Greek Greek-speakers, living and working in Greek cities and in Attica in particular: slaves and those metics whose relevance in Athens whose is attested by, for instance, their presence in theatre audiences.

In *Bacchae,* the god wishes to be worshipped by all, with no distinctions (208–209), as Tiresias declares to Pentheus. The god welcomes the old and the young without distinction (206–207): the old make *thyrsoi*, wear fawnskins and crown their heads with ivy, as the elderly Tiresias and Cadmus remark as they meet to join the festival on the mountain (175–189). Gender and social distinctions are annulled in the cult: Dionysus' special appeal to the female element of the population of Thebes (32–36) reveals the special role reserved for women in the cult. The status of the women stands in sharp contrast to the attitude shown towards them by Pentheus the tyrant, as he considers having to suffer at the hands of mere women beyond everything (785–786). All the polis participates in the god's banquets, as the god ignores human social differences by giving his gift of wine that frees mankind from pain to all, both to the rich and powerful as well as to the poor (421–423). The people who suggest to the ruler and his citizens how to accept Dionysus and his cult are poor and low on the social scale: a herdsman (769–770, 776) and a slave (1150–1152). These definitions mirror the wide inclusivity of the mystery cults, wider than that of the fifth-century political demos.

What equality means for Euripides is expressed concisely at the conclusion of *Bacchae*'s first stasimon (370–433), a choral song that develops Tiresias' and Cadmus' evocation of the cult expressed in the play's first episode and which may be defined as the moral and political manifesto of mystery cults in the play. At the end of the stasimon, the chorus of maenads states its civic and religious allegiance to what the humblest in the mass of people (τὸ πλῆθος ὅ τι/τὸ φαυλότερον), believes in and practices (427–432).[4] It is a remark of great importance, and more so because of the emphasis given to it by being at the end of the first stasimon of the play. Euripides stresses the all-inclusiveness of the Dionysiac cult by using the term πλῆθος, a term that traditionally defines the mass of people in opposition to those in power, the lower classes as opposed to the *kaloi kai agathoi*. By adding the notion of the humblest among the mass, Euripides implies a group including foreigners, metics and slaves. It is a radical concept. This political notion, sung by the *thiasos*, is different and more radical than the egalitarian features of the cult that precede it. What are these values? They are summarized in the civic and religious recommendations to the polis of the second messenger after the death of the tyrant: moral and political moderation, coupled with religious devotion (1150–1152). This essential definition summarizes all the choral declarations on mystical and political values in *Bacchae*, and the fact that they are uttered by one of the humblest of citizens is not unintentional.

In *Frogs*, the Eleusinian initiates' community is animated by the same egalitarian principles that animates it in *Bacchae*: the *thiasos* of initiates is explicitly consists of women and men (157), it includes old people (345) and young (352). As is the case for Tiresias and Cadmus in *Bacchae*, in *Frogs* old people dance, in the company of Dionysus, shaking off their griefs and the weariness of their years through worship (345–50). At the end of *Frogs*' parodos, the chorus sings of how initiates alone can enjoy the light of the sun and of the torches of initiation rituals (ἥλιος/καὶ φέγγος ἱερόν). The chorus also rejoice in those who have been initiated and who treat in pious reverence (εὐσέβεια) not only *xenoi*, as the unwritten law of *philia* would command, but also the man in the street (τοὺς ἰδιώτας) (445–460). Mystical initiation is here paired with a civic and moral virtue, that of treating even the humblest people with respect. The use of the concept of εὐσέβεια marks the solemnity and religious tone of the passage, while the term ἰδιώτης has the same connotations as *Bacchae*'s πλῆθος: it designates in general the ordinary man, the private individual, the man in the street, the private individual versus the polis.[5] As Stanford notes, foreigners and *idiotai* were the most vulnerable people in Athens, as they kept away from politics, and so were left aside by politicians.[6] Despite the egalitarian tone of the choral recommendation in *Frogs*, Aristophanes is not as radical as Euripides: respect is not the same thing as the sharing of the same values that the chorus recommends in *Bacchae* 430–732.

Yet, in the play's parabasis, Aristophanes expresses political views that may be called egalitarian and radical (674–737). Unlike some other of his political pleas, Aristophanes' entreaty in this passage is entirely serious and not interspersed with comical elements,[7] marking its intended sober effect on the audience. Despite his own well-known and often expressed aristocratic anti-war and anti-demos views, in *Frogs* Aristophanes chooses to focus on social and political equality in terms not dissimilar to those in *Bacchae*, and made more acute by the partial enfranchisement of the slave element of the fleet crews who had survived the battle of Arginusae a few months earlier.[8] A comparison of the political passages in *Bacchae*'s first stasimon and *Frogs*' parabasis helps to shed some light on the much-discussed question of Aristophanes' political views.

Commentators on *Frogs* have mainly focused on the theme of Aristophanes' political views with regard to his defence of oligarchic circles who had been disenfranchised after the fall of the Four Hundred, on the political reasons that led to the Patrocleides' decree that reinstated them in their citizens' rights the following year, and to the reasons for the play to have been produced again, probably at the Lenaea festival the following year.[9] I believe that these complex but perhaps secondary questions have obscured the main aim of the appeal, the chorus' radical plea for equality in the parabasis. 'We think that all citizens should be made equal and their fears removed (πρῶτον οὖν ἡμῖν δοκεῖ / ἐξισῶσαι τοὺς πολίτας κἀφελεῖν τὰ δείματα) (687–688) ... let us readily accept as our kinsmen and as citizens with full rights, every man who fights in our fleet (συγγενεῖς κτησώμεθα / κἀπιτίμους καὶ πολίτας, ὅστις ἂν ξυνναυμαχῇ)' (701–702).

While it is certain that Aristophanes calls for the right of the disenfranchised aristocrats to plead their cause and clear themselves of any charge, there is a significant connection between Aristophanes' description of the egalitarian Eleusinian *thiasos* in *Frogs*, his approval of the ecclesia's radical decision to give civil rights to the slaves manning the fleet fighting at Arginusae and his call to widen the range of recipients of civil rights to all who fought with the fleet. The acceptance of all who fight in the fleet as family members, citizens with full rights (συγγενεῖς, ἐπιτίμοι καὶ πολῖται), would have included not only slaves, but metics and foreign mercenaries. Given Greek high civic and religious respect for the institution of the family, the *genos*, for the rights and obligations of citizens, and Athenian restrictive laws on citizenship, Aristophanes' political call is in *Frogs* more innovative and egalitarian than most scholars acknowledge. Aristophanes' political posture is thus somehow contradictory: on one hand it is egalitarian and mystical, on the other elitist and aristocratic. But political notions in fifth-century Athens were markedly different from ours, with political opinions being probably more fluid and less ideologically definite than they are in modern times. The notion of claiming a return to a role in serving the polis of the noble, self-controlled and just *kaloi kai agathoi* (727–8), which Aristophanes pleads for in *Frogs*, is not necessarily incongruous with his egalitarian posture in the same play. As de Ste. Croix remarks, the notion of *kaloi kai agathoi* in Aristophanes' days denoted excellence and distinction, marking well-behaved and respectable citizens, and did not define a group of people united by their political views or social milieu.[10] In fact, Aristophanes' view may well have been shared by that part of oligarchic public opinion that accepted democracy, the party, as de Ste. Croix calls it, of a 'conservative, "Cimonian" variety'.[11]

10.2 The plays' political goal

The term 'oneness of mind, civic concord and cohesion' (ὁμόνοια), may define the political objective of Euripides and Aristophanes in the plays, despite the term not appearing in the texts. It is the term Thucydides uses to define the goal of the Four Hundred and of the hoplites in revolt against them in 411, as both sides feared the loss of the city to the enemy. Perhaps not unnaturally, the process of reconciliation during the summer of 411 took place in two of the theatres of Dionysus. After their revolt, the hoplites assembled in the theatre of Dionysus in Munichia, a hillock at the centre of Piraeus, where they were joined by some delegates of the Four Hundred and were convinced to agree to a meeting of the ekklesia at the theatre of Dionysus in Athens on the question of restoring concord to the polis (περὶ ὁμονοίας) (8.93). A few months after the production of the plays, reconciliation between the democrats and oligarchs (διάλλαξις) took place in Athens after the fall of the Thirty.

The plays can thus be read as a prefiguring the reconciliation that renovated civic harmony in Athens. The ultimate moral and political theme of the plays is that of a religious appeasement, under the aegis of the deities Dionysus and Demeter, as the solution to the polis' crisis. Starting with *Bacchae*, there is evidence that Euripides was focusing his political thoughts on the notion of religious and civic reconciliation in the last years of his life. In *Phoenissae*, for instance, a play that was produced in 410 or 409,[12] the polarity between political equality, the welfare of the polis, reconciliation and tyranny (531–558) is at the centre of the play's political reflection as it is in *Bacchae*. The hatred between the brothers Eteocles and Polynices makes reconciliation (διάλλαξις) impossible (374–375). Normal civic life in a pacific polis is associated with Dionysus. In the second stasimon of *Phoenissae* the chorus then defines war (Ares) as the enemy of Dionysus, as warriors prefer preparing for war to dancing and singing in Bacchic rituals. Ares produces strife, the most frightful of gods (798), while Dionysus produces reconciliation, a key concept in the play (376, 436, 515, 701).

Reconciliation, the end of *stasis*, can only happen between people who share the foundations of mutual understanding, which in both plays is based upon the shared values of the Athenians. As we noted, these values are defined for instance by Xenophon's reconciliation speech by Cleocritus, where the Eleusinian *keryx* urges peace and harmony of the Athenian community on the basis of a common participation in Athens' spiritual and civic life.[13] Similarly, in *Frogs*' parabasis (727-729), those Athenians who should be reinserted in Athens' public life are defined as sharing the same participation in public choral dancing and music performances, in athletics and army training and in school education. In Xenophon's Cleocritus' speech, containing deliberate Eleusinian tones and references, the sharing of religious rituals, the communality in participating in choral activities, as schoolmates and comrades in arms, is the basis for a reconciliation between the two factions. 'Thus ended *stasis* in Athens', is Xenophon's concise conclusion of the complex process to reconstitute Athens' cohesion with a democratic constitution.[14]

In *Bacchae*, the theme of civic concord is implicit in the finale that summarizes the moral and political statements made throughout the play by the *thiasos*/chorus and in the first episode by Tiresias and Cadmus. In the reconstructed exodos,[15] Dionysus announces the divine sentence of exile for Cadmus and Harmonia to the polis and to the Asian *thiasos* as well as of Agave and her sisters, sealing the fate of the royal family and opening up a new life for Thebes. Dionysus then proceeds to establish his cult (in the lacuna between 1329 and 1330), fulfilling the mission he had forcefully stated in the prologos (39-40, 47-8, 61).[16] Nothing more needs to be told. The audience would have been left to imagine Thebes as a reunited, harmonic community ruled by the religious precepts of the cult of Dionysus and blissfully happy in the performance of his rituals.

In *Frogs*, the passage describing Aeschylus' victory over Euripides and his return to Athens to save the city, is imbued with the same civic/mystical themes that animate *Bacchae*'s *thiasos* and is interestingly focused on the Athenian institution that represents them: theatre performances. This theme is expressed in *Frogs* through the theme of the need for the polis to put collective rituals, such as (Dionysiac) theatre performances and dithyrambs, back at the centre of the polis' spiritual and civic life (367-368, 386-390, 1419). In *Frogs*, the first invocation of the chorus to Demeter in the parodos calls her to preserve the polis' song and dance choral performances in her honour (386–390). The victory of Aeschylus at the *agon*, a man who wished to be inspired by the goddess Demeter and her mysteries (886–887), marks the political victory of mystical cults and of Athenian traditional civic values over those represented by the innovator and corruptor Euripides (1015, 1053 ff., 1069 ff. etc.). Aristophanes emphasizes the central role of poets declaring the duty and right of the playwright to teach the polis the correct path using the ritual sanctity of theatrical choruses (686–687) and through a poetical mix of serious arguments and comical expressions (391–392). The task of the playwright is to 'preserve the polis', an expression Aristophanes uses repeatedly in the *agon* (1419, 1436, 1448, 1450, 1458, 1501).

The gravity and seriousness of *Frogs*' political message is reinforced through the use of images and concepts of the last part of Aeschylus' *Eumenides*, a reference noted by Dover,[17] Sommerstein,[18] Lada-Richard,[19] Seaford[20] and Sells.[21] The adoption of an Aeschylean model suggests that Aristophanes' intention was to recall to the audience the extraordinary expressions of civic and religious intensity of Aeschylus' glorification of the end of *stasis* and of the birth of the judicial system of the polis of Athens in the finale of *Eumenides*. Similar ritual choral processions escort the *Semnai Theai* to their temples in *Eumenides* and Aeschylus to Athens in *Frogs*, both blessed by two divinities (Athena in *Eumenides* and Pluto in *Frogs*). Similar religious ritual blessings are addressed to the participants of both processions, a *makarismos* in *Frogs* (1482–1499) and an appeal to *euphemia* in *Eumenides* (1035–1038). The definition of the good, *agathos*, that would ensue for the polis is similar in the two plays. In *Eumenides* (1012–1014) Athena wishes that Athenians would show goodwill in return for the good done to them (εἴη ἀγαθῶν/ἀγαθὴ διάνοια) by the *Semnai Theai*. The twice repeated term for 'good' is echoed in *Frogs*, to define those great ideas for great gains that Aeschylus is invited to give to the polis (μεγάλων ἀγαθῶν ἀγαθαὶ ἐπινοίαι) (1530). The term for restraint, self-control (σωφροσύνη), the virtue that the polis finally acquired (*Eumenides* 1000), corresponds to the quality of Aeschylus, a man of good common sense (εὖ φρονεῖν) (*Frogs* 1485), while the reference to an end to *stasis* and a return to communal joy (χάρματα δ' ἀντιδιδοῖεν / κοινοφιλεῖ διανοίᾳ) in *Eumenides* 976–987 is mirrored in *Frogs* by Aeschylus' mission to Athens to end *stasis*, as well as those great woes, painful armed conflicts (μεγάλων ἀχέων … ἀργαλέων τ' ἐν ὅπλοις ξυνόδων) (1531–1532).[22]

The term 'reconciliation' does not appear in either play but would have been perceived by the audiences as a necessary conclusion of the development for the plots. In neither play is the political goal of the *thiasoi* the violent defeat of the opponent/s to the cults and the conquest of power. In *Bacchae*, the sacrificial execution of Pentheus the tyrant together with the exile of the royal family is dictated by their defiant scorn for the divinity of Dionysus' birth (26–31) and helps allow the return of the Theban *thiasos* to the community of the polis. Only by collectively accepting Dionysus and his cult will the polis of Thebes become cohesive again and proceed to follow Dionysus' instructions in adopting his cult and his cult's moral and civic values of equality, moderation and devotion.

Spectators of *Frogs* would have anticipated the result of the return of Aeschylus to Athens. Far from producing a violent conflict with the leaders of the ecclesia and their allies, Aeschylus' return would have been expected to restore theatrical performances in their traditional role as the great collective Dionysiac ritual; choruses would again be easily financed by rich Athenians and continue their singing and dancing acts; youths would embrace again the traditional education curriculum of *choregia* and *mousike*, and the attempts of the new class of political leaders would be ignored by the demos. The polis would have returned to be led and managed by the *kaloi kai agathoi*, by the legendary Athenians of the past, 'noble six-footers, men with an aura of spears, lances, white-crested helmets, green berets, greaves, and seven-ply ox hide hearts' (1014 ff.), by sophisticated theatre-goers, by those opposing the new modern ways and by all those who fought in the fleet, a somewhat paradoxical amalgam.

Conclusions

This work started by exploring the possible reasons for the similarity of mystery cults' themes in Euripides' *Bacchae* and Aristophanes' *Frogs*, a phenomenon unique in extant tragedy and comedy and largely unexplored by scholars. My analysis of the plays' extratextual context focuses on one hand, on the historical period during which the plays were composed and produced and, on the other, on mystery cults and their influence on the Athenian political life. The context provides the focus of my reading of the plays. My main conclusions can be summarized as follows.

Both plays were composed during the period of political and religious strife in Athens opened by the seizure of power by the Four Hundred in 411 and closed by the reconciliation in 403 between the oligarchic circles and democrats after the overthrow of the Thirty. This domestic conflict is the political context of both plays.

Mystery rituals and values appear to have played a greater role in the formation of Athenians' ethical and political self-identity than is commonly recognized. From the legendary episode of Epimenides saving Athens from civic strife in the 590s to the reconciliation of 403, mystery cults and their values represented an essential religious, ethical and civic point of reference for the Athenian polis. The values of mystery cults, religious purity, equality, inclusiveness, respect of others and self-restraint came to form the basis of Athens' civic ideology and are reflected in the *Homeric Hymn to Demeter* and in Aeschylus' *Oresteia*. These values are those of the choruses/*thiasoi* in *Bacchae* and *Frogs*.

During the fifth century, theatre productions and initiation rituals performed a role in the life of Athenians and in the development of their religious, ethical and political concepts. Both rituals involved the polis at large beyond the group of full-rights male citizens; the interaction between rituals and their public happened largely at a non-rational, subliminal level; their powerful effect on their public strengthened the sense of communality and cohesion of the polis. This enlightens the sense of political authority of the choral odes.

Despite the opposite political stances of the authors, *Bacchae* and *Frogs* share a similar ethical and political vision. Political equality, adherence to the traditional values and rituals of mystery cults, class reconciliation and observance of the polis' constitutional system, common to the two plays, are the basis on which the crisis of the Athenian polis can be resolved, and civic cohesion restored.

Notes

Chapter 1

1. Cf. Webster 1967 p. 257, Cantarella 1974 pp. 291–2 n. 2, Kovacs 2002 p. 2.
2. Xenophon *Hellenica* 1.18.6.
3. Lada-Richards 1999 p. 121.
4. Fundamental works on *Bacchae* include, *inter alia*, Dodds 1940 and 1960 (1944), Winnington-Ingram 1948 and 1966, Musurillo 1966, Roux 1972, Foley 1980 and 1985, Segal 1961 and 1982, Oranje 1984, Vernant 1985, Seaford 1996 and 2012, Versnel 1998, Kovacs 2002, Mills 2006, Friesen 2015, Stuttard (ed.) 2016. Works on *Frogs* include Stanford 1958, Segal 1961, Konstan 1986, Dover 1993, Bowie 1993, Sommerstein 1997, Lada-Richards 1999, Henderson 2002, Edmonds III 2004, Marshall and Kovacs 2008, Griffith 2011.
5. Scholarship on Greek mysteries is vast. Fundamental studies on the Eleusinian mysteries include Foucart 1914, Mylonas 1962, Burkert 1983 (1972) and 1985, Richardson 1974, Foley 1994, Clinton 1992 and 2004, Sourvinou-Inwood 2003a, Cosmopoulos 2003 and 2015, Parker 2005, Bremmer 2014. Studies on the Dionysiac cult include Maiuri 1931, Jeanmarie 1951, Lehmann 1962, Seaford 1981, 2006, 1981a, Daraki 1985, De Cazenove 1986, Burkert 1987, Henrichs 1990a, Sabbatucci 1991, Carpenter and Faraone 1993, Csapo 1997, Carpenter 1997, 2013, Scarpi 2002, Acker 2002, Cosmopoulos 2003, Bowden 2010, Bernabé 2013, Bremmer 2014.
6. Among the main studies is Foley 1980, 1985, Seaford 1981, 1993, 1994, 1996, Goldhill 1987, Bierl 1991, Zeitlin 1993, Friedrich 1996, Sourvinou-Inwood 2003.
7. Relevant to the scope of this work would be, *inter alia*, Ostwald 1955 and 1986, de Ste. Croix 1972, Seaford 1994 and 2012, Parker 1998, Price 2001, Raaflaub 2003, Morgan 2003, Lewis 2006, Hornblower 2008.
8. A subject of immense material. Among others, Pickard-Cambridge 1962, Seaford 1981, 1994, 2000, 2012, 2013, Goldhill 1987, Vernant and Naquet 1988, Henrichs 1990 and 1994/5, various contributors to Winkler and Zeitlin (eds.) 1990, Csapo and Slater 1994, McGlew 2002, Henderson 2003, Sourvinou-Inwood 2003, Murray and Wilson 2004, Finkelberg 2006, Kowalzig 2007, Revermann and Wilson 2008, Wilson 2009, Wiles 2011, Kawalko-Roselli 2011, various contributors to Carter (ed.) 2011, Allan and Kelly 2013.

9 Sourvinou-Inwood 2003 pp. 2–5.
10 The Dionysiac content of *Bacchae* is not unique. Several of Aeschylus' non-extant classic tragedies were probably steeped in the Dionysiac cult, such as *Lycurgeia, Bacchae, Edonians, Eleusinians, Pentheus, Bassarai*. Cf. Mills 2006 pp. 34–5.
11 Xenophon *Hellenica* 2.4.20-22.
12 Democritus fr. B 230 D-K.
13 The history, sequence and details of the Eleusinian cult and rituals is the subject of many different reconstructions and debate, cf. amongst others Foucart 1914, Burkert 1983 (1972), 1985, 1987, Clinton 1992 and 2004, Foley 1994, Robertson 1998, Sourvinou-Inwood 2003, Parker 2005, Bremmer 2014, Cosmopoulos 2015.
14 Cosmopoulos 2015 pp. 75–7.
15 Cf. Aristophanes *Frogs* 337–338.
16 Cosmopoulos 2015 p. 165.
17 Cf. Clinton 1974 n. 13 p. 13. Bremmer 2014 p. 4.
18 Cf. Aristophanes *Pax* 374–375. See also Parker 2005 p. 342 n. 65.
19 Cf. Suda under 'Agra'.
20 See 3.1 for an estimate of the number of people undergoing initiation rituals every year at the end of the fifth century.
21 On the role of the *keryx*, cf. Clinton 1974 pp. 76–82. On the use of the two formulae in Aristophanes' *Frogs*, see 8.5.
22 Cf. Ephorus fr. 70F 80 Jacoby, Parker 2005 p. 347 n. 87.
23 A scene alluded to by Aristophanes in *Frogs* 336: as Dionysus and Xanthias come across a thiasos of initiates Xanthias smells the smoke of a sacrifice of piglets and exclaims: O most glorious Lady, O maiden daughter of Demeter, what a lovely smell of pork has wafted its way to me!' (ὦ πότνια πολυτίμητε Δήμητρος κόρη / ὡς ἡδύ μοι προσέπνευσε χοιρείων κρεῶν). See also Scholia on Aristophanes *Acharnians* 747b. Cf. Parker 2005 p. 347 n. 87.
24 The date is disputed, as Euripides mentions the 20th in *Ion* 1074–1077, and the same date is mentioned by Plutarch in *Camillus* 19.6. Robertson 1998 pp. 547–5, Parker 2005 p. 348 and Bremmer 2014 p. 5 ff. argue for two processions taking place on the 19th and 20th Boedromion.
25 Plutarch *Camillus* 19.6.
26 Strabo 10.3.10, Aristophanes *Frogs* 399 ff. See 3.1 on details of the sanctuary. On the identification of the figure of Iacchus with that of Dionysus see Sophocles *Antigone* 1119, 1151, fr. 959. See also Burkert 1983 (1972) p. 279 n. 23.
27 Aristophanes *Wealth* 1013, Demosthenes *Against Midias* 158.
28 Strabo 9.1.24.

29 Strabo 1.38.2.
30 *Anecdota graeca* 1 pp. 273, 25–7, Cosmopoulos 2015 p. 19.
31 The base of the potion Circe gave to some of Odysseus' companions to bewitch them: *Odyssey* 10.234-6.
32 Following Clinton 2004 pp. 92–5, I believe that the Anactoron could not have been an inner cell in the hall of the Telesterium but must have coincided with the great hall.
33 Clemens Alexandrinus *Proprepticus* 2.12.
34 Lucian *De Saltatione* 15, cf. also Hardie 2004 p. 19.
35 A music vividly evoked by Aeschylus in *Edonians* fr. 57. For a reconstruction of the rituals' imagery and light plays see Clinton 1992 pp. 89–90, 2004 pp. 85–109, Parker 2005 pp. 351–63.
36 Plato *Phaedrus* 250c. Imagery of lights in darkness are associated with Eleusinian rituals, see 2.5 and 8.3.
37 Plutarch *Quomodo quis suos in virtute sentiat profectus* 81d-f.
38 Plutarch fr. 178.
39 IG II^{2}3811, 1-2 =I. Eleusis 637, in Clinton 2004 p. 90.
40 Hippolytus *Refutatio omnium haeresium* 5.8.39-40. A thorough discussion of the symbolism of the ear of corn in the Eleusinian rituals is in Sourvinou-Inwood 2003 pp. 35–7.
41 Athenaeus 14.56.647a, Proclus *In Platonis Timaeum commentarii* 40e.
42 A thorough exploration of the Lenaea festival is in Pickard-Cambridge 1968 pp. 25–42.
43 On this subject I have followed Pickard-Cambridge 1968 pp. 57–100 and Csapo 2013 pp. 1–36.
44 Csapo 2013 p. 1.
45 Cf. Scholiast to Aristophanes *Acharnians* 243, Apollodoros *Bibliotheke* 3.14.7, Nonnos *Dionysiaca* 17.34–245, Sourvinou-Inwood 2003 pp. 150–4.
46 Scholiast to Aristophanes *Acharnians* 243, scholiast to Lucian *Dialogi Deorum* 1–5.
47 On the complex theme of Dionysus and the phallus, Csapo 1997 pp. 253–95.
48 Csapo 2013 p. 30.
49 Csapo 2013 p. 5.
50 Csapo 2013 p. 2 n. 8.
51 The expenditure must have been extraordinary, but modest when compared with later ceremonies. Athenaeus 5.196a-203b relates the description of a procession held in Alexandria to celebrate the accession to power of king Ptolemy II in 285. The Dionysiac procession included dozens of silens and satyrs carrying gilded torches, 1,600 carrier boys, a six-metre-long cart pulled by 180 men carrying a five-metre-tall statue of Dionysus, a 300-litre wine mixing bowl, a 75-ton wineskin

on a cart pulled by 300 men, several other carts carrying statues and golden tripods, hundreds of maenads, lions, leopards, panthers, camels, antelopes, wild asses, ostriches, a bear, a giraffe and a rhinoceros etc.
52 Athenaeus 12.47c.
53 The order and number of performances is controversial, cf. Csapo and Slater 1994 p. 107.

Chapter 2

1 Furley 1996 p. 11.
2 Sourvinou-Inwood 2003 p. 1: '... tragedy was perceived by the fifth-century audiences not as a discrete unit, a purely theatrical experience, simply framed by ritual, but as a ritual performance; and that the deities and other religious elements in the tragedies were not insulated from the audience's religious realities, but were perceived to be, to a greater or lesser extent, somehow close to those realities, part of those realities'.
3 Bremmer 2014 pp. 267–86.
4 Bowden 2010 and in particular chapter 11, 'Encountering the Sacred'.
5 Eliade 1994 (1958) dedicates only a short chapter (pp. 109–15) to initiation rituals in ancient Greece.
6 To mention just a few, Phillips 1978, Schmitz 1981, Peterson 1987, the various contributors to Whitehouse and Martin 2004 and Whitehouse and Laidlaw 2004, Bacigalupo 2005, Wallis 2008.
7 Eliade 1994 (1958) pp. 42, 49.
8 Eliade 1994 (1958) p. xiii.
9 According to Whitehouse 2004 p. 63, since Weber 1930.
10 Whitehouse 2004 p. 63.
11 Whitehouse 2004 pp. 63–85.
12 Whitehouse 2004 pp. 114–15.
13 Euripides was knowledgeable on Orphic cults and beliefs.
14 This has produced some distortion in scholarship research, as *Bacchae* have 'all but effaced other sources of information' on Dionysiac cult and rituals, Henrichs 1990a p. 257.
15 Aristophanes *Acharnians* 241–279.
16 Demosthenes 18.259-260.
17 A full selection of passages in ancient literature concerning the cult of Dionysus in Greece can be found in Scarpi 2002 pp. 221–346. Cf. also Bremmer 2014 pp. 55–80.

18 De Polignac 1995 (1984) pp. 81–8 seems to have missed the central role of Eleusis and its rituals in the formation of Athens' civic ideology and religious consciousness, a role which he attributes solely to Athena's cult on the Acropolis.
19 Plutarch *Life of Solon* 8–10.
20 Turner 1982 pp. 42–5. See also the interesting study on three distinct prehistoric liminal places in Ahrlichs, Riehle and Sultanieva 2015 pp. 205–42.
21 In tradition forests, mountains and grottoes were the cult's places of worship. Cf. for instance Homer *Iliad* 6.132-133 where the maenads are depicted to be performing rituals on the holy Mount Niseos; Apollonius 2.904-910, where Dionysus celebrated his dancing rituals in front of his grotto, Theocritus 26.1-9 where Ino, Autonoë and Agave construct altars to Dionysus in the forest.
22 Csapo 1997 p. 254.
23 Turner 1987 pp. 25–6, 102.
24 Theon of Smyrna *Mathematics*, Introduction.
25 For a complete study of the organizational structure of the Eleusinian rituals cf. Clinton 1974.
26 Cf. Dodds 1940 pp. 155–76, Henrichs 1978 pp. 121–60, Bremmer 1984 pp. 267–86.
27 Diodorus 4.3.
28 Demosthenes *De Corona* 18.257-260.
29 Demosthenes in *De Corona* 18.259-260
30 *Pace* Burkert who defines Greek religion as having 'no founding figures and no documents of revelation, no organization of priests and no monastic orders', Burkert 1985 (1977) p. 8. The Dionysiac texts were Orphic and have been explored by several scholars.
31 Parker 2005 p. 354: 'The goal of the mysteries is eschatological'.
32 Sophocles fr. 837: 'Since thrice blessed are those among mortals who have watched these rites before going to Hades; for they alone have life there, while others have every kind of misery'. Cf. also Richardson 1974 pp. 313–14.
33 *Homeric Hymn to Demeter* 480–483.
34 On the apparent contradiction between the agricultural focus of the rituals and their eschatological function in literature, see Bremmer 2014 pp. 18–20.
35 Recent studies on this issue include Bremmer 2014 pp. 70–80.
36 Bremmer 2014 pp. 73–4. Graf and Johnston 2013 pp. 214–16.
37 Graf and Johnston 2013 pp. 4–5.
38 Tablet 30, in Graf and Johnston 2013 pp. 40–1.
39 Tablet 26a, b, in Graf and Johnston 2013 pp. 36–7.
40 Tablet 27 in Graf and Johnston 2013 pp. 38–9
41 Herodotus 8.65.4: 'ὁ βουλόμενος ... μυεῖται'.

42 'That living image of life, as it alone is given by the goods', as for instance Pindar defines the soul in fr. 131b.
43 See on this point Brelich 1969 p. 461.
44 Turner 1982 p. 42.
45 Aristotle *de Philosophia* fr. 15. Cf. also Plato letter 7.341c on the impossibility to express this subject in clear words.
46 For instance, Demosthenes 18. 259, Apuleius *Metamorphoses* 11.23, Dion Chrysostomos *Orations* 12.33, Theon of Smyrna *Mathematics* 1.25, Proclus In *Platonis Rempublicam commentarii* 2.108.17-30, and, in a different key, Clement of Alexandria *Protrepticus* 2.
47 Quoted by Stobaios 4.52.48-49, probably quoting Plutarch's *de Anima*.
48 Plutarch *Quomodo quis suos in virtute sentiat profectus* 81e.
49 Plutarch *Consolatio ad uxorem* 10.
50 The term βόρβορος to denote the life of non-initiates recurs in various texts associated with mystery cults, such as in Plato *Phaedo* 69c and in Aelius Aristides *Orationes* 19.259.
51 Plutarch *Quomodo quis suos in virtute sentiat profectus* 81d-f.
52 A quote from Plato *Laws* 716a.
53 Defined as such by Plato, *Apology* 22a–c.
54 Settings of mystical experiences are often in idyllic natural places. See 2.1, 2.5, 8.2.
55 Well explored by Riedweg 1986 pp. 30–59.
56 The term *mania* (μανία) 'enthusiasm, divine-inspired frenzy' (LSJ), Chantraine 2000 notes, belongs to the same family as the Greek *menos* (μένος), 'spirit, passion' (LSJ), *memona* (μέμονα), 'to be furiously eager' (LSJ) and the Latin *mens* and *memini*. See the thorough treatment of the concept in Ustinova 2018.
57 See Introduction for a definition of the semantic field of *tel-*.
58 An issue well explored, for instance, by Seaford 1981, 2005, 2010, by Patera 2010 and Paleothodoros 2010.
59 A full analysis and sources in Clinton 2004 pp. 85–109. Cf. also Seaford 2005 pp. 602–6.
60 IG II2 3811 (=I. Eleusis 637), in Clinton 2004 p. 90.
61 IG II2 4058 (=I. Eleusis 399), in Clinton 2004 p. 93.
62 We shall analyse this theme of mystery imagery with regard to the *Homeric Hymn to Demeter* in 5.1 and to Aeschylus' *Oresteia* in 5.2.
63 Phaedrus 248b: 'οὗ δ' ἕνεχ' ἡ πολλὴ σπουδὴ τὸ ἀληθείας ἰδεῖν πεδίον οὗ ἐστιν, ἥ τε δὴ προσήκουσα ψυχῆς τῷ ἀρίστῳ νομή'.
64 'τόποι καθαροὶ καὶ λειμῶνες'.
65 Tablets n. 3 and 27, Graf and Johnston 2013 pp. 8–9 and 38–9.

66 Pindar fr. 130: 'ἔνθεν τὸν ἄπειρον ἐρεύγονται σκότον/ βληχροὶ δνοφερᾶς νυκτὸς ποταμοί'.
67 Plato *Phaedo* 69c.
68 'τὸν ἀμύητον ἐνταῦθα τῶν ζώντων καὶ ἀκάθαρτον ἐφορῶν ὄχλον ἐν βορβόρῳ πολλῷ καὶ ὁμίχλῃ'.
69 Aelius Aristides *Orationes* 19.259.
70 Philostratus, *Apollonius of Tyana*, 1.15. Plutarch uses the same terms for the procession to Eleusis under the protection of Alcibiades' army in 407, in orderly fashion and in silence (ἐν κόσμῳ καὶ μετὰ σιωπῆς). Plutarch, *Life of Alcibiades*, 34.3.
71 On this subject, the work of Lewis-Williams, paleo-archaeologist, ethnographer, neuropsychologist, professor emeritus at the South-African University of Witwatersrand, is of great interest, cf. especially Lewis-Williams 2005.
72 Noted, for instance, by Seaford 2010. Evidence is collected, for instance, by Fenwick and Fenwick 1996.
73 Fenwick and Fenwick 1996.
74 Fenwick and Fenwick 1996 pp. 18, 43–4.
75 Plato *Phaedrus* 246 a ff.
76 Fenwick and Fenwick 1996 pp. 73–98.
77 Alexander 2012 pp. 38–9, Pindar *Olympian* 2.71-74.
78 Plato *Republic* 10.614 ff.
79 Plutarch *De Sera Numinis Vindicta* 22.
80 Alexander 2012 p. 29.
81 Aeschylus Edonians fr. 57: 'ταυρόφθογγοι δ᾽ ὑπομυκῶνταί/ποθεν ἐξ ἀφανοῦς φοβεροὶ μῖμοι,/ἠχὼ τυπάνου δ᾽, ὥσθ᾽ ὑπογαίου/βροντῆς, φέρεται βαρυταρβής'.
82 Alexander 2012 p. 49.
83 Aristotle *de Philosophia* fr. 15. I adopt here the interpretation of Burkert 1987 p. 69.
84 Plato *Phaedo* 82e, 91e–92a.

Chapter 3

1 Burkert 1985 (1977) pp. 285–6.
2 Bérard and Bron 1986 p. 27.
3 Parker 2005 p. 343, on the basis of Andocides *De Mysteriis* 111 and on Terence's *Phormio* 49, a Latin version of *Epidicazomenus*, a New Comedy play by Apollodorus of Carystus.
4 Sourvinou-Inwood 2003 p. 249–50. It is a pity that Sourvinou-Inwood did not further her exploration of this theme in her work on Tragedy and Athenian religion.

5 Gomme 1933 p. 47.
6 Raaflaub 1998 p. 29.
7 Scott 2005 p. 520.
8 Hansen 1988 p. 12.
9 Strauss 1986, pp. 80–1.
10 Maenadism was not limited to Attica but was a ritual common to the whole Greek world. See Henrichs 1978 pp. 121–60, and Bremmer 1984 pp. 267–86.
11 Aelius Aristides *Oratio* 19.
12 'Immense chamber (*cella immanis*)' is the way the Roman architect Vitruvius describes it (Vitruvius 7 *Praefactio* 12).
13 A surface area comparable to the that of the Royal Albert Hall in London.
14 Still 2017.
15 I. G., I², 6 and I. G., I², 313. Clinton 1974 pp. 10–14.
16 Clinton 1974 p. 13 n. 13.
17 Cavanaugh 1996 p. 211.
18 Parker 2005 p. 348 n. 91.
19 Bremmer 2014 p. 4.
20 Andocides *De Mysteriis* 1.11-12.
21 Hansen 1976 p.122
22 Cf. Csapo and Slater 1994 p. 105, with sources.
23 'The year in which there was an eclipse of the moon one evening, and the old temple at Athens was burned, Pythias being now ephor at Sparta and Callias archon at Athens', Xenophon *Hellenica*. 1.6.1. Cf. also the *Constitution of the Athenians* 34.1.
24 Cf. MacDowell 1962 pp. 10–11. Callias is often called Callias III by modern historians to distinguish him from his grandfather Callias II, and his grandfather's grandfather Callias I.
25 Xenophon *Hellenica* 6.3.3.
26 Xenophon *Hellenica* 6.3.1-6.
27 Plato *Protagoras* 314e–f, Plutarch *Life of Pericles* 24.5.
28 Plutarch Life of Alcibiades 8.2.
29 Xenophon *Ways and Means* 4.15. One *mina* was equal to one hundred drachmae, in a period when the daily pay of a hoplite was one drachma.
30 Andocides *De Mysteriis* 130.
31 Plato *Protagoras* 337d.
32 Xenophon *Hellenica* 6.3.3-6.
33 Plato *Apology* 20a. Playing the *aulos* was considered at the time as a frivolous and degenerate pastime, see 4.4.
34 Heraclides Ponticus fr. 170 (Wehrli).

35 Cf. Cratinus fr. 360 and Plato *Laws* 659 a-c.
36 Plato *Symposium* 175e.
37 Plato *Ion* 535d.
38 In that sense Herodotus for example uses it in describing a very large force of mercenaries of the pharaoh Apries (2.163) and the crowd of initiates producing a large cloud of dust near Eleusis during the Persian occupation of Attica (8.65.1).
39 Pickard-Cambridge 1968 p. 263.
40 Csapo-Slater 1994 pp. 79–80, 286.
41 Wiles 2000 p. 93.
42 Kawalko-Roselli 2011 p. 74.
43 Gomme 1933 p. 47; Strauss 1986 pp. 70–85.
44 For metics cf. Aristophanes *Acharnians* 501–8; for slaves and foreigners Aristophanes *Peace* 962–7, Plato *Gorgias* 658c-d, Theophrastos *Characters* 9.5, Aelian *Varia Historia* 2.13.
45 Attested, for instance, in Plato *Gorgias* 515e; Plutarch *Pericles* 9.1. See Kawalko-Roselli 2011 pp. 87–117 for a thorough discussion on the subject.
46 Kawalko-Roselli 2011 p. 90.
47 Aristophanes *Frogs* 554.
48 Wine cost an obol for three κοτύλαι (LSJ).
49 Plutarch *De Tranquilitate animi* 10.
50 Plato *Apology* 26de.
51 Aristophanes *Pax* 375.
52 Thucydides 6.31.3; 8.45.2. But Xenophon *Hellenica* 1.5 reports that the pay of Spartan and Athenian ship crews was three obols per day.
53 Aristophanes *Wasps* 300: 'With my small pay, I am obliged to buy bread, wood, and stew!'
54 Kawalko-Roselli 2011 pp. 78–81.
55 Aristophanes *Frogs* 297.
56 Lysias 12.11.
57 Xenophon wrote *Ways and Means* (Πόροι ἢ περὶ Προσόδων) at the end of his life, around 355, at a time of financial distress for the polis of Athens that may have motivated the appeal, cf. Dillery 1993 p. 1. The contribution of metics to the economy of Athens was likely to have been particularly important during the Peloponnesian War, as they manufactured weapons and armoury.
58 On the importance of metics in Athens' economy cf. Plato *Laws* 850a-d.
59 Plutarch *Vitae Decem Oratorum* 3.
60 *Acharnians* 508: 'τοὺς γὰρ μετοίκους ἄχυρα τῶν ἀστῶν λέγω'.
61 For example, a Scythian archer in *Thesmophoriazousae* (1001–1007), in *Birds* a Scythian god, Triballos (1677–1681).

62 Theophrastos *Characters* IX.
63 Aristophanes *Frogs* 157.
64 Plato's *Laws* 658a-d.
65 '(κρινοῦσι) τραγῳδίαν αἵ τε πεπαιδευμέναι τῶν γυναικῶν καὶ τὰ νέα μειράκια καὶ σχεδὸν ἴσως τὸ πλῆθος πάντων'.
66 Plato *Gorgias* 502b-d.
67 'νῦν ηὑρήκαμεν ῥητορικήν τινα πρὸς δῆμον τοιοῦτον οἷον παίδων τε ὁμοῦ καὶ γυναικῶν καὶ ἀνδρῶν, καὶ δούλων καὶ ἐλευθέρων.
68 Plutarch *Consolatio ad uxorem*, 5.
69 *Vita Aeschyli* 9.
70 Athenaeus 12.47: 'εἰσιὼν εἰς τὸ θέατρον, ἐθαυμάζετο οὐ μόνον ὑπὸ τῶν ἀνδρῶν ἀλλὰ καὶ ὑπὸ τῶν γυναικῶν'.
71 Goldhill 1994 pp. 367-8.
72 Kawalko-Roselli 2011 p. 193-4.
73 Goldhill 1994 p. 368.
74 Henderson 1991 p. 143.
75 Cf. the fundamental work of Zeitlin 1982, pp. 129-57, Goff 2004, Parker 2005, in particular pp. 270-89.
76 Clinton 1974 pp. 1-143.
77 Cf. Pausanias 4.17.1 for the exclusive feminine cult of Demeter in Laconia.
78 A scholion to Lucian *Dialogi Meretricii* VII.4.
79 For a discussion of the myth of Icarius and the role played by the Icarius' daughter, Erigone, and the girls of Athens, see Csapo 1997 p. 267.
80 Maenadism was not limited to Attica but was a ritual common to the whole Greek world. Cf. Henrichs 1978 pp. 121-60, Bremmer 1984 pp. 267-86.
81 Euripides *Melanippe* fr. 494.
82 Parker 2005 p. 324.
83 Carpenter 1997 pp. 52-69. See also Parker 2005 pp. 306-12.
84 Dillon 2001 p. 149-52.
85 Museum of Fine Arts in Boston, inv. 90.155.
86 Antiken sammlung Staatische Musee su Berlin, inv. 2290.
87 Parker 2005 p. 321.
88 *Constitution of the Athenians* 3.5 'the union and marriage of of the wife of the king with Dionysus takes place there' (τοῦ βασιλέως γυναικὸς ἡ σύμμειξις ἐνταῦθα γίγνεται τῷ Διονύσῳ καὶ ὁ γάμος). The term σύμμειξις has no sexual implications: it simply designates the ceremonial meeting of the partners before marriage, cf. Rhodes 1993 (1981) pp. 104-5, Dillon 2002 p. 102 n. 190, but the term γάμος is explicit on the purported sexual nature of the encounter. See also Parker 2005 pp. 303-5.

89 Demosthenes (or pseudo-Demosthenes) in *Contra Neaira* 21–23 describes Lysias the orator helping his mistress Metanira, a slave of the brothel keeper Nikaretes of Corinth, to be initiated in the Eleusinian mysteries with no apparent opposition.

Chapter 4

1 Schechner 1985 pp. 20, 117–50.
2 Sourvinou-Inwood 2003, in particular pp. 1–66.
3 Seaford 2013 pp. 261–80.
4 Kowalzig 2007.
5 Lada-Richards 1993, the basis of her development of *Frogs* as parable of mystery initiation in Lada-Richards 1999.
6 On the meaning of this term cf. Plato Cratilus 420a: 'καὶ μὴν 'πόθος' αὖ καλεῖται σημαίνων οὐ τοῦ παρόντος εἶναι ἱμέρου τε καὶ ῥεύματος ἀλλὰ τοῦ ἄλλοθί που ὄντος καὶ ἀπόντος'.
7 Cf. Aristides *Eleusinia*, Themistius *Orationes* 20.235a, Cf. Seaford 2009 pp. 406–14 and Cairns 2016 pp. 2–7.
8 For instance, Sophocles *Elektra* 1402, *Oedipos Tyrannus* 1306, Plato *Phaedrus* 251a, Aristophanes *Frogs* 1336, Aristotle *Poetica*, 1453b, Plutarch *Life of Aratus* 32.1-2 etc.
9 Plato *Ion* 533d-536d
10 Aristotle *Poetica* 1447a.
11 Murray 1997, p. 114.
12 Diogenes Laërtius Lives of Eminent Philosophers 3.5.
13 Plato *Ion*, 535d-e.
14 Plato *Ion* 533e. Cf. Aristophanes *Frogs* 862. The deity Corybantes would revel in honour of was Cybele, as *Bacchae*'s Asian chorus does, cf. *Bacchae* 78–80.
15 Euripides *Bacchae* 142, 704.
16 Plato *Ion* 535b.
17 Plato *Ion* 533b-d. Cf. also Plato *Republic* 373b.
18 Plato *Symposium* 215b-216a.
19 Plato *Phaedrus* 234d.
20 Demetrius of Phaleron, or perhaps a later imitator, Περὶ ἑρμηνείας, 100–101.
21 Rouget 1985 (1980) is still as far as I know the most complete study on music and its effect on the human mind in several world cultures.
22 To the best of my knowledge with the exception of Sifakis 2001 pp. 21–35. Cf. also West 1992.
23 Aristophanes' *Frogs* 862.

24 Plato *Republic* 398d.
25 Isocrates 9.10: 'ταῖς εὐρυθμίαις καὶ ταῖς συμμετρίαις ψυχαγωγοῦσι τοὺς ἀκούοντας'.
26 Plato *Minos* 321a.
27 Cf. Devine and Stephens 1993 pp. 379–403. I am not a musicologist, but some attempts to reconstruct ancient Greek music and poetry singing, such as the ones attempted by d'Angour, Professor of Classics at Oxford University and a musician, available on YouTube (https://www.youtube.com/watch?v=Dc97mwbbMds), seem to me to have no rhythm to inspire dancing. I would rather be inclined to see some continuity in ancient and modern Greek popular music and dancing, cf. Lawler 1927 p. 74 n. 8, and Michaelides 1956 pp. 37–9.
28 Cf. Jilek 1982 p. 328.
29 Some forms of Dionysiac music and dance cathartic rituals may have survived until modern times, such as the 'taranta' in Puglia, where a subject prey to hallucinations and loss of self is revived by therapists dancing and playing fast and rhythmical music, cf. De Martino 1959.
30 Plato *Ion* 533d-534b
31 Lucian *De Saltatione* 8.
32 Aristotle *Politica* Book 8 1342a-b. See also West 1992 p. 180.
33 Strabo 10.3.9.
34 A list in Halliwell 1986 appendix 5.
35 Aristotle *Poetica* 1449b.
36 Fyfe 1932 ad loc.
37 Halliwell 1995 ad loc.
38 When Aristotle defines 'embellishment' as in *Poetica* 1449a30, he uses the term κοσμέω.
39 Cf Sifakis 2001 p. 24.
40 Cf. Homer *Odyssey* 20.391. Cf. also Homer *Odyssey* 3.480: 'σῖτον καὶ οἶνον ἔθηκεν, ὄψα τε'. Fish was often the serving's main component: modern Greek's word for fish, *psari*, derives from it.
41 Plutarch *Quaestiones Conviviales* 713C.
42 Dio Chrysostomos 12. 33.
43 Aristotle *Poetica* 1449b
44 Segal 1996 p. 155.
45 'Cleansing from guilt or defilement, purification' is the definition in LSJ, while Chantraine 2000 pp. 478–9 defines *katharós* as 'propre, pur (dit de l'eau), nettoyé, vanné, (du grain), employé au sens moral ou religieux. La pureté religieuse se trouvant d'ailleurs associée à la propreté du corps'.
46 Aristotle Poetica 1455b 15.
47 Aeschylus *Eumenides* 276–8.

48 Constitution of the Athenians 1.
49 Plato *Phaedo* 67c-69c.
50 Plato Phaedo 69c: 'τὸ δ' ἀληθὲς τῷ ὄντι ᾖ κάθαρσίς τις τῶν τοιούτων πάντων καὶ ἡ σωφροσύνη καὶ ἡ δικαιοσύνη καὶ ἀνδρεία, καὶ αὐτὴ ἡ φρόνησις μὴ καθαρμός τις ᾖ'.
51 Saban 2018 pp. 28–42.
52 Segal 1996 pp. 149–72.
53 See for instance Rouget 1985 (1980) and Agres, Bigo, Herremans 2019 pp. 294–70.
54 Bourguignon 1973 pp. 3–11.
55 West 1992 p. 1. For a thorough review of the *aulos* in classical Greece see West 1992 pp. 81–107.
56 Defined for instance in the *Homeric Hymn to Hermes* 452 as a 'ravishing thrill' (ἱμερόεις βρόμος αὐλῶν).
57 Cf. Anderson 1994 p. 181.
58 An *auletes* is depicted on the Minoan sarcophagus from Aghia Triada at the Heraklion Museum in Crete.
59 Cf. Vargiu 1970 pp. 379–82
60 *Launeddas* music can be listened to on YouTube in https://www.youtube.com/watch?v=BhsBCwCwBU8
61 Cf. Athenaeus 184d.
62 An interesting study of the *aulos* in Athens is in Wilson 1999 pp. 58–95.
63 Sophocles *Trachiniae* 205–223.
64 Plutarch Quaestiones Convivales 704c.
65 Fragment 235 Schroeder, 125 Bowra.
66 Plato *Symposium* 215c.
67 Aristotle *Politics* Book 8 1339a. Euripides' *Bacchae* 370 ff.
68 Aristotle *Politics* Book 8 1342b.
69 Wilson 2000 p. 5. Works on the chorus include Henrichs 1994–5, Foley 2003, Kowalzig 2007, the various contributors to Murray and Wilson 2004, to Billings, Budelmann, Macintosh 2013 and to Gagné, Govers Hopman 2013.
70 Wilson 2000 p. 1.
71 For an introduction to the subject see Burkert 1985 (1977) p. 102–3.
72 See Henrichs 1994–5.
73 Aristotle *Poetica* 1456a 25.
74 See the seminal study on choral self-referentiality in Henrichs 1994–5, pp. 56–111.
75 Kowalzig 2007, particularly pp. 1–55 and 392–401, and Kowalzig 2007a pp. 221–54.
76 Seaford 2013 pp. 261–79.
77 Seaford 2013 p. 264.
78 Revermann 2006 p. 108.
79 Plato *Laws* 665b3-6.

80 Constitution of the Athenians 56.3.
81 Wilson 2000 p. 22.
82 Old Oligarch 1.13.
83 Plato *Laws* 654–655: 'οὐκοῦν ὁ μὲν ἀπαίδευτος ἀχόρευτος ἡμῖν ἔσται, τὸν [654β] δὲ πεπαιδευμένον ἱκανῶς κεχορευκότα θετέον'.
84 The great number of artists needed to fill the choruses each year was only possible by the Athenian cult of *mousike* which played a central part in Athenian education. Apart from their primary role in the performances at the Great Dionysia, choruses played during other religious festivals, such as the Thargelia festival for Apollo, the Panathenaea, the festival at Delphi and Delos, torch-races between the *phylai* for Athena, Prometheus and Hephaistos, a triarchic regatta from the Piraeus to Cape Sounion as well as phyletic banquets. See Wilson 2000 p. 21.
85 Cf. *Constitution of the Athenians* 56.3, Antiphon *On the Choreut* 11–13.
86 Dithyrambs' choruses numbered fifty members, comedy twenty-four and tragedy twelve to fifteen, see Revermann 2006 p. 108.
87 Golder 1996 p. 4.
88 Golder 1996 p. 2.
89 Cf. for instance Xenophon *Symposium* 7.5.
90 Lawler 1927 pp. 69–112, 1964 pp. 22–62.
91 Causing an often-inspiring vision of women's bodies, cf. Aristophanes *Frogs* 411–415. Obviously, this would be difficult to replicate with a male-composed theatrical chorus.
92 See for instance the four bas-reliefs of dancing maenads at the Prado Museum, Madrid n. E00042, E00043, E00045 and E00046, Roman copies of originals attributed to the fifth century sculptor Callimachus and the marble bas-relief n. 1805,0703.128 at the British Museum depicting a similar scene.
93 Seaford 2000 pp. 31–2.
94 Aristophanes' *Frogs* 1109–1118.
95 Revermann 2006 p. 112.
96 Cf. Henrichs 1994–5 p. 59
97 Wiles 2000 p. 112.

Chapter 5

1 See Bowden 2010 p. 26.
2 As Foley 1994 p. 174 notes: 'an archaizing poem would not only have no reason to mention Athens but would enhance the cult's claim to immemorial antiquity by ignoring the city'.

3   Seaford 2012 p. 36: 'This fictional configuration of ritual, myth, cosmology, fertility, and transition to the polis emerged from the process ... in which the inhabitants of Attica created their polis'.
4   Burkert 1985 (1977) p. 8.
5   Strauss Clay 2006 (1989) pp. 202–65, Foley 1994, particularly 'The Hymn and the Polis' pp. 142–50.
6   Richardson 1974 p. 311 n. ad loc.
7   Richardson 1974 pp. 12–20, in particular p. 17.
8   Parker 1991 pp. 1–17. See also Alderink 1982 pp. 1–16.
9   Seaford 1994 pp. 304, 330 n. 6, 383–4, 2012, pp. 24–51.
10 Strauss Clay 2006 (1989) p. 205
11 Seaford 1994 p. 304, Seaford 2012 pp. 33–6.
12 Strauss Clay 2006 (1989) p. 208.
13 'Since the common people lived in the country, the chiefs in the city, the commons, common people ... opposed to βασιλεύς or ἔξοχος ἀνήρ (Homer *Iliad* 1.188 and 198, etc.)' (LSJ s. δῆμος). Chantraine 2000, ad loc. 'δῆμος, d'abord "pays, territoire" ... les gens du people, parce que les gens du people vivent à la campagne et les grands à la ville. Par opposition aux *eudaemones*, aux *dunatoi*. Cf. Herodotus 1. 196'.
14 Homer *Iliad* 13. 108.
15 For instance, in Aristophanes' *Knights* 163.
16 For instance, in Aristophanes *Frogs* 676.
17 Benveniste 1969 II p. 103: 'la Thémis est l'apanage de basileus, qui est d'origine céleste, et le pluriel thémistes indique l'ensemble de ces prescriptions, code inspiré par les dieux, lois non écrites, recueil de dits, d'arrêts rendus par les oracles, qui fixent dans la conscience du juge (en l'espèce, le chef de la famille) la conduite à tenir toutes les fois que l'ordre du génos est en jeu'. See also Ostwald 1986 pp. 84–5.
18 On the term δίκη see for instance Benveniste 1969 II pp. 107–10. A similar judgement is described in *Iliad* 497–508 where a dispute between two warriors is judged by the army's elders before the assembly, where a prize would be given to the elder who 'spoke the straightest opinion (δίκην ἰθύντατα εἴποι)'.
19 On the identity of the Callichoros and the Maidens' Well see Richardson 1974, pp. 326–8 and Calame 2001 (1977) p. 139 n. 142.
20 Seaford 2012 p. 25.
21 I would opt for this translation that connects ὁμοῖοι with ὅς τάδ' ὄπωπεν, rather than Foley's 1994 rather vague 'same lot'.
22 The two terms, ὄλβος and πλοῦτος, are associated in defining spiritual and material wealth, as they embrace the transcendental divine blessing and the material abundance of goods given by the gods. See Hesiod *Works and Days* 300–1 '... φιλέῃ

δέ σ' ἐυστέφανος Δημήτηρ αἰδοίη, βιότου δὲ τεὴν πιμπλῇσι καλιήν'. In Hesiod *Theogony* 971–4 Plutus, the deity who brings wealth (ἀφνειός), and happiness (ὄλβος), to those who find him, is son of Demeter. Cf. Richardson 1974 pp. 313–14.
23 *Constitution of the Athenians* 23–26.
24 Aristocrats were active in that period to end democracy, cf. Thucydides 1.107.4.
25 Plutarch *Life of Cimon* 17.2, Plutarch *Life of Pericles* 9.4.
26 For this reason, the mystical threads in *Oresteia* have been neglected by most scholars, with the exception of the pioneering work by for instance Headlam 1906 pp. 268–77, Thomson 1935 and 1938 and, more recently, by Bowie 1993 pp. 10–13, Widzisz 2010 pp. 461–89 and Seaford 2012 pp. 125–205. It is curious to note that even scholars who have focused on some of the veiled sub-text of *Oresteia*, such as Gantz 1977 pp. 28–38 and Ferrari 1997 pp. 1–45, both of whom explored at length the religious ritual nature of fires and lights in the trilogy, overlook the connection between fires and lights and the mystical ritual references in *Oresteia*.
27 Chantraine 2000 II p. 617.
28 Plato *Phaedo* 70a.
29 Thomson 1938 I pp. 14–16, II pp. 2–3, Aelius Aristides 19.259.
30 MacLeod 1982 p. 127.
31 Headlam 1906 p. 275.
32 Beer 1981 p. 50.

Chapter 6

1 Hopper 1961 pp. 138–51.
2 Andocides *De Mysteriis* 1.111.
3 Foley 1994 pp. 29–30, Sourvinou-Inwood 2003a pp. 26–7.
4 Cosmopoulos 2015 pp. 139–40.
5 Miles 1998 pp. 25–8.
6 For an examination of the modern rendering of the term see for instance Finley 1973 p. 28, Loraux 1997 pp. 21–62.
7 Among the vast literature on *stasis* the following works should be mentioned: Lintott 1981, Loraux 1997 pp. 21–62, Fisher 2000 pp. 83–123, Van Wees 2008 pp.1–39, Berent 1998 pp. 331–62 and 2000 pp. 257–89, B. Gray 2015.
8 On the concept of *homonoia* see West 1977 pp. 307–19.
9 Aristophanes for instance uses a similar weaving metaphor as a way to bring the polis back to cohesion in *Lysistrata* 574–86
10 Translation Henderson 1987.

11 Plato *Laws* 628a-c.
12 Homer *Iliad* 9.1-49.
13 Homer *Iliad* 9.63-64.
14 Hesiod, *Theogony*, 223-230.
15 Solon, Fr. 4, 9.
16 For instance, Theognis 43-52; Herodotus 3.82.
17 Herodotus 8.3.1. The same concept is also used by Demokritos fr. 249 DK.
18 'θυραῖος ἔστω πόλεμος ... ἐνοικίου δ' ὄρνιθος οὐ λέγω μάχην'.
19 As, for instance, Connor 1984 p. 208 puts it in a comment to Thucydides' account of the end of the Sicilian expedition, a 'stern sceptic, enlightened man ... whose theodicy surprises and perplexes'. See also Price 2001 p. 235.
20 Thucydides 3.70-84.
21 Religion in Thucydides is still a controversial issue. Hornblower 1992 p. 170, for instance, writes of Thucydides' 'religious silences or distortions' and that 'the religious silences of Thucydides are as scandalous as the political silences of Xenophon ... Thucydides seriously understated the religious aspects of the war he set himself up to describe', while Jordan 1986 p. 147 correctly notes: 'For Thucydides religion is the underlying fabric which holds human society together and he shows how a prolonged and vicious war gradually destroys that fabric'.
22 Thucydides 3.82.2
23 Herodotus 5.71-2.
24 Thucydides1.126.
25 Plato *Laws* 1.642d
26 *Constitution of Athenians* 1.1-2.3, 5.2-11.1.
27 Plutarch *Life of Solon* 12.
28 Diogenes Laërtius *Lives of Eminent Philosophers*, 10.
29 Dates vary from the early seventh century to a century later. For a discussion of dating in different sources see Rhodes 1993 (1981) pp. 81-2.
30 Herodotus 5.71.
31 Thucydides 1.126.3.
32 Thucydides 1.126.7.
33 Plutarch *Life of Solon* 12.2-3.
34 Epimenides is perhaps more than a legendary figure. According to Diogenes Laërtius, Epimenides wrote a *Theogony*. Bernabé 2007 p. 152 quotes Kern 1888 p. 79 who believes a dating of Epimenides' *Theogony* to the sixth century as '*verisimillimum*'. He also was credited of having written a *Birth of Corybantes* and *Kuretes*.
35 Plato *Laws* 1.642d: 'τῇδε γὰρ ἴσως ἀκήκοας ὡς Ἐπιμενίδης γέγονεν ἀνὴρ θεῖος, ὃς ἦν ἡμῖν οἰκεῖος, ἐλθὼν δὲ πρὸ τῶν Περσικῶν δέκα ἔτεσιν πρότερον παρ' ὑμᾶς κατὰ τὴν τοῦ θεοῦ μαντείαν, θυσίας τε ἐθύσατό τινας ἃς ὁ θεὸς ἀνεῖλεν'.

36 A decision that in itself had a ritual purifying effect on the community. See Parker 1983 p. 114.
37 Plutarch *Life of Solon* 12.3.
38 'τὸ δὲ μέγιστον, ἱλασμοῖς τισι καὶ καθαρμοῖς καὶ ἱδρύσεσι κατοργιάσας καὶ καθοσιώσας τὴν πόλιν.'
39 Keesling 2017 pp. 164–5.
40 Herodotus 6.35-41, 6.132-4, 6.134.2-136.3.
41 An interesting research of the financial cost of running a stable of racehorses in Scott 2005 pp. 513–21 suggests (p. 520) that there were only four families in fifth-century Athens who raced horse teams at Olympia: the Philaïdae, the Alcmaeonidae, and those of Callias and Alcibiades.
42 See Plato *Republic* 567a-e.
43 Eastern autocrats were symbols of tyranny. See Mitchell 2013 pp. 155–6.
44 Herodotus 6.133 ff. Other accounts are in Ephorus, in part of Stephanos Byzantios on Paros, *FGrH* 70 F63, in Cornelius Nepos' *Life of Miltiades* 7 and in four *scholia* to Aelius Aristides. See Scott 2005 pp. 630–47.
45 What Herodotus' public would have known is that Demeter had been one of the main divinities of Paros since archaic times, as for instance in the *Homeric Hymn to Demeter* (491) she is called queen of sea-encircled Paros at par with Eleusis and Antron and in a fragment Archilochus, the seventh-century Dionysiac poet, mentions a festival that was held on the island in honour of Demeter and Kore (fr. 322 West). More evidence of the Parian cult of Demeter is the connection between Archilochus and the cult to which the poet's grandfather Tellis adhered, as noted by Pausanias (10.28.3).
46 De Polignac 1995 (1984) p. 122.
47 Picard 1950 p. 124–5.
48 Herodotus 6.134.2.
49 On the symbolic implications of Miltiades' wound in Herodotus' narrative strategy see Felton 2014 pp. 47–61.
50 Hau 2016 p. 189.
51 Scott 2005 p. 436.
52 A similar expression, to touch the untouchable (τῶν ἀθίκτων θιγγανεῖν), is the definition of the unjust, unholy man in Sophocles' *Oedipus Tyrannus* 891.
53 Herodotus 6.135.3.
54 Some scholars believe instead that the Pythia suggests that Timo was a *phasma*. Hornblower 2017 n. ad loc. for instance, is of the opinion Timo herself was a *phasma* and attributes the expression to the language of epiphanies.
55 Thucydides 6.27-29, 53, 60-61.

56 Thucydides 6.2729; Andocides *De Mysteriis*, Plutarch *Life of Alcibiades*, Xenophon *Hellenica* 1.4.18.
57 In 32.3, starting his narration of the return of Alcibiades to Athens, Plutarch comments on his sources, declaring Duris the Samian as untrustworthy, and Theopompus, Ephorus and Xenophon as his preferred sources.
58 Xenophon *Hellenica* 1.4; Plutarch *Alcibiades* 33-4.
59 See Furley 1996 pp. 13-17 for a full survey of Athens' public Herms. Herms were found in gymnasia, and a famous Herm sculpted by Alkamenes stood at the entrance of the Acropolis (Pausanias 1.22.8).
60 Their faces were destroyed: as Thucydides put it clearly 'περιεκόπησαν τὰ πρόσωπα'.
61 See Furley 1996 pp. 13-30, Crawley Quinn 2007 pp. 90-3, Osborne 2010, in particular pp. 356-66.
62 Thucydides1.98.
63 Aeschines 3.183-5.
64 Osborne 1985 p.67.
65 A famous case was the one of Diagoras of Melos, condemned to death around the same date of the Herms affair for *asebeia* towards the mysteries (Diodorus 13.6).
66 Plutarch *Life of Alcibiades* 22.
67 Thucydides 6.24.3.
68 MacDowell 1962 p. 9 notes that Hermes was also the god of travellers, and the consequences of his wrath would have been an ominous sign (οἰωνός), for the expedition, the defacement being perhaps an open warning to Athenians not to venture to Sicily across the open sea.
69 Thucydides 6.27.
70 Plutarch Life of Alcibiades 18.
71 Thucydides 6.60.1.
72 Xenophon *Hellenica*1.4.12-20; Plutarch *Life of Alcibiades* 33-34.
73 Plutarch *Life of Alcibiades* 22.4.
74 Thucydides 8.53.
75 Plutarch *Life of Alcibiades* 33.3.
76 Plutarch *Life of Alcibiades* 34.2.
77 A highly likely fact: in 408/7 the sanctuary revenues were still high, cf. 3.1.
78 Plutarch *Life of Alcibiades* 34.3.
79 Herodotus 8.65.
80 Plutarch *Life of Alcibiades* 34.4.
81 Xenophon *Hellenica* 1.4.20.
82 Plutarch *Life of Alkibiades* 34.5.

83 'ἀσέβεια μὲν ἡ περὶ θεοὺς πλημμέλεια καὶ περὶ δαίμονας ἢ καὶ περὶ τοὺς κατοιχομένους, καὶ περὶ γονεῖς καὶ περὶ πατρίδα', Aristotle *De Virtutibus et Vitiis* 1251a30.
84 See Gagné 2009 pp. 215–17.
85 'οὐκ εἰδέναι ὅτι ἀπόρρητα ἦν', Aristotle *Ethica Nicomachea* 1111a Bekker.
86 Clemens Alexandrinus *Stromata* 2.14.60.
87 The scholiast in the above passage comments that Aeschylus alluded to the secret parts of the Eleusinian mystical rituals in several plays: *Female Archers, Priestesses, Sisyphus the Stoneroller, Iphigeneia* and *Oedipus* (*Tragicorum Graecorum Fragmenta* Nauck 86, p. 28), see also Wright 2019 p. 33.
88 Aristophanes *Frogs* 886–887.
89 Rubel 2000, pp. 157–77.
90 Gagné 2009 p. 223.
91 Aristophanes *Clouds* 828–831.
92 Aristophanes *Birds* 184, 1072 ff.
93 Aristophanes *Frogs* 318–320.
94 Janko 2001 p. 8, on the evidence of the eleventh-century Arab scholar Al-Mubaššir, *Life of Zeno the Eleatic*.
95 Scholia to Aristophanes *Birds* 1073, FGH 326 F3a-b.
96 Diodorus Siculus 13.6.7. See also Pseudo Lysias 6.17.
97 Xenophon *Hellenica* 1.6.26-1.7.35, Diodorus Siculus 13.97-103.
98 Xenophon 1.5.16-17. Diodoros 13.74.4.
99 Xenophon 1.6.19.
100 Xenophon 1.6.24.
101 Today Kalem and Garip Adasi.
102 Strauss 1986 pp. 179–82 puts the losses at 500 hoplites and 1,147 rowers.
103 Xenophon *Hellenica* 1.6.34.
104 Six of the eight fleet generals originally in charge at the battle: Aristokrates, Diomedon, Pericles junior, Erasinides, Thrasyllus, and Lysias. Protomachos and Aristogenes wisely did not return to Athens.
105 Xenophon *Hellenica* 1.6.35.
106 Xenophon *Hellenica* 1.7.9.
107 See for a discussion of sources Andrewes 1974 pp. 119–20, 1992 pp. 481–2.
108 Diodorus Siculus 13.100.1-2.
109 Diodorus Siculus 15.35.
110 Plato *Menexenus* 243c.
111 Among them Andrewes 1974, Roberts 1977, Lang 1992, Rubel 2000, Asmonti 2006, Gish 2012.

112 Andrewes 1992 p. 493.
113 Ostwald 1986 p. 441.
114 Roberts 1977 p. 111.
115 With the exception for instance of Seaford 1994 p. 83 n. 34 and Rubel 2000 pp. 137–45.
116 Andrewes 1992 p. 492 n. 60.
117 See the ethic/political debate on the subject in Sophocles' *Antigone* and Sourvinou-Inwood's 1989 pp. 134–48 innovative interpretation of the play, see also Parker 1983 chapter 2.
118 Diodorus Siculus 13.101.4
119 Thucydides 6.60.2.
120 For a discussion of *miasma* versus death rituals see Parker 1983 chapter 2 and Seaford 1994 chapter 3.
121 Cf. Brelich 1969 pp. 288–9, Schmitt 1977 pp. 1059–73.
122 Xenophon *Hellenica* 1.8.8.
123 Diodorus Siculus 13.101.6
124 Grote 1850 Vol. VIII pp. 279–80.
125 Still, as Gish notes, the details of the trial in Xenophon's thorough account show that the demos moved with great attention to legal institutions and democratic procedures (Gish 2012 p. 202).
126 Xenophon *Hellenica* 1.7.12.
127 Hunt 2001 pp. 359–80.
128 Asmonti 2006 pp. 1–21.
129 *Frogs* 1422-1423: περὶ Ἀλκιβιάδου τίν' ἔχετον /γνώμην ἑκάτερος; ἡ πόλις γὰρ δυστοκεῖ.
130 Plato *Gorgias* 472.
131 Thucydides 8.89, 92.
132 Andrewes 1953 p. 3.
133 Xenophon *Hellenica* 7.1.2.
134 Asmonti 2006, p. 21.
135 Who was known to have convinced the ecclesia not to accept the Spartans' peace proposal after Cyzicus, cf. Aeschynes 2.39, Diodorus 13.53, *Constitution of the Athenians* 28.3. Cf. also Aristophanes *Frogs* 679, 1504, 1532.
136 Lysias 13.5-12.
137 See for instance Stem 2003 p. 18 for a discussion on the date.
138 Xenophon *Hellenica* 2.3.11-2.4.43. It was probably written after the battle of Mantinea (362), see Dillery 1995 p. 14.
139 Cf. Krentz 1995 p. 122. See also Dillery 1995 pp. 146–63.

140 Cf. V. Gray 1989 p. 7.
141 Dillery 1995 p. 8.
142 Bowden 2004 p. 229.
143 Loraux 1997 and 1997a, Azoulay 2014 pp. 689–719 produces a critique of Loraux's approach to a reading of the episode from a political theory angle but overlooks entirely its religious inspiration and implications. Other useful studies on Xenophon's political and religious outlook include Krentz 1995, Skoczylas Pownall 1998, Seager 2001, and Gray 1989 and 2003.
144 Xenophon *Hellenica* 2.3.2.
145 Xenophon *Hellenica* 2.4.17.
146 Xenophon *Memorabilia* 1.2.12.
147 Andocides *de Mysteriis* 47, 68.
148 Lycurgus *Leokrates* 1.112-13.
149 Lysias 12.43-6.
150 Xenophon *Hellenica* 2.3.13.
151 Interestingly analysed by Dillery 1995 pp. 148–56.
152 Xenophon *Hellenica* 2.3.16 'εἰ δέ, ὅτι τριάκοντά ἐσμεν καὶ οὐχ εἷς, ἧττόν τι οἴει ὥσπερ τυραννίδος ταύτης τῆς ἀρχῆς χρῆναι ἐπιμελεῖσθαι, εὐήθης εἶ'.
153 Cf. for instance, Solon fragment 4; Plato *Republic* 351d.
154 Xenophon *Hellenica* 2.3.24-26.
155 Xenophon *Hellenica* 2.3.21.
156 Lysias 12.
157 See for instance *The Constitution of the Athenians* 15.3-5 on Peisistratos' disarming the Athenians, Aristotle *Politics* 5.1311.10 ff., Herodotus 1.59.5 on Peisistratos' personal bodyguard and Thucydides 6.55.3 and 6.56.2 on Hippias'.
158 Xenophon *Hellenica* 2.3.48 'σὺν τοῖς δυναμένοις καὶ μεθ' ἵππων καὶ μετ' ἀσπίδων ὠφελεῖν'.
159 Xenophon *Hellenica* 2.3.50.
160 Xenophon *Hellenica* 2.3.53. See Gould 1973 p. 83. Gould too falls in the trap of considering Xenophon as a neutral observer of historical events.
161 Thucydides 8.73.4-6.
162 Thucydides 8.75.2.
163 Thucydides, 8.105-6, Xenophon *Hellenica* 1.1, Diodorus Siculus 13.50.4-7. Cf. also Rhodes 1993 (1981) pp. 429–30.
164 *Constitution of the Athenians* 40.2.
165 *Constitution of the Athenians* 40.2.
166 Xenophon *Hellenica* 2.4.25.
167 See Ostwald 1986 p. 503-4: see also Raubitschek 1941 pp. 284–95, Taylor 2002 pp. 377–97.

168 Diodorus 14.32.4; Lysias 12.52.
169 Xenophon *Hellenica* 2.4.8-10.
170 Krentz 1995 p. 142 estimates the figure of 584 as the number of full Athenian citizens in Eleusis, and Lysias mentions the figure of 300 being arrested.
171 Xenophon *Hellenica* 2.4.13-17.
172 Divine interventions are viewed by Xenophon as punishing the impious, cf. for instance *Hellenica* 5.4.1. Cf. also Skoczylas Pownall 1998 pp. 251-77 and Krentz 1995 pp. 144-5.
173 Possibly on Ephorus' evidence, as it is mentioned by Diodorus in 14.32.2.
174 Xenophon *Hellenica* 2.4.17. Cf. for instance Aeschylus *Seven against Thebes* 1.
175 Xenophon *Hellenica* 2.4.18.
176 Foucart 1914 p. 203.
177 Xenophon *Hellenica* 2.4.20.
178 In *Birds* 876-87 Aristophanes invokes the Great Mother of gods and men, Cybele the Ostrich, mother of Cleocritus, δέσποινα Κυβέλη, στροῦθε, μῆτερ Κλεοκρίτου.
179 Xenophon *Hellenica* 2.4.20-22.
180 Gray 1989 pp. 101-3.
181 Not unlike in its conciliatory tone the speech Xenophon puts in the mouth of another *keryx*, Callias, in Xenophon *Hellenica* 6.3.1-6.
182 Xenophon *Hellenica* 2.4.20. See Plato's definition of the comradeship between people who have shared the experience of being entertained, going through initiation and being initiated (ξενίζειν τε καὶ μυεῖν καὶ ἐποπτεύειν) as the basis of *philia*, in letter 7.333e.
183 Xenophon *Hellenica* 2.4.39-42
184 Xenophon *Hellenica* 2.4.38.
185 Cf. Krentz 1995 p. 154.
186 Heraclitus fr. 116: 'ἀνθρώποισι πᾶσι μέτεστι γινώσκειν ἑωυτοὺς καὶ σωφρονεῖν'.
187 Xenophon *Hellenica* 2.4.43.
188 Xenophon *Hellenica* 3.1.1.
189 Plato *Menexenos* 243e-244b.
190 ὁ δὲ τᾶς ἡσυχίας βίοτος καὶ τὸ φρονεῖν ... ξυνέχει δώματα, 'a life of tranquillity holds households together' (389-392).
191 Xenophon *Hellenica* 2.4.38 and detailed in the *Constitution of Athenians* 39.1-6. Cf. Rhodes 1993 (1981) pp. 462-72.
192 See for instance Lysias 6.39, Isocrates 5.111, Rhodes 1993 (1981), p. 463.
193 Cf. Xenophon *Hellenica* 2.4.38, *Constitution of Athenians* 39.1-6, Rhodes 1993 (1981) pp. 462-472.
194 Isocrates *De Bigis* 6.

Chapter 7

1. Hellenica *Oxyrhynchia* 1176. See Stevens 1956 pp. 87–94. A full list of testimonia in Kovacs' *Euripidea* 1994.
2. Dodds 1960 (1944) p. xivii.
3. Roux 1972 Vol I pp. 8–9.
4. Revermann 1999–2000 pp. 451–67.
5. Mills 2006 p. 8.
6. Hanink 2008 pp. 115–35.
7. Stewart 2019 pp. 1–23, Lewis (ed.) 2005.
8. Fairweather 1974 pp. 231–75.
9. Lefkowitz 1978 pp. 459–69
10. Lefkowitz 1979 pp. 187–210.
11. Scullion 2003 pp. 389–400.
12. It is of course entirely possible that Euripides was kept informed of events in Athens. The circle of prime Athenian artistic personalities who were at Archelaus' court with Euripides comprised the tragedian Agathon, his lover Pausanias, the painter Zeuxis, the poet Timotheus and the epic poet Choerilus of Samos (Stewart 2019 p. 1, with ancient sources). Land and sea communications between Athens and Macedonia would have been regular, at least until the battle of Aegospotami.
13. Plato *Gorgias* 525c-e.
14. Aristotle *Politics* 1311a-b.
15. Lada-Richards 1999 p. 121.
16. Sourvinou-Inwood 2003 pp. 2–5.
17. Kowalzig 2007 p. 225.
18. Pascal 1911 p. 48, Segal 1961 p. 227, Carrière 1966 pp. 121–2, Cantarella 1974 pp. 292–301.
19. There is no evidence that Aristophanes was aware of the text of *Bacchae* when he wrote *Frogs*. In the play Aristophanes quotes from a large number of Euripides' plays or parodies them. The plays include *Hypsipyle, Andromeda, Oineus, Alcmene, Melanippe the Wise, Alexander, Hippolytus, Philoctetes, Orestes, Theseus, Antigone, Sthenoboia, Phrixos, Iphigenia in Taurica, Meleager, Iphigenia in Aulis, Electra, Hecabe, Temenidae, Cretans, Medea, Aiolos,* and *Polydos* (Schlesinger 1937 pp. 303–8). He never quotes *Bacchae*.
20. Segal 1961 pp. 227–8.
21. Dover 1993 p. 38. I tend to agree with Dover. I suspect that Aristophanes may have had read the manuscript and that *Frogs* may have been intended as an encrypted homage to his dead friend Euripides.
22. Foley 1985 p. 229.

23 Dodds 1960 (1944) p. xxxix.
24 Dodds 1960 (1944) p. xxiii.
25 Foley 1980 p. 108.
26 Foley 1985 p. 244.
27 Foley 1985 p. 255.
28 Foley 1985 p. 206.
29 Versnel 1998 pp. 96–212.
30 Versnel 1998 pp. 100–1.
31 Versnel 1998 pp. 99–100.
32 Seaford 1996 pp. 46–7.
33 Seaford 1996 p. 51.
34 Stuttard 2016 pp. 4–7.
35 Stanford 1958 pp. xiv–xvii. Yet Athenians were still optimistic on their chances to win the war, and the lack of food presumably started after the loss of control over the Black sea passage after the battle of Aegospotami.
36 Segal 1961 p. 213.
37 Segal 1961 p. 224.
38 Segal 1961 p. 230.
39 Dover 1993 pp. 69–76.
40 Sommerstein 1997 pp. 1–9.
41 Lada-Richards 1999 p. 327.
42 The supply of corn to Athens probably only ceased after the defeat as the polis was besieged by Lysander (Xenophon *Hellenika* 2.2.11). In 405, the polis was not yet in a mood to surrender (Xenophon *Hellenika* 2.215).
43 Wiles 2011 pp. 33–41.
44 Griffith 2013 p. 200.
45 Halliwell 2015 pp. 508–10.
46 Norwood 1908.
47 Versnel 1998.
48 A work Nietzsche later (1886) however partially recanted: 'I call it something poorly written, ponderous, embarrassing, with fantastic and confused imagery, sentimental, here and there so saccharine it is effeminate, uneven in tempo, without any impulse for logical clarity, extremely self-confident and thus dispensing with evidence, even distrustful of the *relevance* of evidence,... an arrogant and rhapsodic book.' Nietzsche 1999a (1886), pp. 5–6.
49 Rohde 1925 (1898), Henrichs 1984 pp. 205–40, in particular pp. 223–8, Seaford 1995 p. 6, Seaford 1996 pp. 30–5.
50 Dodds 1960 (1944).
51 Winnington-Ingram 1948.

52 Girard 1988 (1972).
53 Roux 1972.
54 Oranje 1984.
55 Vernant 1985.
56 Versnel 1998.
57 Henrichs 1984 p. 224.
58 Nietzsche 1999 (1872) p. 52.
59 Nietzsche 1999 (1872) p. 20.
60 Nietzsche 1999 (1872) p. 18.
61 Dodds 1960 (1944) p. xliv.
62 Dodds 1960 (1944) p. xxvii.
63 Winnington-Ingram 1948 pp. 178–9.
64 Winnington-Ingram 1948 pp. 4–5.
65 Segal 1961 pp. 227–8.
66 Segal 1982 p. 17.
67 Segal 1982 pp. 340–1.
68 Musurillo 1966 pp. 300 and 309.
69 Girard 1988 (1972) p. 235.
70 Girard 1988 (1972) pp. 139–41.
71 Versnel 1998 p. 173.
72 Versnel 1998 pp. 131–7.

Chapter 8

1 Thucydides 8.63.3 ff.
2 Thucydides 8. 69.4 ff.
3 Thucydides 8.65.
4 Thucydides 8.73.
5 Andocides *De Mysteriis* 95–98,
6 Xenophon *Hellenika* 1.4.12-20; Plutarch *Life of Alkibiades* 33–34.
7 Xenophon *Hellenika* 1.4.18-19.
8 Lysias 13.12.
9 Xenophon *Hellenica*, 2.2.3, 2.2.10.
10 Thucydides 5.116.4.
11 Aristophanes *Frogs* 33. Cf. Hellanikos' fragments, Fr. 80, p. 56 *Fragmenta Historicorum Graecorum* Müller.
12 Cf. Chantraine 2000 vol. II p. 926 ad loc., and LSJ ad loc., oppose the term to ἄστυ, which denotes the physical dwelling place of a community.

13 The secession of women from the community on political grounds is also the theme of Aristophanes' *Lysistrata* and *Thesmophoriazousae*. A comparative study of the role of the mystical community of women in *Bacchae* and these plays awaits serious treatment, further to Levine 1987.
14 Norwood 1905, pp. 434–5.
15 Dodds 1960 (1944) n. ad loc.
16 See Alcaeus Fr. 208, part of a body of work significantly known as *Stasiotika*, where he compares the state of his polis of Mytilene to a ship in a storm. 'I fail to understand the turmoil (*stasis*) of the winds: one wave rolls in from this side, another from that, and we in the middle are carried along in company with our black ship, much distressed in the great storm' (ἀσυννέτημμι τῶν ἀνέμων στάσιν· / τὸ μὲν γὰρ ἔνθεν κῦμα κυλίνδεται, / τὸ δ' ἔνθεν, ἄμμες δ' ὂν τὸ μέσσον / ναΐ φορήμμεθα σὺν μελαίνᾳ / χείμωνι μόχθεντες μεγάλῳ μάλα·).
17 On the subject of the enemies of the polis in *Frogs* see 8.5.
18 Aristophanes' satirical portraits of democratic leaders should not of course be taken at face value: the disparagement of political adversaries was common in Old Comedy. Cf for instance the description of Cleon in *Wasps* 1030 ff. and *Knights* 217–9, 247–249, 258–263, 303–312 etc. and the abuse of Cleophon, soon to be a victim of oligarchs, in *Frogs* 679, 1504, 1532–1533.
19 On the characteristics of the *kaloi kai agathoi* see Finley 1973 p. 19.
20 See for instance Herodotus well-known depiction of the figure of the tyrant in the Otanes' speech (3.80); Aeschylus' anti-tyrannical stance includes *Persae*, where he contrasts Athenian democracy with Persian tyranny as Athenians are not slaves (δοῦλοι) or subjects (ὑπήκοοι) to anybody, and for this reason are stronger in arms than the army of people subject to tyranny (242–244); Sophocles' *Antigone* (507), where the tyrant Creon has unchecked freedom of action and has a great greed for money (1056); Euripides' *Heracles* (141, 251), where the relationship between the tyrant and the Heraklids is that of master and slaves; Sophocles' *Ajax*, where Agamemnon declares 'it is not easy for a tyrant to be pious (εὐσεβεῖν)' (1350); Sophocles' famous second stasimon of *Oedipos Tyrannus*, where the tyrant and his impious hubris are the ruin of the polis (873–896) etc. Cf. Lanza 1977, particularly chapters 2 and 4 and Seaford 2003.
21 Raaflaub 2003 p. 59.
22 Mitchell 2013 p. 162.
23 Henderson 2003 p. 156.
24 On its location cf. Azoulay 2017 (2014) pp. 36–7.
25 See for a full treatment of the subject Azoulay 2017 (2014).
26 Azoulay 2017 (2014) pp. 6–7.

27 Andocides *De Mysteriis* 95–97. The *Constitution of the Athenians* 8.4 refers to a similar law promoted by Solon.
28 Attributed to Drako by Ostwald 1955 pp. 103–28, Rhodes 1993 (1981) pp. 220–1 lists in chronological order the evidence of the legislation.
29 Andocides *De Mysteriis* 95–98.
30 *Constitution of Athenians* 16.10.
31 Andocides *De Mysteriis* 97.
32 Lycurgus *Against Leokrates* 79.
33 Andocides *De Mysteriis* 98.
34 Shear 2007 pp. 148–60.
35 The *Proagon* (Pre-contest) took place in the building next to the theatre of Dionysus, the Odeion. There the playwright, accompanied by his actors and members of the chorus, would present to the public the new play they intended to compete with at the festival of Dionysus.
36 Hansen 1988 p. 12.
37 *Constitution of the Athenians* 7.1.
38 Sourvinou-Inwood 2003 pp. 92–8, Seaford 2012 pp. 79–85, Shear 2007 p. 157.
39 Thucydides 1.98. Cf. Thompson and Wycherley 1972 pp. 94–6.
40 Thompson and Wycherley 1972 p. 132.
41 When the Plataeans sought the protection of the Athenians from the Thebans they came to Athens while the polis was performing sacrifices at the Altar. There they sat down at the Altar and offered themselves to the Athenians. See Herodotus 6.108.4.
42 Cf. for instance Herodotus 2.7.1.
43 Xenophon for instance in *Hipparchicus* 3.2 recommends the head of the cavalry to parade around the agora during festivals starting at the Herms and around the Altar of the Twelve Gods, as the chorus would do at the Dionysia.
44 Sourvinou-Inwood 2003 pp. 69–70, Wilson 2000 p. 135 n. 34.
45 Pindar fr. 75. I believe that the context of this dithyramb is definitely the *xenismos* at the Altar of the Twelve Gods, as the only occasion of the altar coming into play was during the Dionysia. Furthermore, Pindar refers to the unnamed altar as the navel of Athens, which is further evidence he referred to this altar. Cf. Sourvinou-Inwood 2003 pp. 96–8.
46 Morwood 2007 p. 27.
47 Morwood 2007 pp. 20–2.
48 FGrHist. 239AI2-15, in Robertson 1996 p. 320.
49 Sourvinou-Inwood 2003 pp. 313–4.
50 'Le mot κράτος, qui relève d'une racine exprimant la notion de "dureté", signifie "force", notamment force physique qui permet de triompher', Chantraine 1990 (1968) p. 578.

51 Segal 1982a pp. 82-3.
52 Heraclitus fr. 43 D-K.
53 Thucydides 6.15.
54 Sophocles *Oedipus Tyrannus* 872.
55 Aristophanes in *Frogs* does not use the noun 'demagogue', and only uses the verb once (419), to mean simply 'to lead the demos'.
56 Thucydides 2.65.7-11, cf. also the *Constitution of the Athenians* 28.3.
57 Aristophanes had used a similar religious formula, a curse (ἀρά), in *Thesmophoriazousae* (331-351) to invoke the gods against a comical mix of people whom the women of Athens are opposed to, combining would be tyrants and their abetters with deceiving lovers and cheating prostitutes.
58 Isocrates *Panegyricus* 157 describes the ritual of the proclamation by the Eumolpidae and Kerykes barring all barbarians and those guilty of murder from the sacred mystical rituals of Eleusis. See also Foucart 1914 pp. 308-13, Mylonas 1962 p. 247 n. 116, Parker 1983 pp. 281-6.
59 In *Bacchae*, Euripides shares Aristophanes' denunciation of the catastrophic effects of giving heed to the powers of persuasion of political orators. In *Bacchae* (270-271), in what may well be Euripides' direct address to Athenians, Tiresias too warns the polis on the dangers a community faces when under the influence of a bold man with a fluent tongue, (δυνατὸς καὶ λέγειν οἷός), but no sense, as he is a bad citizen. This political warning is made stronger by being emphasized by the chorus with a triple alpha privative definition a few lines later: disaster (δυστυχία), is the result of intemperate mouths (ἀχαλίνων στομάτων), and of lawless folly (ἀνόμου τ' ἀφροσύνας) (386-8). Perhaps this was a traditional notion: cf. Sophocles' *Antigone* 127-128: 'Ζεὺς μεγάλης γλώσσης κόμπους ὑπερεχθαίρει'.
60 For an analysis of the impact of coinage on the development of the polis see Seaford 2004.
61 Seaford 2003a p. 97.
62 Chantraine 2000 ad loc.
63 Homer *Iliad* 10.223-226.
64 Solon fr. 4.

Chapter 9

1 Demeter, writes the author of the Derveni Papyrus quoting an earlier Orphic theogony, was the same deity as Rhea, Ge, Meter, Hestia, Deio: Derveni Papyrus Column XXII 11-12: 'ἔστι δὲ καὶ ἐν τοῖς Ὕμνοις εἰρ[η]μένον· "Δημήτηρ [Ρ]έα Γῆ Μήτηρ Ἑστία Δηιώι"'. Kouremenos 2006 pp. 105 and 137.

2 Related for instance in Herodotus 4.76.4.
3 Plato *Ion* 533d-534a, translation Lamb 1925.
4 Cf. Herodotus 8.45.
5 Graf and Johnston 2013 pp. 66–93.
6 West 2003 pp. 109–33.
7 Fragment 27, West 2003 p. 245–6: 'διδαχθεὶς τὰς τελετὰς καὶ λαβὼν πᾶσαν παρὰ τῆς θεοῦ τὴν διασκευήν.'
8 Tablet 28, in Graf and Johnston 2013 pp. 38–9. It should be noted that the term 'Bacchus' was reconstructed as a conjecture.
9 Pindar *Isthmian Odes* 7. 1–5.
10 Sophocles *Antigone* 1115–1121.
11 Callimachus *Hymn to Demeter* 69–70.
12 Strabo 10.3.10.
13 Clinton 1992 p. 125.
14 Clinton 1992 p. 125.
15 'The recent reassessment of both the archaeological and literary evidence has established firm Dionysiac connection with Eleusis already in the sixth century BC', Versnel 1998 p. 153 with sources; also, Seaford 1994 pp. 263, 381–2.
16 ABV 331/13. Currently at Musée Livenel in Compiègne.
17 Reggio Calabria, National Archaeological Museum. As Sourvinou-Inwood 1978 pp. 108–9 interestingly notes, the presence of pomegranates among the terracotta fruit found at Locri attests a Locrian knowledge of the *Homeric Hymn to Demeter*. Persephone's cockerel is also related to Hades and the underworld: see Cosentino 2016 pp. 189–212.
18 Carpenter 1997 pp. 90–1.
19 Mark 1984 p. 291, Carpenter 1997 pp. 90–1.
20 Clinton 1992, pp. 124–5. The evidence is in four vase paintings of the fifth century: a *hydria* from Crete currently at the National Museum in Athens (n. 1443), a *hydria* from Capua currently in the museum of Lyon, a volute crater in Stanford University Museum of Arts attributed to the Cleophon painter (70.12, Beazley n. 8110), and a *skyphos* attributed to the painter Makron at the British Museum (Reg. n. 1873,0820.375, Beazley n. 204683).
21 Pausanias 1.2.4.
22 The only classical source is the scholiast to Lucian 279-81. See Parker 1979 p. 256–7.
23 Plutarch *Life of Demetrius* 12.1.
24 Apollodoros 3.14.7.
25 Seaford 1994 pp. 250–7. Seaford 2012 pp. 36–8.

26 On the subject of Dionysus coming to Greek cities as *xenos* see also Lada-Richards 1999 pp. 123–5; Petridou 2015 pp. 302–5
27 Pickard-Cambridge 1968 (1953) p. 57.
28 Seaford 1994 p. 241.
29 Seaford 1994 pp. 7–10.
30 Massenzio 1969 p. 56; see also Seaford 1994 pp. 301–5.
31 In myth, the dominant kinship relationship of women is with their fathers, which also gives them their collective name (Proitides, Minyades) and comes above their relationship as individuals, sisters, wives and mothers: Massenzio 1969 p. 95.
32 The *hierophant* showed an ear of corn to the congregation at the very acme of the ritual, 'the mighty, and marvellous, and most perfect secret suitable for one initiated into the highest mystical truths: an ear of grain in silence reaped' (ἐν σιωπῇ τεθερισμένον στάχυν): Hippolytus *Refutatio Omnium Haeresium* 5.3.
33 See Isocrates *Panegyricus* 28: 'When Demeter came to our land, ... she gave these two gifts, the greatest in the world – the fruits of the earth, which have enabled us to rise above the life of the beasts, and the holy rite (τὴν τελετήν) which inspires in those who partake of it sweeter hopes regarding both the end of life and all eternity.' See also Apollodoros *Bibliotheca* 1. 32, Callimachus *Hymn 6 to Demeter* 17 ff.
34 Mair 1921 p. 31.
35 Callimachus *Hymn to Demeter* 134–7.
36 Herodotus 8.65.
37 The number of 30,000 cannot be interpreted literally as some scholars do; it often simply indicated a great multitude: see for instance the number applied to the voting demos in Herodotus 5.97, and a numerous troop in 2.163; cf. also Aeschylus *Persians* 315, Aristophanes *Birds* 1179.
38 Cf. Turner 1987 p. 55.
39 Sommerstein 1997 p. 170 n. 155.
40 Where Aphrodite describes Hippolytus going to watch and celebrate Demeter's mysteries (σεμνῶν ἐς ὄψιν καὶ τέλη μυστηρίων). See Seaford 1996, n. ad loc.
41 *Orphic Hymns* 45 and 52.
42 Parker 1983 p. 227.
43 The mystical connotation of the passage has been largely ignored by commentators. Winnington-Ingram 1948 p.85 for instance thinks that 'earthquake, volcano, flood and fire are as truly part of nature as flowers and woods, as milk and honey ... nature in her fury'.
44 Reinstating the manuscript reading φῶς. Cf. Seaford 1996 n. ad loc.
45 Calame 2004 pp. 158–61.

46 Henrichs 1994-5 p. 68.
47 Ferrari 1979 p. 79.
48 Ferrari 1979 p. 70, Seaford 1996 n. 64-169 pp. 155-6, Sommerstein 1997 p. 184 n. 323-53.
49 Stanford 1958 p. 101 n. ad loc., Dover 1993 n. ad loc. 235-6, Seaford 1996 pp. 155-6 n. ad loc.
50 Cf. Sommerstein 1997 p. 184.
51 A similar cultic definition of sacred and easy pain in the sacred service of Dionysus can be found in Euripides' *Ion* 128, 131, 134-135.
52 Stehle 2004 p.130.
53 Aristophanes uses *euphemia* formulae in in other plays, see *Acharnians* 237, 241, *Peace* 1316, and Euripides in *Ion* 98 with nearly identical wording. See Ferrari 1979 pp. 69-70.
54 Cameron 1970 pp. 95-118, Burkert 1985 (1977) pp. 250-4.
55 Seaford 1996 p. 155.
56 Dodds 1960 (1944) p. 75 n. 68-70, notes the similarity, commenting that Aristophanes in *Frogs* uses the formula as a parody. In view of the seriousness and centrality in the play of the parodos' *prorrhesis*, I would doubt this.
57 Aristophanes had used a similar religious formula, a curse (ἀρά), in *Thesmophoriazousae* (331-351) to invoke the gods against a comical mix of people whom the women of Athens are opposed to, combining would be tyrants and their abetters with deceiving lovers and cheating prostitutes.
58 Cf. the *Homeric Hymn to Demeter* 480: 'Happy is he among men upon earth who has seen these mysteries' (ὄλβιος, ὅς τάδ' ὄπωπεν ἐπιχθονίων ἀνθρώπων). Other instances of mystical *makarismoi* are in for instance Pindar fr. 137: 'Blessed is he who sees them [the Eleusinian mysteries] and goes beneath the earth:he knows the end of life and knows it is a Zeus-given beginning' (ὄλβιος ὅστις ἰδὼν κεῖν' εἶσ' ὑπὸ χθόν'·/οἶδε μὲν βίου τελευτάν/οἶδεν δὲ διόσδοτον ἀρχάν), and Sophocles fr. 837: 'Thrice blessed are thtose among mortals who have seen these ritualsbefore going to Hades, for they alone have life there, while others have every kind of misery' (ὡς τρισόλβιοι/κεῖνοι βροτῶν, οἳ ταῦτα δερχθέντες τέλη/μόλωσ' ἐς Ἅιδου· τοῖσδε γὰρ μόνοις ἐκεῖ/ζῆν ἔστι, τοῖς δ' ἄλλοισι πάντ' ἔχειν κακά).
59 Cf. Bernabé 1996 p. 17.
60 Plato *Euthydemus* 277.
61 Plato *Cratinus* 406c.
62 Cf. Aristophanes *Wasps* 1361-1363.
63 Cf. Halliwell 2008 pp. 155-214.
64 Scholars have been discussing extensively the term τὸ σοφὸν and σοφία and their meaning in *Bacchae*, see Willink 1966 pp. 229-31, Cropp 1981 pp. 39-42,

Leinieks 1984 pp. 178-9, pp. 39-42, Reynolds-Warnhoff 1997 pp. 77-103, Schein 2016 pp. 257-73.
65 Leinieks 1984 pp. 178-9.
66 Arthur 1972 pp. 159-79.
67 Willink 1966 p. 230 n. 3: 'We should not repine at our inability to find a perfect equivalent: the whole point is that τὸ σοφόν is an "unknown" which it is one purpose of the drama to evaluate.'
68 See Seaford 1996 pp. 169-70 n. ad loc.
69 For its use to define the state of quiet of the Pythagorean initiates see Lucian *Vitarum Auctio* 3. See also Seaford 1996 p. 183 n. 389-9.
70 This use of the term σοφία is not uncommon in Euripides, cf. for instance *Heraclidae* 615.
71 An echo perhaps of Protagoras' famous note on the difficulty of exploring the nature of divinity in Diogenes Laërtius 9.8.
72 In Euripides, a similar connection between mystical rituals, peace, prosperity and their opposites, *stasis* and strife, can also be found in fragment 453 of his tragedy *Cresphontes*, where he calls Peace βαθύπλουτε, identifying her with mystical rituals (καλλιχόρους ἀοιδὰς/φιλοστεφάνους τε κώμους), invoking her to ban the enemy, *stasis* (ἐχθρὰ Στάσις), and raging strife, (μαινομένα Ἔρις) from homes.
73 An old proverb, cf. Theognis 15-18.
74 Central to the choral messages of *Bacchae*, the concept of εὐδαιμονία is often misinterpreted by scholars who have been consciously or unconsciously under the influence of Nietzsche's vision. De Romilly 1963 pp. 361-80 writes of εὐδαιμονία as an essentially irrational, emotional liberation, 'un bonheur d'évasion', and misses entirely the relationship between εὐδαιμονία and the religious/political implications of *Bacchae*'s choral odes.
75 Dodds 1960 (1944) n. ad loc.
76 In this sense used by Pindar *Pythian* 8, 1-12. An association echoed by Plato in *Menexenus* 243e-244b.
77 Dodds 1960 (1944), n. ad loc.
78 Cf. Plato *Phaedrus* 247d, 250b-c. The most complete study of the notion of σωφροσύνη in Greek literature is still, I believe, North 2019 (1966).
79 A concept that accompanied the development of the collective sentiment of the polis. See Heraclitus fr. 43: hubris needs to be extinguished more than a house on fire (ὕβριν χρὴ σβεννύναι μᾶλλον ἢ πυρκαϊήν).
80 Seaford 1994 p. 405.
81 See Seaford 1996 p. 183 n. 389-9.
82 For instance, Homer *Iliad* 1.16; 1.375.

83 Thucydides 1.84.3.
84 Homer *Iliad* 16.130ff. and 19.369ff.
85 Seaford 1988 p. 134.
86 Dodds 1960 (1944) p. 198 n. ad loc.
87 Damen and Richards 2012 p. 365, n. 72.
88 Bernabé 1996 p. 17.
89 Winnington-Ingram 1948 pp. 176–8.
90 Dodds 1960 (1944) pp. 128–30 n. 430–3.
91 Musurillo 1966 pp. 299–309.
92 Seaford 1996 n. 430 p. 185.
93 Di Benedetto 2004 pp. 107–14.
94 See Buckley 1850 ad loc., Sandys 1880 p. 872 n. ad loc., Murray 1904 ad loc., Grube 1935 ad loc.
95 Dodds 1960 (1944) pp. 186–8.
96 Nagy in Buckley 1850 revision.
97 Vellacott 1973 p. 223.
98 Kovacs 2002 p. 97.
99 Di Benedetto 2004 p. 241.
100 Mills 2006 pp. 45, 70.
101 Winnington-Ingram 1948 p. 113.
102 Winnington-Ingram 1966 p. 35.
103 Blake 1933 pp. 361–8. 'What is what is wise? Or what is the most beautiful gift of the gods to mortals? Is it to keep one's winning hand over the heads of one's enemies? What is beautiful and honest is always dear'.
104 Roux 1972 II pp. 514–17.
105 Leinieks 1984 pp. 178–9.
106 See Seaford's commentary on his restoration of the text and translation, in Seaford 1994 pp. 402–4, and Seaford 1996 pp. 218–19.
107 To Seaford's various examples I would be tempted to add Sappho's answer to the same question in fr. 16, on the nature of ἐπὶ γᾶν μέλαιναν κάλλιστον that concludes it is not armies or fleets, but whomever one loves.

Chapter 10

1 The character is mocked in *Frogs* 679, 1504 and 1532–1533 and his trial is mentioned by Lysias *In Nicomachum* 10–11 and *In Agoratum* 8–12. On Aristophanes' aristocratic opinions see for instance de Ste. Croix 1972 pp. 355–76.

2 The term 'mixed together' (μιγάς) suggests also mixed marriages, and mixed blood progenies.
3 See Seaford 1996 p. 151 n. ad loc. See also Roux 1972 p. 247 n. ad loc.
4 Cf. Aristotle *Poetica* 1449a defining comedy as being μίμησις φαυλοτέρων.
5 See Thucydides1.124; Plutarch *Theseus* 24.2. Cf also Plato *Laws* 777 d-e.
6 Stanford 1958 pp. 112–3 n. 454–9.
7 As for instance in *Lysistrata* 1114–77.
8 Xenophon, *Hellenica*, 1.6.24.
9 Stanford 1958 p. 131 n. 686 who focuses on Aristophanes' plea on behalf of the oligarchs as 'perhaps some of Aristophanes' friends were among those he pleads for'. Dover 1993 pp. 73–6 and Sommerstein 1997 pp. 19–22 focus on the political success of the play and on its effect on Patrocleides' decree. Wiles 2011 p. 40, rightly calls the revival of the play because of its parabasis alone 'a detail that sounds like a scholarly surmise'. See also McGlew 2002 pp. 163–70 for a discussion on the passage and the critique of some scholars' interpretations.
10 De Ste. Croix 1972 pp. 372, 375.
11 De Ste. Croix 1972 p. 371.
12 Kovacs, 2002 p. 203.
13 Xenophon *Hellenica* 2.4.20.
14 Xenophon *Hellenica* 3.1.1.
15 As convincingly reconstructed by Seaford 1996 pp. 252–3 n. ad loc.
16 Seaford 1996 pp. 252–3 n. ad loc.
17 Dover 1993 pp. 383–4 n. 1528–33.
18 Sommerstein 1997 p. 298, n. 1525 and 1528–33.
19 Lada-Richard 1999 pp. 326–9.
20 Seaford 2012 p. 276.
21 Sells 2012 pp. 91–4.
22 I believe that the reference here is not the war with Sparta as most interpreters would have it, but to *stasis* as in *Thesmophoriazusai* 788: στάσις ἀργαλέα.

References

Acker, C. (2002), *Dionysus en Transe: La voix des femmes*, Paris, L'Harmattan.

Agres, K., Bigo, L., Herremans D. (2019), 'The Impact of Musical Structure on Enjoyment and Absorptive Listening States in Trance Music', in Clarke, D. and Clarke, E., pp. 254-70.

Ahrlichs, J.J., Riehle, K., Sultanieva, N. (2015), 'The Production of Liminal Places – An Interdisciplinary Account', EAZ, Waxmann, pp. 205-42.

Alderink, L.J. (1982), 'Mythical and Cosmological Structure of the Homeric Hymn to Demeter', *Numen*, Vol. 29, pp. 1-16.

Alexander, E. (2012), *Proof of Heaven: A Neurosurgeon's Journey into the Afterlife*, New York, Simon & Schuster.

Allan, W., Kelly, A. (2013), 'Listening to Many Voices; Athenian Tragedy as a Popular Art', in Marmodoro, A., and Hill, J. (eds.).

Anderson, W.D. (1994), *Music and Musicians in Ancient Greece*, Ithaca, Cornell University Press.

Andrewes, A. (1953), 'The Generals in the Hellespont', *The Journal of Hellenic Studies*, Vol. 73, pp. 2-9.

Andrewes, A. (1974), 'The Arginusae Trial', *Phoenix*, Vol. 28, pp. 112-22.

Andrewes, A. (1992), 'The Spartan Resurgence', *The Cambridge Ancient History*, Vol. 5, pp. 464-96.

Arthur, M. (1972), *The Choral Odes of the* Bacchae *of Euripides*, Yale Classical Studies, pp. 159-65, 176-9.

Asmonti, L.A. (2006), 'The Arginusae Trial, the Changing Role of "Strategoi" and the Relationship between Demos and Military Leadership in Late Fifth-Century Athens', *Bulletin of the Institute of Classical Studies*, Vol. 49, pp. 1-21.

Azoulay, V. (2017, originally published 2014), *The Tyrant-Slayers of Ancient Athens*, Oxford, Oxford University Press.

Azoulay, V. (2014), 'Repolitiser la cite grecque, trente ans après', *Annales, Histoire, Sciences Sociales*, pp. 689-719.

Bacigalupo, A.M. (2005), 'Gendered Rituals for Cosmic Order: Mapuche Shamanic Struggles for Wholeness', *Journal of Ritual Studies*, Vol. 19, pp. 53-69.

Beer, D.G. (1981), 'Tyranny, *Anarkhia*, and the Problems of the Boule in the Oresteia', *Florilegium*, Vol. 3, pp. 47-71.

Benveniste, E. (1969), *Le vocabulaire des institutions indo-européennes*, 2 vols, Paris, Les Éditions de Minuit.

Bérard, C. and Bron, C. (1986), 'Bacchos au cœur de la cité. Le thiase dionysiaque dans l'espace politique', *L'association dionysiaque dans les sociétés anciennes*, Rome, École française de Rome.

Berent, M. (1998), 'Stasis, or the Greek Invention of Politics', *History of Political Thought*, Vol. 19, pp. 331–62.

Bernabé, A. (1996), 'La formula orfica "Cerrad las puertas, profanos"', *'Ilu*, Vol. 1, pp. 14–37.

Bernabé, A. (2007), *Poetae Epici Graeci*, Pars II, Berlin, de Gruyter.

Bierl, A.F.H. (1991), *Dionysus und die Griechische Tragödie*, Tübingen, Gunter Narr.

Bierl, A. (2009, originally presented as the University thesis 1998), *Ritual and Performativity, The Chorus in Ancient Comedy*, Center of Hellenic Studies, Harvard University.

Billings, J., Budelmann, F., Macintosh, F. (2013), *Choruses, Ancient and Modern*, Oxford, Oxford University Press.

Bishop, P. and Gardner, L. (2018), *The Ecstatic and the Archaic*, London, Routledge.

Blake, W.E. (1933), 'Euripidis Baccharum interpretatio secundum versus 877-881', *Mnemosyne*, Vol. 60, pp. 361–8.

Bourguignon, E. (1973), *Religion, Altered States of Consciousness and Social Change*, Columbus, Ohio University Press.

Bowden, H. (2004), 'Xenophon and the Scientific Study of Religion', in Tuplin, C. and Azoulay, V., pp. 229–46.

Bowden, H. (2010), *Mystery Cults in the Ancient World*, London, Thames & Hudson.

Bowie, A.M. (1993), *Aristophanes, Myth, Ritual and Comedy*, Cambridge, Cambridge University Press.

Brelich, A. (1969), *Paides e Parthenoi*, Rome, Edizioni dell'Ateneo.

Bremmer, J.N. (2014), *Initiation into the Mysteries of the Ancient World*, Berlin/Boston, de Gruyter

Buckley, T.W.A. (1850), *Euripides' Bacchae*, London, Bohn.

Burkert, W. (1983, originally published 1972), *Homo Necans*, Berkeley, University of California Press.

Burkert, W. (1985, originally published 1977), *Greek Religion*, Oxford, Blackwell.

Burkert, W. (1987), *Ancient Mystery Cults*, Cambridge, Harvard University Press.

Cairns, D. (2016), 'Mind, Body and Metaphor in Ancient Greek Concepts of Emotion', *L'Atelier du centre de recherche historique*, Vol. 16, pp. 2–17.

Calame, C. (2001, original edition 1977), *Choruses of Young Women in Ancient Greece*, Oxford, Rowan & Littlefield.

Calame, C. (2004), 'Choral Forms in Aristophanic Comedy', in Murray, P. and Wilson, P. (eds.), *Music and the Muses, the Culture of Mousike in the Classical Athenian City*, Oxford, Oxford University Press.

Cameron H.D. (1970) 'The Power of Words in the Seven against Thebes', *Transactions and Proceedings of the American Philological Association*, Vol. 101, pp. 95–118.

Cantarella, R. (1974) 'Dioniso, fra Baccanti e Rane', in Heller, J.L. (ed.) *Serta Turyniana*, Chicago, University of Illinois Press, pp. 291–310.

Carpenter, T.H. and Faraone, C.A. (eds.) (1993), *Masks of Dionysus*, Ithaca, Cornell University Press.

Carpenter, T.H. (1997), *Dionysiac Imagery in Fifth-Century Athens*, Oxford, Clarendon Press.

Carrière, J. (1966) 'Sur le message des *Bacchantes*', *L'Antiquité Classique*, Fasc. 1, pp. 118–39.

Carter, D.M. (2011), *Why Athens? A Reappraisal of Tragic Politics*, Oxford, Oxford University Press.

Cavanaugh, M.B. (1996), *Eleusis and Athens: Documents in Finance, Religion and Politics in the Fifth Century B.C.*, Atlanta, Scholars Press.

Chantraine, P. (1990, originally published 1968), *Dictionnaire de la langue grecque*, Paris, Klincksieck.

Christopoulos, M., Karakantza, E.D. and Levaniouk, O. (eds.) (2010), *Light and Darkness in Ancient Greek Myth and Religion*, Lanham/Plymouth, Lexington Books.

Clinton, K. (1974), 'The Sacred Officials of the Eleusinian Mysteries', *Transactions of the American Philosophical Society*, Vol. 64, pp. 1–143.

Clinton, K. (1992), *Myth and Cult, the Iconography of the Eleusinian Mysteries*, Athens, Svenska Institutet.

Clinton, K. (2004), 'Epiphany in the Eleusinian Mysteries', *Illinois Classical Studies*, Vol. 29, pp. 85–109.

Connor, W.R. (1984), *Thucydides*, Princeton, Princeton University Press.

Cosentino, A. (2016), 'Persephone's Cockerel', in Johnston, P.A., Mastrocinque, A., Papayoannou, S. (eds.), *Animals in Greek and Roman Religion*, Cambridge, Cambridge Scholars Publishing, pp. 189–212.

Cosmopoulos, M.B. (2003) (ed.), *Greek Mysteries*, Abingdon, Routledge.

Cosmopoulos, M.B. (2015), *Bronze Age Eleusis and the Origins of the Eleusinian Mysteries*, Cambridge, Cambridge University Press.

Crawley Quinn, J. (2007), 'Herms, Kouroi and the Political Anatomy of Athens', *Greece and Rome*, Vol. 54, pp. 82–105.

Cropp, M. (1981), 'ΤΙ ΤΟ ΣΟΦΟΝ?', *Bulletin of the Institute of Classical Studies*, N. 28, pp. 39–42.

Csapo, E. (1997), 'Riding the Phallus for Dionysus: Iconology, Ritual and Gender/Role De/Construction', *Phoenix*, Vol. 51, pp. 253–95.

Csapo, E. (2013), 'The Dionysian Parade and the Poetica of Plenitude', *UCL Housman Lecture*, pp. 1–36.

Csapo, E. and Slater, W.J. (1994), *The Context of Ancient Drama*, Ann Arbor, Michigan University Press.

Damen, M.L., Richards, R.A. (2012), '"Sing the Dionysus": Euripides' *Bacchae* as a Dramatic Hymn', *The American Journal of Philology*, Vol. 133, pp. 343–69.

Daraki, M. (1985), *Dionysus et la Déesse Terre*, Paris, Flammarion.

De Cazenove, O. (ed.) (1986), *L'Association Dionysiaque dans les Sociétés Anciennes*, Rome, École Française de Rome.

De Martino, E. (1959), *La terra del rimorso*, Milan, Il Saggiatore.

De Polignac, F. (1995, originally published 1984), *Cults, Territory, and the Origins of the Greek City-State*, Chicago and London, University of Chicago Press.

De Romilly, J. (1963), 'Le thème du bonheur dans les Bacchantes', *Revue des Études Grecques*, Vol. 76, pp. 361–80.

De Ste Croix, G. E.M. (1972), *The Origins of the Peloponnesian War*, London, Duckworth.

Devine, A.M., Stephens, L.D. (1993), 'Evidence of Experimental Psychology for the Rhythm and Metre of Greek Verse', *Transactions of the American Philological Association*, Vol. 123, pp. 379–403.

Di Benedetto, V. (2004), *Le Baccanti*, Milan, Rizzoli.

Dillery, J. (1993), 'Xenophon's "Poroi" and Athenian Imperialism', *Historia: Zeitschrift für Alte Geschichte*, Bd. 42, pp. 1–11.

Dillery, J. (1995), *Xenophon and the History of His Times*, Abingdon, Routledge.

Dillon, M. (2001), *Girls and Women in Classical Greek Religion*, Cambridge, Routledge.

Dodds, E.R. (1940), 'Maenadism in the *Bacchae*', *The Harvard Theological Review*, Vol. 33, pp. 155–76.

Dodds, E.R. (1960, first edition 1944), *Euripides* Bacchae, Oxford, Clarendon Press.

Dover, K. (1993), *Aristophanes* Frogs, Oxford, Clarendon Press.

Edmonds III, R.G. (2004), *Myths of the Underworld Journey*, Cambridge, Cambridge University Press.

Eliade, M. (1994, originally published 1958), *Rites and Symbols of Initiation*, Putnam, Spring Publications.

Fairweather, J. (1974), 'Fiction in the Biographies of Ancient Writers', *Ancient Society*, Vol. 5, pp. 231–75.

Felton, D. (2014), 'The Motif of the "Mutilated Hero" in Herodotus', *Phoenix*, Vol. 68, pp. 47–61.

Fenwick, P. and Fenwick, E. (1996), *The Truth in the Light*, Guildford, White Crow Books.
Ferrari, F. (1979), 'La parodo delle *Baccanti*: moduli e composizione', *Quaderni Urbinati di Cultura Classica*, Vol. 3, pp. 69–79.
Ferrari, G. (1997), 'Figures in the Text: Metaphors and Riddles in the Agamemnon', *Classical Philology*, Vol. 92, pp. 1–45.
Finkelberg, M. (2006), 'The City Dionysia and the Social Space of Attic Tragedy', *Bulletin of the Institute of Classical Studies*, pp. 17–26 n. 87.
Finley, M.I. (2019, originally published 1973), *Democracy, Ancient and Modern*, New Brunswick, Rutgers.
Fisher, N. (2000), 'Hybris, Revenge and Stasis in the Greek City-States', in Van Wees (ed.), pp. 83–123.
Foley, H.P. (1980, drawn from her 1975 Harvard doctoral dissertation), 'The Masque of Dionysus', *Transactions of the American Philological Association*, Vol. 110, pp. 107–33.
Foley, H.P. (1985), *Ritual Irony, Poetry and Sacrifice in Euripides*, Ithaca, Cornell University Press.
Foley, H.P. (1994), *Homeric Hymn to Demeter*, Princeton, Princeton University Press.
Foley, H.P. (2003), 'Choral Identity in Greek Tragedy', *Classical Philology*, Vol. 98, pp. 1–30.
Foucart, P. (1914), *Les Mystères d'Éleusis*, Chartres, Picard.
Friedrich, R. (1996), 'Everything to Do with Dionysus? Ritualism, the Dionysiac and the Tragic' in Silk, M.S. (ed.) 1996.
Friesen, C.J.P. (2015), *Reading Dionysus*, Tubingen, Mohr Siebeck.
Furley, W.D. (1996), 'Andocides and the Herms: A Study of Crisis in fifth-century Athenian Religion', *Bulletin of the Institute of Classical Studies*, Supplement N. 65, pp. 1–162.
Fyfe, W.H. (1932), *Aristotle* Poetica, Cambridge, Harvard University Press.
Gagné, R. (2009), 'Mystery Inquisitors: Performance, Authority, and Sacrilege at Eleusis', *Classical Antiquity*, Vol. 28, pp. 211–47.
Gagné, R. and Govers Hopman, M. (eds.) (2013), *Choral Mediations in Greek Tragedy*, Cambridge, Cambridge University Press.
Gantz, T.N. (1977), 'The Fires of the Oresteia', *The Journal of Hellenic Studies*, Vol. 97, pp. 28–38.
Girard, R. (1988, originally published 1972), *Violence and the Sacred*, trans. P. Gregory, London, Continuum.
Gish, D. (2012), 'Defending *demokratia*: Athenian Justice and the Trial of the Arginusae Generals in Xenophon's Hellenica', in Hobden F. and Tuplin, C. (eds.), *Xenophon, Ethical Principles and Historical Enquiry*, Leiden-Boston, Brill, pp. 161–212.

Goff, B. (2004), *Citizen Bacchae*, Berkeley, University of California Press.

Golder, H. (1996), 'Making a Scene: Gesture, Tableau, and the Tragic Chorus', *Arion*, Vol. 4, pp. 1–19.

Goldhill, S. (1987), 'The Great Dionysia and Civic Ideology', *The Journal of Hellenic Studies*, Vol. 107, pp. 58–76.

Goldhill, S. (1994), 'Representing Democracy', in Osborne, R. and Hornblower S. (eds.), pp. 347–69.

Gomme, A.W. (1933), *The Population of Athens in the Fifth and Fourth Centuries B.C.*, Oxford, Clarendon Press.

Graf, F. and Johnston, S.I. (2013), *Ritual Texts for the Afterlife: Orpheus and the Bacchic Gold Tablets*, London, Routledge.

Gray, B. (2015), *Stasis and Stability, Exile, the Polis and Political Thought, c. 404–146 BC*, Oxford, Oxford University Press.

Gray, V. (1989), *The Character of Xenophon's* Hellenica, London, Duckworth.

Gray, V. (2003), 'Interventions and Citations in Xenophon, Hellenica and Anabasis', *The Classical Quarterly*, Vol. 53, pp. 111–23.

Griffith, M. (2011), *Aristophanes'* Frogs, Oxford, Oxford University Press.

Grote, G. (1850), *History of Greece*, London, Murray.

Grube, G.M.A. (1935), 'Dionysus in the Bacchae', *Transactions and Proceedings of the American Philological Association*, Vol. 66, pp. 37–54.

Halliwell, S. (1986), *Aristotle's* Poetica, Chicago, University of Chicago Press.

Halliwell, S. (1995), *Aristotle's* Poetica, Harvard, Harvard University Press.

Halliwell, S. (2008), *Greek Laughter: A Study of Cultural Psychology from Homer to Early Christianity*, Cambridge, Cambridge University Press.

Halliwell, S. (2015), 'Aristophanes' *Frogs* by Mark Griffith' (Review), *The Classical Journal*, Vol. 110, pp. 508–10.

Hanink, J. (2008), 'Literary Politics and Euripidean Vita', *The Cambridge Classical Journal*, Vol. 54, pp. 115–35.

Hansen, M.H. (1976), 'How Many Athenians Attended the Ecclesia?', *Greek, Roman and Byzantine Studies*, pp. 115–34.

Hansen, M.H. (1988), *Three Studies in Athenian Demography*, Copenhagen, The Royal Danish Academy of Sciences and Letters.

Hardie, A. (2004) 'Muses and Mysteries', in Murray, P. and Wilson, P., pp. 11–38.

Hau, L.I. (2016), *Moral History from Herodotus to Diodorus Siculus*, Edinburgh, Edinburgh University Press.

Headlam, W. (1906), 'The Last Scene of the *Eumenides*', *The Journal of Hellenic Studies*, Vol. 26, pp. 268–77.

Henderson, J. (1987), *Aristophanes'* Lysistrata, Oxford, Oxford University Press.

Henderson, J. (1991), 'Women and the Athenian Dramatic Festivals', *Transactions of the American Philological Association*, Vol. 121, pp. 133–47.

Henderson, J. (2002), *Aristophanes* Frogs, Harvard, Harvard University Press.

Henderson, J. (2003), 'Demos, Demagogue, Tyrant in Attic Old Comedy', in Morgan, K.A.

Henrichs, A. (1978), 'Greek Maenadism from Olympias to Messalina', *Harvard Studies in Classical Philosophy*, Vol. 82, pp. 121–60.

Henrichs, A. (1984), 'Suffering, Violence: The Modern View of Dionysus from Nietzsche to Girard', *Harvard Studies in Classical Philology*, Vol. 88, pp. 205–40.

Henrichs, A. (1990), 'Drama and Dromena: Violence and Sacrificial Metaphor in Euripides', *Harvard Studies in Classical Philosophy*, Vol 100, pp. 173–88.

Henrichs, A. (1990a), 'Between City and Country: Cultic Dimensions of Dionysus in Athens and in Attica', *Classics*, Berkeley, University of California.

Henrichs, A. (1994–5), '"Why Should I Dance?" Choral Self-Referentiality in Greek Tragedy', *Arion*, Vol. 3, pp. 56–111.

Herbert, R., Clarke, E. and Clarke D. (2019), '*Music and Consciousness 2*', Oxford, Oxford University Press.

Hopper, R.J. (1961), 'The Mines and Miners of Ancient Athens', *Greece & Rome*, Vol. 8, pp. 138–51.

Hornblower, S. (1992), 'The Religious Dimension to the Peloponnesian War, or, What Thucydides Does Not Tell Us', *Harvard Studies in Classical Philology*, Vol. 94, pp. 169–97.

Hornblower, S. (2008), *A Commentary on Thucydides*, Oxford, Oxford University Press.

Hunt, P. (2001), 'The Slaves and the Generals of Arginusae, *The American Journal of Philology*, Vol. 122, pp. 359–80.

Jeanmarie, H. (1951), *Dionysus, Histoire du culte de Bacchus*, Paris, Payot.

Jilek, W. G. (1982), 'Altered States of Consciousness in North American Ceremonials', *Ethnos* Vol. 10, pp. 326–43.

Jordan, O. (1986), 'Religion in Thucydides', *Transactions of the American Philological Association*, Vol. 116, pp. 119–47.

Kawalko-Roselli, D. (2011), *Theatre of the People. Spectators and Society in Ancient Athens*, Austin, University of Texas Press.

Keesling, C.M. (2017), *Early Greek Portraiture*, Cambridge, Cambridge University Press.

Kern, O. (1888), *De Orphei Epimenidis Pherecydidis Theogoniis Quaestione Criticae*, Berlin, Libraria Nicolai.

Konstan, D. (1986), 'Poésie, politique et rituel dans les Grenouilles d'Aristophane', in *Métis*, Vol. 1, pp. 291–308.

Kouremenos, Y., Parassoglu, G., Tsantsasanoglu, K. (eds.) (2006), *The Derveni Papyrus*, Firenze, Leo S. Olschki.
Kovacs, D. (1994), *Euripidea*, Leiden, Brill.
Kovacs, D. (2002), *Euripides Tragedies*, Harvard, Harvard University Press.
Kowalzig, B. (2007), *Singing for the Gods, Performance of Myth and Ritual in Archaic and Classical Greece*, Oxford, Oxford University Press.
Kowalzig, B. (2007a), '"And now all the world shall dance!" (Eur. *Bacch*. 114), Dionysus' Choroi between Drama and Ritual' in Csapo E. and M.C. Miller (eds.), *The Origins of Theater in Ancient Greece and Beyond*, Cambridge, Cambridge University Press.
Krentz, P. (1995), *Xenophon* Hellenica II.3.11-IV.2.8, Oxford, Aris and Phillip.
Lada-Richards, I. (1999), *Initiating Dionysus, Ritual and Theatre in Aristophanes' Frogs*, Oxford, Clarendon Press.
Lang, M.L. (1992), 'Theramenes and Arginusae', *Hermes*, Vol. 120, pp. 267–79.
Lanza, G. (1997, French translation of Italian original published in 1977), *Le tyran et son public*, Paris, Belin.
Lawler, L.B. (1927), The Maenads: 'A Contribution to the Study of the Dance in Ancient Greece', *Memoirs of the American Academy in Rome*, pp. 69–112.
Lawler, L.B. (1964), *The Dance of the Ancient Greek Theatre*, Iowa City, University of Iowa Press.
Lefkowitz, M.R. (1978), 'The Poet as Hero: Fifth-Century Autobiography and Subsequent Biographical Fiction', *The Classical Quarterly*, Vol. 28, pp. 459–69.
Lefkowitz, M.R. (1979), 'The Euripides Vita', *Greek, Roman and Byzantine Studies*, Vol. 20, pp. 187–210.
Lehmann, K. (1962), Ignorance and Search in the Villa of Mysteries', *The Journal of Roman Studies*, Vol. 52, pp. 62–8.
Leinieks, V. (1984), 'Euripides *Bacchae* 887–81=897–901', *The Journal of Hellenic Studies*, Vol. 104, pp. 178–9.
Levine, D. (1987), '*Lysistrata* and *Bacchae*: Structure, Genre, and "Women on Top"', *Helios*, Vol. 11, pp. 29–38.
Lewis, S. (ed.) (2006), *Ancient Tyranny*, Edinburgh, Edinburgh University Press.
Lewis-Williams, D. and Pearce, D. (2005), *Inside the Neolithic Mind*, London, Thames & Hudson.
Lintott, A. (1981), *Violence, Civil Strife and Revolution in the Classical City*, Baltimore, Johns Hopkins University Press.
Loraux, N. (1997), *La cité divisée*, Paris, Payot.
Loraux, N. (1997a), 'La guerre dans la famille', *Clio*, No 5, pp. 2–62.
MacDowell, D.M. (1962), *Andocides and the Mysteries*, Oxford, Clarendon Press.

MacLeod, C.W. (1982), 'Politics and the *Oresteia*', *The Society for the Promotion of Hellenic Studies*, Vol. 102, pp. 124–44.

Mair, A.W. (1921, revised edition 1955), *Callimachus Hymns and Epigrams*, Harvard, Harvard University Press.

Maiuri, A. (1931), *La Villa dei Misteri*, Rome, Libreria della Stato.

Mark, I.S. (1984), 'The Gods on the East Frieze of the Parthenon', in *Hesperia: The Journal of the American School of Classical Studies at Athens,* Vol. 53, pp. 289–342.

Marmodoro, A., Hill, J. (eds.) (2013), *The Authors' Voice in Classical and Late Antiquity*, Oxford, Oxford University Press.

Marshall, C.W. and Kovacs, G. (2008), *No Laughing Matter*, Bristol, Bristol Classical Press, 2012.

Massenzio, M. (1969), 'Cultura e crisi permanente: la "xenia" dionisiaca', *Studi e materiali di storia delle religioni* Vol. XL, pp. 27–113.

McGlew, J.F. (2002), *Citizens on Stage*, Ann Arbour, University of Michigan Press.

Michaelides, S. (1956), 'Greek Song-Dance', *Journal of the International Folk Music Council*, pp. 37–9.

Michelini, A.N. (1994), 'Political Themes in Euripides' Suppliants', *The American Journal of Philology*, Vol. 115, pp. 219–52.

Miles, M.M. (1998), 'The Athenian Agora', *The American School of Classical Studies at Athens*, pp. iii–v, vii, ix–xxii, 1–9, 11–33, 35–103, 105–85, 187–209, 211–15, 217–21, 223–33.

Mills, S. (2006), *Euripides:* Bacchae, London, Duckworth.

Mitchell, L. (2013), *The Heroic Rulers of Archaic and Classical Greece*, London, Bloomsbury.

Morgan, K.A. (ed.) (2003), *Popular Tyranny*, Austin, University of Texas Press.

Morris, I. (2005), 'The Growth of Greek Cities in the First Millennium BC', *Princeton/Stanford Working Papers in Classics*, pp. 1–29. https://www.princeton.edu/~pswpc/pdfs/morris/120509

Morwood, J. (2007), *Euripides' Suppliant Women*, Oxford, Aris and Phillips.

Murray, G.G.A. (1904), *The* Bacchae *of Euripides*, London, Allen & Unwin.

Murray, P. (1997), *Plato on Poetry*, Cambridge, Cambridge University Press.

Murray, P. and Wilson, P. (eds.) (2004), *Music and the Muses, the Culture of Mousike in the Classical Athenian City*, Oxford, Oxford University Press.

Musurillo, H. (1966), 'Euripides and Dionysiac Piety', *Transactions and Proceedings of the American Philological Association*, Vol. 97, pp. 299–309.

Mylonas, G.E. (1962), *Eleusis and the Eleusinian Mysteries*, Princeton, Princeton University Press.

Nietzsche, F. (1999, originally published 1872), *The Birth of Tragedy*, R. Speirs (trans.), Cambridge, Cambridge University Press.

Nietzsche, F. (1999a, originally published 1886), *An Attempt at Self-Criticism*, Speirs R. (trans.), Cambridge, Cambridge University Press.

North, H. (2019, originally published 1966), *Sophrosyne, Self-Knowledge and Self-Restraint in Greek Literature*, Ithaca, Cornell University Press.

Norwood, G. (1905), 'On Two Passages in the *Bacchae*', *The Classical Review*, Vol. 19, pp. 334–5.

Norwood, G. (1908), *The Riddle of the Bacchae, The Last Stage of Euripides' Religious Views*, Manchester, Manchester University Press.

Oranje, H. (1984), *Euripides' Bacchae, the Play and its Audience*, Leiden, Brill.

Osborne, R. (1985), 'The Erection and Mutilation of the Hermai', *Proceedings of the Cambridge Philological Society*, N. 211, pp. 47–73.

Osborne, R. (1987), *Classical Landscape with Figures: The Ancient Greek City and its Countryside*, London, Philip.

Osborne, R., and Hornblower, S. (eds.) (1994), *Ritual, Finance, Politics*, Oxford, Oxford University Press.

Osborne, R. (2010), *Athens and Athenian Democracy*, Cambridge, Cambridge University Press.

Ostwald, M. (1955), 'The Athenian Legislation Against Tyranny and Subversion', *Transactions and Proceedings of the American Philological Association*, Vol. 86, pp. 103–28.

Ostwald, M. (1986), *From Popular Sovereignty to the Sovereignty of Law*, Los Angeles, University of California Press.

Paleothodoros, D. (2010), 'Light and Darkness in Dionysiac Rituals as Illustrated on Attic Vase Paintings of the 5th Century BCE', in Christopoulos, M., et al. (eds.), pp. 237–53.

Parker, R. (1979) 'Dionysus at the Haloa', *Hermes*, Vol. 107, pp. 256–7.

Parker, R. (1983), *Miasma: Pollution and Purification in Early Greek Religion*, Oxford, Clarendon Press.

Parker, R. (1991), 'The Hymn to Demeter and the Homeric Hymns', *Greece & Rome*, Vol. 38, pp. 1–17.

Parker, R. (2005), *Polytheism and Society at Athens*, Oxford, Oxford University Press.

Parker, V. (1998), '*Tyrannus*: The Semantics of a Political Concept from Archilochus to Aristotle', *Hermes*, 126 Bd, pp. 145–72.

Pascal, C. (1911), *Dioniso, Saggio sulla religione e la parodia religiosa in Aristofane*, Catania, Battiato.

Patera, I. (2010), 'Light and Light Equipment in the Eleusinian Mysteries' in Christopoulos, M., et al. (eds.), pp. 254–68.

Peterson, T.V. (1987), 'Initiation Rite as Riddle', *Journal of Ritual Studies*, Vol. 1, pp. 73–84.
Petridou, G. (2015), *Divine Epiphany in Greek Literature and Culture*, Oxford, Oxford University Press.
Picard, C. (1950), 'La tentative sacrilège de Miltiade au sanctuaire parien de Déméter', *Revue Archéologique*, Vol. 36, pp. 124–5.
Pickard-Cambridge, A.W. (1968, originally published 1953), *The Dramatic Festivals of Athens*, Oxford, Clarendon Press.
Price, J.J. (2001), *Thucydides and Internal War*, Cambridge, Cambridge University Press.
Raaflaub, K.A. (1998). 'The Transformation of Athens in the Fifth Century', in Boedeker, D. and Raaflaub, K. (eds.), *Democracy, Empire, and the Arts in Fifth-Century Athens*, Cambridge, Harvard University Press.
Raaflaub, K.A. (2003), 'Stick and Glue: The Function of Tyranny in Fifth-Century Athenian Democracy', in Morgan, K.A. pp. 59–116.
Raubitschek, A.E. (1941), 'The Heroes of Phyle', *Hesperia: The Journal of the American School of Classical Studies at Athens*, Vol. 10, pp. 284–95.
Revermann, M. (1990–2000), 'Euripides, Tragedy and Macedon: Some Conditions of Reception', *Illinois Classical Studies*, Vol. 24/25, pp. 451–67.
Revermann, M. (2006), 'The Competence of Theatre Audiences in Fifth- and Fourth-Century Athens', *The Journal of Hellenic Studies*, Vol. 126, pp. 99–124.
Revermann, M. and Wilson, P. (eds.) (2008), *Performance, Iconography, Reception*, Oxford, Oxford University Press.
Reynolds-Warnhoff, P. (1997), 'The role of τὸ σοφόν in Euripides' *Bacchae*', *Quaderni Urbinati di Cultura Classica*, Vol. 57, pp. 77–103.
Rhodes, P.J. (1993, originally published 1981), *A Commentary on the Aristotelian Athenaion Politeia*, Oxford, Clarendon Press.
Richardson, N.J. (1974), *Homeric Hymn to Demeter*, Oxford, Clarendon Press.
Riedweg, C. (1986), *Mysterienterminologie bei Platon, Philon und Klemens von Alexandrien*, Berlin, New York, de Gruyter.
Roberts, J.T. (1977), 'Arginusae Once Again', *The Classical World*, Vol. 71, pp. 107–11.
Robertson, N. (2003), 'Orphic Mysteries and Dionysian Ritual', in Cosmopoulos, M.B., pp. 218–40.
Robertson, N.D. (1996), 'New Light on Demeter's Mysteries: The Festival Proerosia', *Greek Roman and Byzantine Studies*, pp. 319–79.
Robertson, N.D. (1998), 'The City Centre of Archaic Athens', *Hesperia: The Journal of the American School of Classical Studies at Athens*, pp. 283–302.
Robertson, N.D. (1998a), 'The Two Processions to Eleusis and the Program of the Mysteries', *The American Journal of Philology*, Vol. 119, pp. 547–75.

Rohde, E. (1925, original edition 1898), trans. W.B. Hillis, *Psyche, the Cult of Souls and Belief in Immortality among the Greeks,* London, Kegan Paul, Trench, Trubner.

Rouget, G. (1985, originally published 1980), *Music and Trance*, Chicago, University of Chicago Press.

Roux, J. (1972), *Euripide Les Bacchantes*, Paris, Les Belles Lettres.

Rubel, A. (2000), *Fear and Loathing in Ancient Athens*, Durham, Acumen.

Saban, M. (2018), 'The Characters Speak Because They Want to Speak: Jung, Dionysus Theatre and Therapy', in Bishop, P. and Gardner, L., pp. 28–42.

Sabbatucci, D. (1991), *Saggio sul Misticismo Greco*, Rome, Edizioni dell'Ateneo.

Sandys, J.E. (1904), *The* Bacchae *of Euripides*, Cambridge, Cambridge University Press.

Scarpi, P. (2002), *Le Religioni dei Misteri*, Milan, Mondadori.

Schein, S.L. (2016), 'The Language of Wisdom in Sophocles' *Philoctetes* and Euripides' *Bacchae*', in Kyriakou, P. and Rengakos, A. (eds.), *Wisdom and Folly in Euripides*, Berlin, de Gruyter.

Schechner, R. (1985), *Between Theater and Anthropology*, Philadelphia, University of Pennsylvania Press.

Schlesinger, A.C. (1937), 'Identification of Parodies in Aristophanes', *The American Journal of Philology*, Vol. 58, pp. 294–305.

Schmitt, P. (1977), 'Athéna Apatouria et la ceinture: les aspects féminins des Apatouria a' Athènes', *Annales*, Vol. 6, pp. 1059–73.

Schmitz, K.L. (1981), 'Ritual Elements in Community', *Religious Studies*, Vol. 17, pp. 163–77.

Scott, L. (2005) *Historical Commentary on Herodotus Book 6*, Leiden, Boston, Brill.

Scullion, S. (2003), 'Euripides and Macedon, or the Silence of the Frogs', *The Classical Quarterly*, Vol. 53, pp. 389–400.

Seaford, R. (1981), 'Dionysiac Drama and the Dionysiac Mysteries', *The Classical Quarterly*, Vol. 31, pp. 252–75.

Seaford, R. (1981a), 'The Mysteries of Dionysus at Pompeii', *Pegasus*, University of Exeter.

Seaford, R. (1988), 'The Eleventh Ode of Bacchylides: Hera, Artemis, and the Absence of Dionysus', *The Journal of Hellenic Studies*, Vol. 108, pp. 118–36.

Seaford, R. (1993), 'Dionysus as Destroyer of the Household', in Carpenter, T. H. and Faraone, C.A. (eds.).

Seaford, R. (1994), *Reciprocity and Ritual*, Oxford, Clarendon Press.

Seaford, R. (1996), *Euripides'* Bacchae, trans. and notes Seaford, R., Oxford, Aris and Phillips.

Seaford, R. (2000), 'The Social Function of Greek Tragedy: A Response to Jasper Griffin', *The Classical Quarterly*, Vol. 50, pp. 30–44.

Seaford, R. (2003), 'Tragic Tyranny', in Morgan, K.A., pp. 95–115.

Seaford, R. (2003a), 'Dionysus, Money and Drama', *Arion* Vol. 11, pp 1–19.
Seaford, R. (2004), *Money and the Early Greek Mind*, Cambridge, Cambridge University Press.
Seaford, R. (2005), 'Mystical Light in Aeschylus' *Bassarai*', *The Classical Quarterly*, Vol. 55, pp. 602–6.
Seaford, R. (2006), *Dionysus*, Abingdon, Routledge.
Seaford, R. (2009), 'The Fluttering Soul', in Dill, U. and Walde, C. (eds.) *Antike Mythen. Medien, Transformationen und Konstructionen*, Berlin, de Gruyter, pp. 406–14.
Seaford, R. (2010), 'Mystical Light and Near-Death Experience', in Christopoulos, M., et al., pp. 201–6.
Seaford, R. (2012), *Cosmology and the Polis*, Cambridge, Cambridge University Press.
Seaford, R. (2013), 'The Politics of the Mystical Chorus', in Billings, J. Budelmann, F. and Macintosh, F. (eds.), *Choruses, Ancient and Modern*, Oxford, Oxford University Press, pp. 261–80.
Seager, R. (2001), 'Xenophon and Athenian Democracy', *The Classical Quarterly*, Vol. 51, pp. 385–97.
Segal, C.P. (1961), 'The Character and Cult of Dionysus and the Unity of the *Frogs*', *Harvard Studies in Classical Philology*, Vol. 65, pp. 207–42.
Segal, C. (1982), *Dionysiac Poetica and Euripides*' Bacchae, Princeton, Princeton University Press.
Segal, C. (1982a), 'Etymologies and Double Meanings in Euripides' *Bacchae*', *Glotta*, 60, pp. 81–93.
Segal, C. (1996), 'Catharsis, Audience and Closure', in Silk, M.S. (ed.).
Sells, D. (2012), 'Eleusis and the Public Status of Comedy in Aristophanes' *Frogs*', in Marshall, C.W. and Kovacs, G., pp. 83–100.
Shear, J.L. (2007), 'The Oath of Demophantus and the Politics of Athenian Identity', in Sommerstein, A.H. and Fletcher, J. (eds.), *Horkos: The Oath in Greek Society*, Bristol, Bristol Phoenix Press, pp. 148–60.
Sifakis, G.M. (2001), 'The Function and Significance of Music in Tragedy', *Bulletin of the Institute of Classical Studies*, Vol. 45, pp. 21–35.
Silk, M.S. (ed.) (1996), *Tragedy and the Tragic*, Oxford, Clarendon Press.
Skoczylas Pownall, F. (1998), 'Condemnation of the Impious in Xenophon's *Hellenica*', *The Harvard Theological Review*, Vol. 91, pp. 251–77.
Sommerstein, A.H. (1997), *Aristophanes*' Frogs, Oxford, Oxbow.
Sourvinou-Inwood, C. (1978), 'Persephone and Aphrodite at Locri: A Model for Personality Definition in Greek Religion', *The Journal for Hellenic Studies*, Vol. 98, pp. 101–21.
Sourvinou-Inwood, C. (1989), 'Assumptions and Creation of Meaning: Reading Sophocles' *Antigone*', *The Journal of Hellenic Studies*, Vol. 109, pp. 134–48.

Sourvinou-Inwood, C. (2003), *Tragedy and Athenian Religion*, Lanham, Lexington Books.

Sourvinou-Inwood, C. (2003a), 'Aspects of the Eleusinian Cult', in Cosmopoulos, M.B., pp. 25–49.

Stanford, W.B. (1958), *Aristophanes'* Frogs, London, Macmillan.

Stehle, E. (2004), 'Choral Prayer in Greek Tragedy', in Murray, P. and Wilson, P. (eds.), pp. 121–56.

Stem, R. (2003), 'The Thirty at Athens in the Summer of 404', *Phoenix*, Vol. 57, pp. 18–34.

Stevens, P.T. (1956), 'Euripides and the Athenians', *The Journal of Hellenic Studies*, Vol. 76, pp. 87–94.

Stewart, E. (2019), 'Tragedy and Tyranny: Euripides, Archelaus of Macedon and Popular Patronage', in Lewis, S. (ed.), *Tyranny: New Contexts*, Paris, Presses Universitaires de Franche Comté, pp. 1–23.

Still, G.K. (2017), http://www.gkstill.com

Strauss, B.S. (1986), *Athens after the Peloponnesian War*, New York, Cornell University Press.

Strauss Clay, J. (2006, originally published 1989) *The Politics of Olympus*, London, Bristol University Press.

Stuttard, D. (2016) (ed.), *Looking at* Bacchae, London, Bloomsbury.

Taylor, M.C. (2002), 'One Hundred Heroes at Phyle?' *Hesperia*, Vol. 71, pp. 377–97.

Thomson, G. (1935), 'Mystical Allusions in the *Oresteia*', *The Journal of Hellenic Studies*, Vol. 55, pp. 20–34.

Thomson, G. (1938), *Aeschylus* Oresteia, Cambridge, Cambridge University Press.

Thompson, H.A. and Wycherley, R.E. (1972), 'The Agora of Athens', *The American School of Classical Studies*, Vol. 14, pp. ii–v, vii–xxiii, 1–257.

Tuplin, C. and Azoulay, V. (eds.) (2004), *Xenophon and his World*: papers from a conference held in Liverpool in July 1999, Stuttgart, Franz Steiner.

Turner, V. (1982), *From Ritual to Theatre*, New York, PAJ Publications.

Turner, V. (1987), *The Anthropology of Performance*, New York, PAJ Publications.

Ustinova, Y. (2018), *Divine Mania: Alteration of Consciousness in Ancient Greece*, Abingdon, Routledge.

Van Wees H. (2008), '*Stasis*, Destroyer of Men. Mass, Elite, Political Violence and Security in Archaic Greece', in Brélaz, C. and Ducrey, P. (eds) *Sécurité Collective et ordre public dans les sociétés anciennes*, pp. 1–39.

Vargiu, A. (1970), 'Note su uno strumento primitivo: "Is launeddas"', *Lares*, Vol. 36, pp. 379–82.

Vellacott, P. (1973), 'The *Bacchae* and Other Plays: *Ion, The Women of Troy, Helen, The Bacchae*', London, Penguin Classics.

Vernant, J.-P. and Vidal-Naquet, P. (1988, French originals 1972 and 1986), *Myth and Tragedy in Ancient Greece*, New York, Zone Books.

Vernant, J.-P. (1985), 'Le Dionysus masqué des *Bacchantes* d'Euripide', *L'Homme*, tome 25, pp. 31–58 n. 93.

Versnel, H. (1998), *ΕΙΣ ΔΙΟΝΥΣΟΣ, The Tragic Paradox of the Bacchae*, Leiden, Brill.

Von Wilamowitz-Moellendorff, U. (1872), *Future Philology!* Postl, G, Babich, B. and Schmid H. (trans.) 2000, Fordham. http://fordham.bepress.com/phil_babich/3

Webster, T.B.L. (1967), *The Tragedies of Euripides*, London, Methuen.

West, M.L. (1974), *Studies in Greek Elegy and Iambus*, Berlin, de Gruyter.

West, M.L. (2003), *Greek Epic Fragments*, Harvard, Harvard University Press.

West, W.C. (1977), 'Hellenic Homonoia and the Decree from Plataea', *Greek, Roman and Byzantine Studies*, Vol. 18.

Whitehouse, H. (2004), *Modes of Religiosity*, Walnut Creek, Altamira Press.

Whitehouse, H. and Laidlaw, J. (eds.) (2004), *Ritual and Memory*, Walnut Creek, Altamira Press.

Whitehouse, H. and Martin, L.M. (2004), *Theorizing Religious Past*, Walnut Creek, Altamira Press.

Widzisz, M. (2010), 'The Duration of Darkness and Light of Eleusis in the Prologue of Agamemnon and the Third Stasimon of *Choephoroe*', *Greek, Roman and Byzantine Studies*, Vol. 50, pp. 461–89.

Wiles, D. (2000), *Greek Theatre Performance*, Cambridge, Cambridge University Press.

Wiles, D. (2011), *Theatre and Citizenship*, Cambridge, Cambridge University Press.

Wilson, P. (1999), 'The Aulos in Athens', in Goldhill, S. and Wilson, P. (eds.), pp. 58–95.

Wilson, P. (2000), *The Athenian Institution of the Khoregoia*, Cambridge, Cambridge University Press.

Wilson, P. (2009), 'Tragic Honours and Democracy: Neglected Evidence of the Politics of the Athenian Dionysia', *The Classical Quarterly*, Vol. 59, pp. 8–29.

Winkler, J.J. and Zeitlin, F.I. (eds.) (1990), *Nothing to Do with Dionysus?* Princeton, Princeton University Press.

Winnington-Ingram, R.P. (1948), *Euripides and Dionysus*, Cambridge, Cambridge University Press.

Winnington-Ingram, R.P. (1966), 'Euripides *Bacchae* 877–881=897–901', *Bulletin of the Institute of Classical Studies*, No. 13, pp. 3–7.

Zeitlin, F.I. (1982), 'Cultic Models of the Female: Rites of Dionysus and Demeter', *Arethusa*, Vol. 15, pp. 12–57.

Zeitlin, F.I. (1993), 'Staging Dionysus between Thebes and Athens', in Carpenter, T.H. and Faraone, C.A. (eds.).

Index

Acharnians (Aristophanes) 16
Aeschylus 40
   Agamemnon 74–5, 77, 79, 175
   asebeia 98
   Choephoroe 74, 75–6, 77
   democracy/tyranny 79
   Edonians 33
   Eumenides. See Eumenides
   light/darkness imagery 74–6, 80
   metics 43
   Oresteia 40, 43, 73–80, 98
   Persians 178
afterlife, the 31–3, 144–5
Agamemnon (Aeschylus) 74–5, 77, 79, 175
agriculture 159
Alcibiades 12, 38, 100, 104, 130
   Eleusinian mysteries' scandal 92, 94, 95–7
Alcmaeon (Euripides) 4
Alexander, E. 32–3
Andocides 38
Anthesteria festival 47, 48
Antigone (Sophocles) 151, 156, 163, 187
Apaturia festival 102–3
archaeology 157
Archelaus (king of Macedonia) 118–19
Arginusae, battle of 99–105
Aristides, Aelius 30, 37
   evil, deliverance from 77
Aristocrates 104
Aristogiton, statue of 139–40, 141
Aristophanes
   Acharnians 16
   Birds 99
   Clouds 99
   equality 190–2
   Frogs. See Frogs
   Lysistrata 83
   metics 43
   Pax 43
   politics 149–50, 187, 190–2, 194
   Thesmophoriazousae 47, 150
Aristotle
   Didascaliae 4
   Ethica Nicomachea 98
   Poetica 51, 55–6, 57
   Politica 55
   Politics 61
   tragedy 55–6, 58, 59, 62
asebeia 97–9
atheism 99
Athena 77–8
Athens 17
   agora, the 141–2
   Attica 82
   civic concepts 81
   ecclesia, the 38–9, 46
   economy 130, 151
   eschara 141–2
   hierarchy 42
   inclusion 6–7, 68–70
   initiates in 35–40
   metics 42–3
   military power 130
   money 81
   monuments 139–40, 141
   politics. See politics
   population 36
   religion. See religion
   religious festivals 6–12
   theatre 12, 44
   theatre audiences in 40–8
   women 46, 48
Attica 82
aulos 60–1
Australia
   initiation rituals 15

Bacchae (Euripides) 3–5, 16, 22, 197–8
   audiences 40, 117–19
   aulos 61

catharsis 57
chorus, the 63, 64, 119–20, 138, 165–70, 181–5
dancing 169
Demeter and Persephone, cult of 153–4
Dionysus 158
Dionysus, cult of 120, 132, 133–6, 138, 153–4, 156, 187, 192
Dodds, E.R. 121, 125–6
equality 69, 188–9
ethics 170–9, 181–5
Foley, H.P. 121–2
Frogs, similarities with 119–20, 126, 168–9
Girard, R. 126–7
happiness 174–5
inclusion 69, 188–9
initiates 40
light/darkness polarity 163, 164
Macedonia 117–19
maenadism 19
makarismos 168
metre 166
money 152
mountains 162
music 61, 166, 169
Musurillo, H. 126, 181
Nietzsche, F. 125
orderly behaviour 177–9, 184
paradox of 121, 122, 124–7
Pentheus. *See* Pentheus
plot 3–4
poetry 52
polis 112, 131–6, 138, 147, 178
politics 121–2, 131–6, 138–9, 177, 181–2, 197–8, 227 n. 59
production 4–5
reconciliation 192–3, 194
religious and civic content 5, 119–20, 122, 126, 132–3, 153
religious spaces 161, 162–3
Rohde, E. 125
scholarship 5, 121–2, 124–7
Seaford, R. 122
Segal, C.P. 126
stasima interpretation 181–5
stasis 131–2
Stuttard, D. 122
success 35
tyranny 142–9, 152, 175, 179, 185
Versnel, H. 122, 127
violence 126–7, 184–5
virtues 176–7
war 131
Winnington-Ingram, R.P. 126
wisdom 170–3, 182–4, 185
women 44, 132–3
Bacchus. *See* Dionysus
bewitching 54
Birds (Aristophanes) 99
Birth of Tragedy (Nietzsche, F.) 125
Blake, W.E. 183
blessedness 174–5, 179
blood feuds 78, 80
Bourguignon, E. 59

Callias III (archon *eponymos*) 39–40
catharsis 9, 57–9
Choephoroe (Aeschylus) 74, 75–6, 77
choregoi 63
chorus, the 62–5
  Agamemnon 75
  aulos 61
  Bacchae 63, 64, 119–20, 138, 165–70, 181–5
  Demeter 71
  Frogs 63, 64, 119–20, 149–51, 154–5, 165–70, 179–80
  joy 169
  politics 79
  women 71
citizenship 180–1
civic content 5
civic harmony 175
Cleocritus 39, 106, 110–11
Cleophon 130
Clinton, K. 37, 158
Clouds (Aristophanes) 99
collectivity 159–60
community, the 71–2 *see also* polis
  gifts 159–60
  order 31
  religion 13–15, 71–2
  ritual 49
  stasis 83
  theatre 49

Conon 100
consciousness, states of 59
Constitution of the Athenians 86–7, 107, 113
cosmic crisis 69, 71, 73
Cresphontes (Euripides) 231 n. 72
Critias 106–7
Cybele 153
Cylon 85–6

dancing 54, 154, 169 *see also* music
   chorus, the 62–5, 71
   spectacle 64
   tragic 64
darkness/light polarity. *See* light/darkness polarity
De Corona (Demosthenes) 16, 33
De latenter vivendo (Plutarch) 30
De sera numinis vindicta (Plutarch) 29
death 33
   burial 100–1, 102–3, 143, 144–5
Decelea 96
decree of Demophantus 130, 140–1
Demeter 6–10, 67–73, 155, 158 *see also* Demeter and Persephone, cult of
   food 160
   gifts 159–60
   peace 160
   theophany 91
Demeter and Persephone, cult of 6–10, 13, 16, 155–60
   agriculture 159, 160
   Bacchae 153–4
   chorus, the 168
   cosmic crisis 69, 71, 73
   democracy 73
   Dionysus, merging with cult of 21, 153–61
   Eleusis 6–9, 16–17, 96–7
   equality 71, 190
   eschatology 20, 82
   Frogs 154–5
   gifts 159–60
   Homeric Hymn to Demeter 67–73
   inclusion 68–70
   initiates 37
   initiation rituals 18, 19–20, 22
   laughter 169
   Paros 90
   polis 92, 153

politics 81
prorrhesis 150
sanctuaries 7, 16–17, 37, 89–91, 113, 157
Supplices 144
Telesterium, the 9–10, 17, 37, 87
women 47
Demetrius 53
democracy 73, 79 *see also* equality
   decree of Demophantus 130, 140–1
   Solonian law 140
   Thirty, the 105–13
   threats to 92–6
   Xenophon 112
demos, the
   Arginusae, battle of 99–105
   leaders 149–50
   Thirty, the 105–13
   threats to 92–6, 129–30
Demosthenes
   De Corona 16, 33
Di Benedetto, V. 182
Diagoras of Melos 98–9
Dicaeus 160
Didascaliae (Aristotle) 4
diet 9, 56
Dio Chrysostomus 56–7
Diodorus Siculus 100–1, 102–3
Diomedon 104
Dionysus 11, 157–8 *see also* Dionysus, cult of
   Bacchae 158
   Dodds, E.R. 125–6
   gifts 159
   Nietzsche, F. 125
   Rhea 153, 156
   Segal, C.P. 126
   women and 47–8, 159, 189
Dionysus, cult of 11, 13, 16, 17–18, 155–9
   agora, the 141
   agriculture 159
   Bacchae 120, 132, 133–6, 138, 153–4, 156, 187, 192
   choral performances 62, 167–8
   decree of Demophantus 141
   Demeter and Persephone, merging with cult of 21, 153–61
   Dodds, E.R. 125–6
   equality 188

eschara 141–2
eschatology 21
Frogs 120, 187, 195
initiation rituals 18–20, 22
light/darkness polarity 163
music 61, 167
Musurillo, H. 126
Nietzsche, F. 125
Orphic tablets 21–2
Pentheus 147–8
Pindar 142
polis 140, 141–2, 153, 187
politics 81, 140
Rohde, E. 125
sanctuaries 11–12, 157
Segal, C. 126
tyranny 140, 142–3
violence 126
war 192
Winnington-Ingram, R.P. 126
women 47–8, 159, 189
divine favour 174–5
divine justice 70–1
divine power 173–4
divinity 52–3, 174–5, 179
    Demeter 91
    music 53–7
Dodds, E.R. 117–18, 121, 125–6, 181, 182
Dover, K. 120, 123

ecclesia, the 38–9, 46
economy 130, 151, 159
ecstasy 59–61
Edonians (Aeschylus) 33
Eleusinian mysteries' scandals 92, 93–4, 95–7, 99
Eleusis 16–17, 82, 157
    festival 6–9, 16–17, 96–7, 144 *see also* Demeter and Persephone, cult of
    rulers 70–1
    society 70
    Solon 82
    Thirty, the 108–9, 110
Eliade, M. 15
Encomium of Helen (Gorgias) 50–1
Ephialtes 74
Epimenides 86–8
equality 71, 188–92 *see also* inclusion

Erasinides 104
erōs 25
eschara 141–2
eschatology 20–1, 82 *see also* afterlife, the
    catharsis 57–8
    Plato 25–7, 57–8
    Plutarch 23–4
    Supplices 144–5
Ethica Nicomachea (Aristotle) 98
ethics 22
    Bacchae 170–9, 181–5
    Frogs 179–81
Eumenides (Aeschylus) 43, 45
    chorus, the 167
    equality 188
    light/darkness polarity 165
    mystical/political values 74, 76, 77, 78, 79–80, 194
    polis 194
    religion 194
    revenge 106
    self-control 194
    stasis 84, 194
    tyranny, rejection of 112
    virtues 176
Euripides 117–18
    Alcmaeon 4
    Bacchae. See Bacchae
    Cresphontes 231 n. 72
    equality 189
    Helen 156–7
    Hippolytus 29
    Ion 156, 163
    Iphigeneia in Aulis 4
    in Macedonia 117–19
    Phoenissae 192
    politics 142–5, 187, 192
    religion 153
    Supplices 142–4
    tyranny 142–5
Euryptolemus 104
evil, deliverance from 77, 175
extraordinary passion 52–3

fasting 9
Fenwick, P. 32
festivals 6–10 *see also under individual names*
    laughter 169

Foley, H.P. 120, 121–2
  'Masque of Dionysus, The' 121
  'Poetry and Sacrifice in Euripides' 121
Four Hundred, the 129–30, 192
fragment 3.33 (Solon) 3.33 178
fragment 4 (Solon) 88–9
fragment 36 (Solon) 89
fragment 43 (Plutrach) 156
fragment 129 (Pindar) 28, 29, 32
fragment 178 (Plutarch) 23–4, 28, 29, 30, 32
Frogs (Aristophanes) 4, 5, 16, 22, 197–8
  Alcibiades 104
  audiences 40, 43
  Bacchae, similarities with 119–20, 126, 168–9
  chorus, the 63, 64, 119–20, 149–51, 154–5, 165–70, 179–80
  dancing 169
  Demeter and Persephone, cult of 154–5
  Diagoras of Melos 99
  Dionysus, cult of 120, 187, 195
  Dover, K. 123
  equality 190–2
  ethics 179–81
  Griffith, M. 124
  Halliwell, S. 124
  happiness 179
  initiates 40
  Lada-Richards, I. 50, 123–4
  light/darkness polarity 164–5
  makarismos 168
  metre 166
  money 152
  music 53–4, 166, 169
  plot 4
  poetry 52
  polis 131–2, 136–8, 150, 193–4, 195
  politics 123–4, 131–2, 136–9, 149–51, 194, 197–8
  production 5
  prorrhesis 150
  reconciliation 192, 193–4
  religious and civic content 5, 119–20, 123–4, 153, 194
  religious spaces 161–2, 163
  scholarship 5, 121, 123–4
  Segal, C. 123, 126
  self-control 194
  Sommerstein, A.H. 123
  Stanford, W.B. 123
  stasis 131–2, 137–8, 152
  success 35
  vegetation polarity 29
  war 131
  Wiles, D. 124
  wisdom 180–1
  women 44–5
funeral rituals 100–1, 102–3, 143, 144–5

Gela 92
gifts 159–60
Girard, R. 126–7
god-inspired 51
Goldhill, S. 46
Gorgias 51, 58
  Encomium of Helen 50–1
Gorgias (Plato) 45
Great Dionysia festival 6, 10–12
  chorus, the 63
Greater Mysteries festival 8
greed 151–2
Griffith, M. 124
Grote, G. 103

Hades 28–9, 72
Halliwell, S. 124
Haloa festival 47
happiness 169, 174–5, 179
Harmodius, statue of 139–40, 141
Helen (Euripides) 156–7
Hellenica (Xenophon) 105
Henrichs, A. 165–6
Heraclides Ponticus 40
Herms 141
  defacement of 92, 93, 94–5
Herodotus 84, 89–92, 160, 207 n. 38
Hesiod 84
  Shield of Heracles 155
  Theogony 155
  Works and Days 155
hierophant 10, 28
Hippolytus (Euripides) 29
Homer 178
  Iliad 29, 83–4
  Odyssey 29

Homeric Hymn to Demeter 7, 10, 16, 82, 91, 155, 158
    equality 188
    eschatology 20
    gifts 159–60
    laughter 169
    politics 67–73
    social change 160
    vegetation polarity 29
hubris 149, 174

Iacchus *see* Dionysus
Iliad (Homer) 29, 83–4
imagery 27–31, 161–2
impiety 97 *see also* asebeia
inclusion 6–7, 68–70 *see also* equality
individuality 21–2
initiates 15, 20–5, 27, 30–1, 180
    in Athens 35–40
    Homeric Hymn to Demeter 72
    light/darkness polarity 28
    Plato 25–7
    Plutarch 23–5
    in theatre audiences 40
    vegetation polarity 28–9
initiation rituals 7–10, 14–15, 18–20, 22–3, 197–8
    costs 7–8
    Dio Chrysostomus 56–7
    extraordinary passion 53
    Herodotus 160–1
    light/darkness polarity 27–8, 163–5
    music and dancing 54, 57
    Plato 25–7
    Plutarch 23–5
    scandal 92, 93–7
    secrecy 72
    spaces 161–3
    theatre performances and 49–50
    vegetation polarity 28–9
Ion (Euripides) 156, 163
Ion (Plato) 41, 51–2, 54, 58
Iphigeneia in Aulis (Euripides) 4
Isocrates 54

joy 169
Jung, C. 58
justice 72
    divine 70–1

Kawalko-Roselli, D. 46
kerdos 151–2
Kowalzig, B. 62–3

Lada-Richards, I. 50, 123–4
launeddas 60
Laws (Plato) 45, 83
Lenaea festival 10–11, 47
Lenaea vases 47
Lesser Mysteries festival 8
Life of Alcibiades (Plutarch) 93
Life of Solon (Plutarch) 86, 87
light/darkness polarity 27–8, 72–3, 74–6, 80, 163–5
liminality 17–18, 161
Locri Epizephyrii 157
Loraux, N. 106
love 26
Lucian of Samosata 54
Lysistrata (Aristophanes) 83

maenadism 19, 47, 134, 147–8, 177, 178–9
makarismos 20, 21, 168, 174–5
mania 26
'Masque of Dionysus, The' (Foley, H.P.) 121
Massenzio, M. 159
meadows 161–2
Menexenos (Plato) 101, 112
mercenaries 152
metics 42–3
metre 166
military order 177–9
military power 130, 152
Miltiades 89–91
money 81, 151–2
monuments 139–40, 141, 158
mountains 162
mousike 55
music 10, 20, 166, 169
    Aristotle 55–6
    aulos 60–1
    divinity 53–7
    elements of 56
    Gorgias 51
    Phyrgian mode 55, 166
    Plato 51–2, 54, 154
    states of consciousness 59

Musurillo, H. 126, 181–2
mystery cults 13–14 *see also* religion
    Demeter and Persephone, cult of. *See*
        Demeter and Persephone, cult of
    Dionysus, cult of. *See* Dionysus,
        cult of

nature 28–30, 161–2
near-death experiences (NDE) 32–3
Nietzsche, F. 125
    Birth of Tragedy 125

Odyssey (Homer) 29
Oedipus Tyrannus (Sophocles) 62, 187
oligarchs
    Four Hundred, the 129–30, 192
    Thirty, the 105–13
Olympian (Pindar) 28, 29, 32, 180
oneness of mind, civic concord and
    cohesion 192 *see also* reconciliation
order/disorder polarity 30–1
orderly behaviour 177–9, 184, 194
Oresteia (Aeschylus) 40, 43, 73–80, 98
Orpheus 156
Orphic Hymns 163
Orphic tablets 21–2
Orphism 153, 155–6

Parker, R. 69
Paros 90
Pax (Aristophanes) 43
Pentheus 3–4, 145–9, 174, 184–5
    Bacchae, paradox of 125, 127
    greed 152
    polis 125, 132–6
Pericles junior 104
Persephone 6–10, 67–8 *see also* Demeter
    and Persephone, cult of
    sanctuary of 157
Persian invasion 160
Persians (Aeschylus) 178
Phaedo (Plato) 25, 27, 29–30, 57
Phaedrus (Plato) 25, 28, 30, 32, 52–3
Phoenissae (Euripides) 192
Phyrgian mode 55, 166
Pickard-Cambridge, A.W. 41
Pindar 142
    fragment 129 28, 29, 32
    Olympian 28, 29, 32, 180

Plato 23, 25–7, 169
    aulos 61
    catharsis 57–8
    Epimenides 87
    evil, deliverance from 77
    Gorgias 45
    Ion 41, 51–2, 54, 58
    Laws 45, 83
    light/darkness polarity 28
    Menexenos 101, 112
    music 51–2, 54, 61, 154
    order/disorder polarity 30
    Phaedo 25, 27, 29–30, 57
    Phaedrus 25, 28, 30, 32, 52–3
    poetry 51–2, 54
    Politicus 83
    Republic 51
    Symposium 41, 52, 61
    tragedy 54
    vegetation polarity 29–30
Plutarch 23–5, 45
    aulos 61
    De latenter vivendo 30
    De sera numinis vindicta 29
    Eleusinian mysteries' scandal 94, 97
    Epimenides 87–8
    fragment 43 156
    fragment 178 23–4, 28, 29, 30, 32
    Herms, defacement of 95
    Life of Alcibiades 93
    Life of Solon 86, 87
    light/darkness polarity 28
    music 56, 61
    order/disorder polarity 30–1
    polis 87–8
    Quomodo quis suos in virtute sentiat
        profectus 23, 24, 30–1
    silence/noise polarity 30–1
    vegetation polarity 29, 30
Poetica (Aristotle) 51, 55–6, 57
poetry 50–3
    music and 53–4
'Poetry and Sacrifice in Euripides' (Foley,
    H.P.) 121
polarities 28–31, 49, 72–3
polis 77–8, 79, 141, 187, 195, 197–8
    Aristophanes 83
    Bacchae 112, 131–6, 138, 147, 178
    Cylon 85–6

decree of Demophantus 130, 140–1
Demeter and Persephone, cult of 92, 153
Dionysus, cult of 140, 141–2, 153, 187
Epimenides 86–8
Eumenides 194
Frogs 131–2, 136–8, 150, 193–4, 195
historical context 81–2
hubris 149
money and 151–2
Plato 83, 112
purification rituals 86–8
Solon 88–9
stasis 83–4, 86–7, 92, 131
Thirty, the 105–13
tyranny 139–42, 143, 147–8
Politica (Aristotle) 55
political content 5–6
political hierarchy 42
politics 5–7, 73–4, 81–2, 197 *see also* democracy *and* polis
Aristophanes 149–50, 187, 190–2
Bacchae 121–2, 131–6, 138–9, 177, 181–2, 192–3, 195, 227 n. 59
changes 159
chorus, the 62–3
decree of Demophantus 140–1
Euripides 142–5, 187
Four Hundred, the 129–30, 192
Frogs 123–4, 131–2, 136–9, 149–51, 194
harmony 175
Homeric Hymn to Demeter 67–73
oligarchs 105–13, 129–30, 192
Oresteia 73–80
reconciliation 192–4
religion and 111
scholarship 121–4
Solonian law 140
stasis 82–5, 86, 92, 105–6, 131
Thirty, the 105–13
violence 129–30
Xenophon 110
Politics (Aristotle) 61
Politicus (Plato) 83
prorrhesis 150
Psyche (Rohde, E.) 125
psychotherapy 58
purification rituals 86–8, 164

Quomodo quis suos in virtute sentiat profectus (Plutarch) 23, 24, 30–1

racehorses 216 n. 41
reconciliation 192–4
religion 13–14, 68 *see also* initiation rituals
asebeia 97–9
atheism 99
Bacchae 5, 119–20, 122, 126, 132–3, 153
Demeter and Persephone, cult of. *See* Demeter and Persephone, cult of
Dionysus, cult of. *See* Dionysus, cult of
doctrinal mode 15–16, 19, 20
emotional intensity 15
Frogs 5, 119–20, 123–4, 153, 194
imagistic mode 15, 19, 20, 59
music 55
politics and 111
spaces 161–3
Thucydides 215 n. 21
women 46–7
Xenophon 109–11
religious content 5
religious festivals 6–12
choruses 212 n. 84
Republic (Plato) 51
revenge 196
Revermann, M. 65
Rhea 153, 156
rhythm 54
Richardson, N.J. 68–9
Rohde, E.
Psyche 125
Roux, J. 118, 183

Saban, M. 58
sanctuaries
Demeter and Persephone, cult of 7, 16–17, 37, 89–91, 113, 157
Dionysus, cult of 11–12, 157
Telesterium, the 9–10, 17, 37, 87
Satyrus 117
Vita 118
Schechner, R. 49
scholarship 121–4
Seaford, R. 63, 69, 122, 183–4
secrecy 20, 72
Segal, C.P. 58, 120, 123, 126
self-control 177–9, 184, 194

Semnai Theai 76, 78, 80
sexual desire 25
Shear, J.L. 140–1
Shield of Heracles (Hesiod) 155
shuddering 51, 53
silence/noise polarity 30–1
slaves 44
society 159, 160
    chorus, the 63–4
    equality 188–92
    hierarchy 42
    inclusion 68–70
Socrates 25–6
Solon 82, 84, 88
    fragment 3.33 178
    fragment 36 89
    fragment 4 88–9
Solonian law 140
Sommerstein, A.H. 123
Sophocles
    Antigone 151, 156, 163, 187
    Oedipus Tyrannus 62, 187
    Trachiniae 61
souls 26–7
sounds 33
Sourvinou-Inwood, C. 50
spaces 161–3
Sparta 39, 96
Stanford, W.B. 123
stasis 82–5, 86, 92, 105–6
    Bacchae 131–2
    Eumenides 84, 194
    Frogs 131–2, 137–8, 152, 194
    kerdos 151, 152
    money 151, 152
    Xenophon 111, 112
statues 139–40, 141, 158
Ste. Croix, G.E.M. de 192
Strabo 55, 157
Stuttard, D. 122
Supplices (Euripides) 142–4
Symposium (Plato) 41, 52, 61

Telesterium, the 9–10, 17, 37, 87
Telines 92
theatre 12, 44, 49, 150, 193–4, 197–8 *see also* theatre audiences
    catharsis 57–9
    chorus, the. *See* chorus

initiation rituals and 49–50
Plato 52
poetic inspiration 50–3
psychotherapy and 58
states of consciousness and 59–60
terms 52
tragedy. *See* tragedy
theatre audiences 40–4, 48, 65
    Bacchae 40, 117–19
    catharsis 58–9
    chorus, the 64–5
    initiates 40
    metics 43
    seat allocation 42
    slaves 44
    ticket prices 42
    tragedy 58–9
    women 44–8
theatre of Dionysus 41–2
Thebes 142–3
Theogony (Hesiod) 155
Theon of Smyrna 18
theophany 91
theorika 42
Theramenes 106, 107–8
Thesmophoria festival 47
Thesmophoriazousae (Aristophanes) 47, 150
thiasoi 5, 145
Thirty, the 105–13
Thomson, G. 77
Thrasybulus 106, 107, 109, 111–12
thronosis 57
Thucydides 84–5, 92–3, 94–6
    Cylon 86
    oneness of mind, civic concord and cohesion 192
    politics 149, 192
    religion 215 n. 21
Trachiniae (Sophocles) 61
tradition 173
tragedy 45–6, 51
    Aristotle 55–6, 58, 59, 62
    chorus, the 62–5
    dancing 64
    music and 55–6, 61
    Plato 54
    Segal, C.P. 58

tragic dancing 64
'Tragic Paradox of *Bacchae*' (Versnel, H.) 122
Two Goddesses, cult of the. *See* Demeter and Persephone, cult of
tyranny 79
    Archelaus 118–19
    Bacchae 142–9, 152, 175, 179, 185
    Critias 106–7
    Cylon 85–6
    decree of Demophantus 140–1
    Dionysus, cult of 140
    Euripides 142–5
    Euripides 142–9
    hubris 149
    Pentheus 3–4, 125, 145–9, 174
    polis, the 139–42, 143, 147–8
    Thirty, the 105–13
    wealth 152

uninitiated, the 4, 22, 23, 29–31
    Homeric Hymn to Demeter 20, 72
    light/darkness polarity 28
    mire, the 24, 27, 28, 29–30, 31
    Plato 25, 27, 57
    Plutarch 24
    vegetation polarity 28–9

vases 47–8
vegetation polarity 28–30 *see also* nature

Versnel, H. 122, 127
    'Tragic Paradox of *Bacchae*' 122
violence 126–7, 130, 184–5
virtues 176–81
Vita (Satyrus) 118
Vita Aeschyli 45

war 78, 111, 112, 130–1, 160 see also *stasis*
    Dionysus 192
Ways and Means (Xenophon) 42–3
wealth 151–2
Whitehouse, H. 15
Wiles, D. 124
Winnington-Ingram, R.P. 126, 181, 182–3
wisdom 170–3, 180–1, 182–4, 185
women 44–8
    Bacchae 132–3
    choruses 71
    Dionysus, cult of 47–8, 159, 189
    funeral rituals 143
    maenadism 19, 47, 134, 147–8, 177, 178–9
    thiasoi 5, 145
Works and Days (Hesiod) 155

xenoi 158–9
Xenophon 39
    Arginusae, battle of 100, 101, 102
    Hellenica 105
    Thirty, the 105, 106–12, 113
    Ways and Means 42–3

www.ingramcontent.com/pod-product-compliance
Lightning Source LLC
Chambersburg PA
CBHW062123300426
44115CB00012BA/1790